The Documentary Filmmaker's Roadmap

The Documentary Filmmaker's Roadmap is a concise and practical guide to making a feature-length documentary film—from funding to production to distribution, exhibition and marketing. Using her award-winning film *Musicwood*—a *New York Times* Critics' Pick—as a case study, director Maxine Trump guides the reader through the complex lifecycle of the documentary film. Her interviews with lawyers, funders, distributors, TV executives and festival programmers provide a behind-the-scenes look that will assist readers on their own filmmaking journey.

Written from the perspective of a successful documentary filmmaker, the book covers mistakes made and lessons learned, a discussion on the documentary genre, crowdfunding, pre-production through post, test screenings, the festival circuit distribution, legal pitfalls, fair use and more. Perfect for documentary filmmaking students and aspiring filmmakers alike, this book emphasizes the skills needed to succeed in a competitive production market. An appendix includes useful web links for further study, a list of films for recommended viewing and sample release forms.

This concise guide is ideal for the classroom or as a quick reference out in the field, at a budget meeting or in the editing room.

Maxine Trump got her start in radio and television, working for seven years in development and commissioning for BBC Comedy in the UK. She emigrated to the US in 2003 to become a director of television commercials and has received both Gold and Silver BDA awards for her work. She went on to direct short documentaries and TV shows for various networks including TNT, the Sundance Channel and Discovery.

The Documentary Filmmaker's Roadmap

A Practical Guide to Planning, Production and Distribution

Maxine Trump

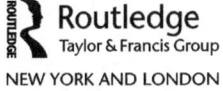

NEW YORK AND LONDON

First published 2019
by Routledge
711 Third Avenue, New York, NY 10017

and by Routledge
2 Park Square, Milton Park, Abingdon, Oxon OX14 4RN

Routledge is an imprint of the Taylor & Francis Group, an informa business

© 2019 Maxine Trump

The right of Maxine Trump to be identified as the author of this work has been asserted by him/her in accordance with sections 77 and 78 of the Copyright, Designs and Patents Act 1988.

All rights reserved. No part of this book may be reprinted or reproduced or utilised in any form or by any electronic, mechanical, or other means, now known or hereafter invented, including photocopying and recording, or in any information storage or retrieval system, without permission in writing from the publishers.

Trademark notice: Product or corporate names may be trademarks or registered trademarks, and are used only for identification and explanation without intent to infringe.

Library of Congress Cataloging-in-Publication Data
Names: Trump, Maxine, author.
Title: The documentary filmmaker's roadmap : a practical guide
    to planning, production and distribution / Maxine Trump.
Description: New York : Routledge, 2018. | Includes index.
Identifiers: LCCN 2018006726| ISBN 9781138070875 (hardback) |
    ISBN 9781138070882 (pbk.) | ISBN 9781315114873 (e-book)
Subjects: LCSH: Documentary films—Production and
    direction—Handbooks,   manuals, etc.
Classification: LCC PN1995.9.D6 T78 2018 | DDC 070.1/8—dc23
LC record available at https://lccn.loc.gov/2018006726

ISBN: 978-1-138-07087-5 (hbk)
ISBN: 978-1-138-07088-2 (pbk)
ISBN: 978-1-315-11487-3 (ebk)

Typeset in Warnock Pro
by Apex CoVantage, LLC
Printed and bound by CPI Group (UK) Ltd, Croydon, CR0 4YY

Contents

Introduction   ix

1 Research: Choosing Your Story   1
    Archive Or Third Party Materials   6

2 Pre-production   8
    Inspiration/Early Analysis and Prep   8
    Equipment   18

3 How to Choose Documentary Genres   20
    The Essay Film   25

4 Budget   38
    Filmmakers' Costs   38
    Production Insurance and Legal   39
    Finishing Costs   39
    Example Budgets   40

5 Production   46
    Releases   47
    The Look of the Production   47
    Crew   48
    Filming   49
    BTS   50
    Interviews   50
    Tracking the Details   52
    Editing While Filming   52

vi Contents

6 Funding   55

In Kind   56
Deferred   56
Foundations and Film Funds   57
Individuals/Crowdfunding/Fundraisers   60
Our Goal   63
Sponsors and Individual Investors   64
Non-profits   65
TV Pre-sales   65

7 Social Media and Print Assets   67

Social Media   68
Key Art   71
Website   71
Trailer   72

8 Crowdfunding   73

Think Of Your Strategy and What Crowdfunding Can Do For You   73
Lead Time   74
Outreach/Reaching People   74
Making Strangers Your Funders and Your Audience   75
Then and Now   77
Pre-Launch   77
Launch   86
Results   92

9 The Edit   96

Story Beats and Structure   100
Voice Over   103
Good Narration   105
Music and Sound   105
Finishing and Assembly   109

10 Case Study: *Cartel Land* Edit   110

11 Copyright Law, Third-party and Archive Material   129

    Music   131
    Third-party Materials   132
    Public Domain   133
    Fair Use   133
    Privacy   135
    Releases   137
    When a Release Isn't Possible   137
    Errors and Omissions Insurance   139
    Journalism   140
    Hidden Cameras, Phone Calls and Door Stepping   141
    Satirical Works   142
    Trespassing   144
    Recreations   144

12 Brain Trusts, Test Screenings and Outreach   146

13 In Conversation With: Fork Films Funder, Women Make Movies Distributor, DOC NYC Festival, PBS POV Television Strand Exhibitor   151

    Funder: Fork Films   151
    DOC NYC Festival   157
    Women Make Movies Distributor   159
    TV Network—PBS and POV   163

14 Festivals   169

    Applying/Premiering   170
    Premiere Night   172
    Distributors At Film Festivals   174
    The Festival Circuit   175
    Press at Festivals   176
    25 Tips for the First-Time Feature Director on the Festival Circuit   177

viii Contents

15 Distribution (or Selling and Income)   184
    National   188
    International   190
    Our Deal   192
    Semi-Theatrical/Non-Theatrical Distribution   194
    Educational   194

16 Theatrical   196
    Theaters In Our Theatrical Run   200

17 Press and Marketing   202
    Theatrical Marketing and Press   204
    Reviewers   206
    Blogs   206
    Overall   206

18 TV and Streaming   208
    Digital Streaming   208
    US TV Networks   211
    European TV Networks   214
    BBC Storyville   214

19 In Conclusion   216
    Special Thanks   218

    Appendix   220
    About the Author   236
    Index   237

Introduction

I'm a filmmaker and after five years of production, two more years of festival tours, and theatrical openings and community screenings, I have finished my feature documentary, *Musicwood*. After all that time, I can finally say I'm a feature filmmaker, and that feels good.

In full confession I have worked in the media all my life. I started in radio comedy for the BBC almost straight out of university, after a small stint working for a film composer agent, and then worked my way up to a Development Executive. Wanting to be involved in production rather than stay in development, I emigrated to America with BBC America, where I learned how to write, produce, direct and edit TV trailers. I finally left in 2005 for the freelance world. It was then that I started making branded content, otherwise known as short form documentaries for TV networks (that were financed by certain paid sponsors). It was here that I found my love for documentaries.

In 2000 whilst still at the BBC in London (and in the comedy development world) I remember having a life-changing experience. I watched the documentary *Dark Days*, which changed my perception of documentaries forever and was my favorite film for a very long time. I would talk to everyone and anyone about it.

But what made the most significant change in my career? After all it's unusual to move from scripted and fiction development to non-fiction; often it's the other way round, if at all. So after being freelance in the US for three years, I had a period of time where I was waiting for my work visa and couldn't be contracted for any paid employment. As a short commercial filmmaker I offered my services for free to a large non-profit organization, and there I found the story of my first feature film, *Musicwood*.

I'd like to give a moment of pause here to reflect on that a little bit. I moved from my normal working environment (in the media) to a new experience, which meant I was also stuffing envelopes for this nonprofit and that's when

I found my story. There is a reason that John Berger's book *Ways of Seeing* is so popular: we all have our own vision; that comes from our own experiences and everyone is in different places of opportunity. I was once told by a brilliant comedy writer that he would often take a break from his writing world and do something completely different. Once he taught basketball for a high school. Story ideas often come to you when you're off experiencing something else entirely not just stuck in the process of production all the time. Make sure to make those opportunities in your life and get out and meet those amazing characters or make room to hear their stories.

The production and making of *Musicwood* took five years. Don't balk at that figure as I was working on other projects, on other TV documentaries throughout that time. And we were following a story, a story unfolded for the characters over that period of time.

I was told many times that after production ends, and you've finished the edit of the film, the work doesn't end there. As a novice feature filmmaker I don't think I understood quite what meant, and it would have been really useful if I had fully comprehended that statement. This book aims to fill in those gaps. It will give you a full and detailed journey from early research through to production, editing and distribution. I needed this book when I was making my film and I couldn't find one out there that wasn't a tome and too heavy to carry around with me all the time. A book that would take me through the "whole" journey. All the steps from budgeting, funding, production through to distribution. So much of our time is spent raising funds for our films, that I deliberately provide a lot of details in that chapter of the book.

So how did this book come about? I am an avid note taker – notes, notes, notes, on backs of envelopes, on the back of my hand, on scraps of scraps. And I keep every one of them, every word of advice, every film festival panel I attended, every consultation I paid for, every book I read and every film I analyzed. This book is a distillation of all of my notes, which I see as cheat-sheets in a way. As long as I knew that I had checked off and checked in with all of these notes, I would be ok. And then my Producer thought someone else might benefit from these notes, other novice filmmakers, perhaps you?

I wrote two articles with my producer for the great film website *IndieWire* about what I'd learned. So this book is really a continuation of these articles. Of course, there are books out there that do a much more detailed job and in-depth analysis of documentary "making." Books that I have dipped in and

Introduction xi

out of all the time, like Sheila Curran Bernard's *Documentary Storytelling* and Michael Rabiger's *Directing the Documentary*. They are thorough, thick and film-saving books: read them.

I'm thinking of this as a companion of sorts to those books, as a brief and focused reference for practical advice, the kind of advice I would have loved to have been given while making my film.

Also, the only reason I have all of these notes in the first place is that the documentary community is amazing. I have to thank some of the best directors and editors in the world who met with us and sent us their scripts and gave us amazing advice in the production of *Musicwood* and afterwards.

I am lucky enough to live and work in New York City and hence have been able to meet with many of the contributors to the "In Conversation With section" of the book. We chat with the generous Kat Vechio of Fork Films, Debra Zimmerman of Women Make Movies, Justine Nagan of POV, Raphaela Neihausen of DOC NYC and Pam Torno of ITVS Digital. What a great list of fabulous film women.

I also want to thank the fantastic editor Matt Hamacheck who kindly reviewed my analysis of his editing of *Cartel Land*, the brilliant lawyer Chris Perez whose section on "Fair Use" is the best advice you can get. And I can't ignore Marshall Curry for his kind words about *Musicwood* that really encouraged us back when we were making the film. Surround yourselves with those people whose work you respect. And then all of our amazing Kickstarter supporters and funders (thank you Patagonia) who make most of our films possible.

For the purposes of this book, in each chapter, I will outline the practical information I think you'll need and that I used for my last film. I use *Musicwood* as a case study to analyze (it's available on iTunes and Amazon if you haven't seen it). I'll let you know what we did that worked, what didn't work so well and what I would do differently next time.

Musicwood is an adventure-filled journey, a political thriller with music at its heart. We follow an unusual band of the most famous guitar-makers in the world (Bob Taylor of Taylor guitars, Chris Martin of Martin Guitars and Dave Berryman of Gibson Guitars) as they travel together into the heart of one of the most primeval rain forests on the planet. Their mission: to negotiate with Native American loggers and change the way this forest is logged before it's too late. Enter Greenpeace, a radical environmental group, and soon all are battling over a forest that is the last of its kind on the planet.

Musicwood has had a lot of success: it screened in over 100 cities and towns, got distribution both in the US and internationally, and had a limited theatrical engagement. We screened in theaters, film and music festivals, libraries, on TV and on airplanes. We won festival awards, it was a *New York Times* Critics' Pick and was often chosen as a Critics' Choice by other outlets. We're even at 100% on Rotten Tomatoes!

But like all films, it took a ton of work to get there. *Musicwood* I have to admit is a social issue documentary and was very hard to market. But through determined perseverance, after our premiere, the film continued its life for the following four years, we're still getting royalty checks for rentals, purchases and screenings.

We dove headfirst into the deep end of feature documentary making—yes, my Producer had TV documentary experience and I had made short and hour long documentaries for various TV networks, but this experience was completely different and totally immersive. Sometimes it felt like we were barely keeping our heads above water. But don't despair, everyone feels like this and this book should help.

If someone had given me all these notes at the outset, taught me some of these practical methods, we would have made fewer mistakes, maybe the film would have been better, maybe. But then again I never think what I do is that great, but that's what keeps all of us hungry to learn more and push ourselves, it's the artists Achilles heel.

As novice filmmakers we learned to doggy paddle and eventually swim; we refined our style and technique as we went along. I can say I am now really happy with the film we made.

Think of these notes as your own personal inflatable water wings: if you're learning to swim in the documentary deep end, these are here to help keep you afloat. So let's dive in!

1

Research: Choosing Your Story

Filmmaking is hard. Know that, recognize it, you are about to embark on a process that you will be committing much of your free time. But, it is the most rewarding work I have ever done. I love the Sean Penn quote, "If it doesn't end up on screen it will end up in you." For many of the films I have made I have as many stories to tell about them.

It's not only a journey of making a film; it will have a profound effect on your life too. So why have you chosen the story you are about to tell? Will it be a story you will remain passionate about for years to come? Is there a story to follow, where things change over time? Can you imagine talking to everyone you know about it? Have you already started? These are all good questions to ask yourself before you start embarking on your film journey. Your why, your need, to make the film, and why should it be you.

My why for *Musicwood* was no one was telling this Native American story that was so shocking and surprising, and I was the only one who had access and was willing to give these people a voice. Was it some white colonial guilt that I was itching, making recompense, maybe, mixed in with being always interested in stories about the underdog. Peppered with being very passionate about rain forests, and this huge rain forest in America that no one knew about. And then there is music and fine craft making. Meditative, magical, full of drama and surprise, with a tremendous backdrop. I was in.

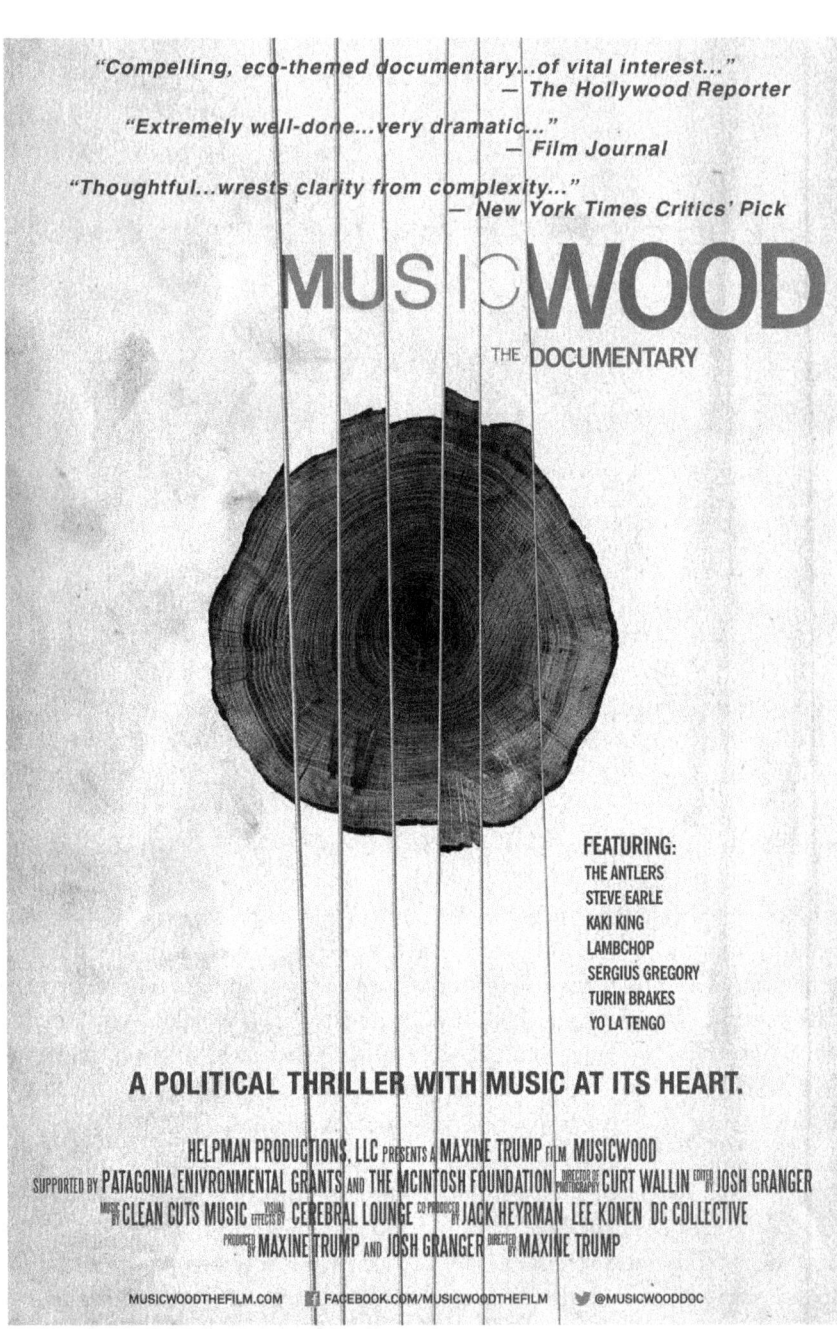

FIGURE 1.1 *Musicwood* theatrical poster

I once heard Kristen Johnson (cinematographer and acclaimed director of *Camera Person*) talk about the three needs of filmmaking. The need of the person that is being filmed, the need of the person taking the image, and the third need, of those who will be watching these images. All great needs to be conscious of when beginning your research journey, you need all three if you want your film to be seen. The third being just as important as the first and second.

Then what about the first need, the characters themselves, the people in your film. Do they have struggles? Do they want something badly and are actively pursuing it? The adage is very true of "character is action" and "drama is conflict." You may have to start developing skills where you can tell if a character has charisma. Is there something you can like about them (because you will be spending months of your life with them)?

The filmmaker Robert Greene told Tribeca Film festival that he looks for characters who have layers to their personalities or performative qualities. The director Jesse Moss talks about finding subjects who are natural performers, but also conflicted characters who have strong contradictions and impulses. But the key word is "natural" performers; be careful of people lighting up just for the camera—you don't want actors in your documentaries unless of course there is a reason for it.

Other filmmakers won't pick up the camera until they've hung out with their characters first. Yet others will do it straight away. Ramona Diaz does test shoots, even filming in moments of silence. Diaz told Tribeca that she considers how characters handle silence as very telling and unpredictability is key. Will your characters surprise you? Chris Hegedus talks about the optimal character being the person who is often risking all to pursue a dream.

Don't be put off in telling a difficult story. Research the best material, or best contact, that will make the best film. Go to secondhand bookshops, research online articles, of course, but you'll be surprised what you find from browsing, in libraries, that's how the hugely successful Netflix documentary series Wild Wild Country came about, from researching in libraries. Watch all the videos you can find on the subject—anything that can help inform you about the story you are trying to tell. Talk to people on the phone, be as informed as possible, but don't be afraid to ask people what they think, or how they can help, or whom they might know. With the best research you will be armed with the easiest access points to your story.

4 Research: Choosing Your Story

With our last film *Musicwood* we found characters that we thought would be the people we would follow but they then led us to better characters with more impactful stories. They had more extreme personality traits, or had the most to lose, or the most to gain. So be flexible and listen to your gut instinct; we're all individual and we may be drawn to different subjects for different reasons—that's why there are so many different films out there.

With *Musicwood*, it was going to be a difficult story to navigate: filming in a remote location with inaccessible characters like CEOs of huge US corporations, Native American tribes, tough-as-nails loggers and radical environmentalists.

Heads of companies or CEOs can often be the most media trained, so be aware of that when thinking of following their story. They may not offer the character revelations on camera that make for exciting films. We were lucky in that the head of Taylor Guitars for example, had built his guitar company from scratch. Had so much charisma, was a musician himself but also made himself available to us when we needed to film. Rare for a founder, CEO or president of a company.

As a female white British filmmaker, I hadn't picked the easiest of stories to tell. A Native American story that brought my own white woman guilt and colonial ancestry to the table. I made sure to reach out to the Native American Museum and other tribal members that weren't associated with a Native American corporation and asked them to be on my advisory board. We brought on a consultant from one of the tribes early on in production. If we were fully funded at that time, we would have made sure to have a member of production also Native American. We used contacts to make introductions rather than reaching out to the tribes themselves, so there could be a level of trust from the beginning.

Some of our experts in forest ecology were very nervous about the film we were making. They would take a phone call, give me material, or lead us to a great contact but then would quite vehemently tell us our film was a mistake as it could adversely affect this threatened forest. I read a ton of books on the issues presented in *Musicwood* before I approached specialists on the subject. This way, I didn't sound like a complete idiot on the phone, and I could express knowledge about the issues. I think this definitely did win over a number of people who were hesitant to talk to us.

Later, when the film was finished, some of these same initial skeptics sent us wonderful emails, telling us it was the best film they had ever seen on the area. That felt amazing.

Remember as you're researching stories or "casting" characters you are not only building trust with these people but they might become the best patrons for your film, word of mouth is often the best way to get anyone to watch your film, so treat everyone with respect. Whether they will be your antagonist or protagonist in your film.

It can be hard if you are making a film in another country or another state to meet with a character before you shoot. If someone hasn't recommended them, if you haven't spoken on the phone with them (which would be incredibly rare) or there are no you tube interviews with them on camera then make sure to fly in early and meet with them before shooting. They may have a great phone voice, but are shy in person and unbearably shy in front of the camera.

You also never want to agree to payment for any participation in a documentary film. The characters will feel compromised and because you are paying them they may very well only tell you what they think you want to hear. It won't be authentic and you may experience editorial problems because the information isn't factual.

I like to learn by my mistakes, or at least be prepared for the situation happening again. I like to interview in situ, in the environment that the character dwells in. I say "dwell" rather than "work" or "live" because then it's open to interpretation, what environment best emulates who your character is everyday or the role they play in your film. Because whatever appears in the shot will be read symbolically by the audience. So if for whatever reason you can't control the environment, carry some duvetyne (black material that absorbs light, so doesn't show wrinkles) and clips with you so that you may be able to dress a set quickly. This isn't ideal but if you've had a character that is integral to your film but hard to pin down maybe this is the perfect solution. It keeps the background neutral but black. Not the best backdrop color but if this is the only chance to interview this subject, that you have tried hard to secure then maybe this is your only option. There are also seamless papers that you can purchase, but they are bulky and heavy and not easy to carry.

My favorite films for in situ interviews happen to both be films that involve teenagers: *Rich Hill* and *Racing Dreams*. The directors filmed in the teenagers' bedrooms, in the streets where they hang out, underneath bridges, while they're smoking, etc. It really gives you a flavor of who the characters are just by the location and what is in the scene.

Marshall Curry talked about casting for *Racing Dreams*; he spent time with a lot of children before deciding on the three characters he would follow. When casting he would ask them questions about anything else but what he needed for the film to get a sense of their character, bearing in mind they *are* the film. He would ask questions like: Is their bedroom tidy? or What do they think of God?

And remember sound. Especially in locations. If you want to film scenes externally in South East Alaska (where *Musicwood* takes place), sea planes are very popular and they make a lot of noise; so do boats. You may have gone to the location to scout in the early evening but what happens at 11am in the morning when you're trying to film? Are you on a flight path? Is there construction?

ARCHIVE OR THIRD PARTY MATERIALS

Research can also include trying to secure third party materials—that is, any material not owned or shot by you. We explore Fair Use and copywriting etc. in more detail later in the book. When you begin casting characters or speaking to your experts you may begin to start building a research bank of media they have, can send you (or where you might find it) and who owns it.

Start creating a clearance log sheet (see Figure 11.1) and see if they can send you the material straight away. One filmmaker takes a scanner with him to his interviews so that there is no need to chase photos etc., as it can be an arduous process.

If you think you need media from a TV network archives they may have a minimum duration, I had a quote for one piece of archive that would cost US$1,500. An expensive line item in your budget so are there creative solutions you can use that might be the ephemera of the story? What was the weather like that day? Where are we? How are we feeling at this point of the film?

An archive producer can definitely negotiate better rates for you if you do need that certain clip as they have relationships with these libraries. And don't forget many libraries provide archive material for free—National Archives, Congress—if they are owned by the government. What about government departments like NOAA (National Oceanic and Atmospheric Administration)? They provided me with some amazing submersibles footage. If your film is heavy on archive it may be worth spending a day at these libraries in DC. Embassies, The Federal Reserve, President libraries—if you tell them you are conducting research they tend to be more approachable. And at the end of the day it might be cheaper to use a graphic designer and maybe create your own text headlines or simple, low cost, motion graphics.

If there is some great archive online that you can download that gives credence to your argument in the film then that can possibly allow you to use it for free if used correctly. See the chapter regarding "Fair Use" for details (Chapter 11).

2
Pre-production

I want to start this chapter with some advice, something that filmmakers often overlook: if you want an audience, you have to think of your audience. Now that I work as a consultant, I see filmmakers neglecting to think of this all the time. What do I mean by that? I mean think about who you're trying to reach. Michael Moore believes that you should never forget that you are entertaining people. I often think of someone who works for Greenpeace; they don't necessarily want to come home and in their own time turn on a film about forest destruction unless there is a surprising and startling story behind it. If you are passionate about an issue think about how you can tell a story to make people care. This doesn't mean you can't be creative, but with feature documentaries we're trying to get our work widely seen. With short documentaries you have more ability to not work within limitations, and that can be their inventive beauty. I'm not saying box yourself in with your feature, but do consider where you want it to go, and that will help with funding.

INSPIRATION/EARLY ANALYSIS AND PREP

Marc Singer's 2000 film *Dark Days* was the film that made me want to make documentaries. His black-and-white photography, extraordinary characters and access, and DJ Shadow-written score made for a documentary that was extremely cinematic. I honestly don't think I had seen a theatrical documentary before. It set me on a path of seeking out documentaries that were exciting, electrifying, absorbing, thought provoking and as cinematic as possible.

So when it came time to make *Musicwood*, my Producer and I constantly analyzed documentaries that we loved. We watched them over and over, in pre-production, during production and while in the edit. We broke them down scene by scene, and examined what tricks they used to make their films come alive. For us, any of Marshall Curry's or Amir Bar-Lev's films were good places to start; you probably have your own favorites. We watched many films, and thoroughly analyzed three (*If A Tree Falls*, *The Pat Tillman Story* and *Daughter from Danang*, in case you're curious). I mean we got the scripts, annotated them and even loaded the films into an editing program timeline to manually diagram the cuts and music and VO (voice over)—anything to really see how these excellent films were structured.

Try to think of the tone of your film when in pre-production as that will really dictate how you will work. How do you want the film to look? Are there special techniques involved (animation, graphics, recreations)? Whose POV (point of view) will it be from? How will it *feel*?

If you can really identify the major plot points of the story you want to tell, it will help you to define the most important aspects of filming your documentary.

But what is a plot point or story beat? I can best describe this by any element of a story that puts pressure on your character.

When we break down the story structure of *Cartel Land* later in the book (Chapter 10), you will even see how finding out someone is a father is a plot point because where it is placed in the story puts pressure on our character. If we find out a character is unsafe for example, we care even more in the next scene if we find out he has three young children. Or if he's fighting a drug war and find out later that he was an addict himself.

With *Musicwood*, it was hard to plot the storyline because the story really changed direction as time went on (this is true of many documentaries). There was also much we didn't know; for example, the complex history of the Native Alaskan Corporation or how this corporation had fought *against* environmental protections for their land. However this could be found out easily by taking time to research, conflicts already existed in the story. We decided to start our film when a new piece of the forest (in protected areas) contentiously was possibly going to be made available to log.

At one point, we were told by a biologist that it was easier to get environmental protection standards agreed with oil corporations, in Alaska, than to get them from the Native Corporation featured in our film; we're not sure if this is true but the passionate comment made an impression. We heard incredible stories from other biologists who constantly lived in fear, had their cars destroyed, had been bullied and even shot at for their published reports.

This helped give us a full and detailed backstory for some of our characters before we met them. Which really helped us think of scenes. Also the more time you spend with your characters the better idea of whether these are people you believe and trust. What struggles and obstacles do they have? Start mapping out scenes you want to capture that can express these moments that will reveal character.

Write a synopsis of the film you want to make, or the story you think you are telling. This can be a half page and is a short explanation of what you will putting on screen (roughly about 500 words is often the length grant proposals expect, longer than a logline). Or maybe write a more involved treatment of roughly two pages long. This will help you really understand how you will tell the story. Who are the characters? How will you show us their struggles? What locations will you take us to? How will the scenes make us feel? What does your protagonist want? Who will they meet along the way that will aid or abet them on their journey.

Here is our synopsis example for *Musicwood*:

> The Musicwood *documentary follows a Coalition of the world's foremost guitar-makers (Martin, Gibson, Taylor, Fender) as they attempt to save the old-growth trees of Alaska's Tongass National Forest, the largest contiguous coastal rain forest in the world.*
> *To do this they have had to drop their competitive differences, unite as the* Musicwood *coalition and travel to Alaska to deal with the largest*

privately owned logging company in the area, Sealaska. A logging company of Native Americans who have been in the area for 10,000 years. Native Americans who've notoriously been given a raw deal from the US government. So cultures will clash. To get them to change won't be easy, as it's their livelihood that's also at risk. "It will be as close to a miracle as we are likely to see in our lifetime." — Chris Martin, CEO Martin Guitars.

So the stakes are high.

At risk is the heart and soul of the acoustic guitar ...

the fate of a rare forest ...

and the survival of our world itself.

Musicwood is the story of a journey, the building of a relationship that will cross boundaries and prejudices in an attempt to solve an issue that affects us all. We join the Musicwood Coalition on their journey to Alaska and go behind-the-scenes in their negotiations. As we watch the cutting down of 700 year-old Spruce trees to make baby diapers in China, we hear how important these trees are to people that live in the forest. It is a rare chance to hear the Native American perspective, the film documents the guitar-makers' struggle to build a relationship with the Native Americans that acknowledges the injustices of their past, but fights to preserve the forest for the future.

Featuring exclusive performances with some of the most exciting acoustic musicians of the day, Musicwood gives the guitar and the forest its own voice. The footage of the forest is breathtaking as is the craftsmanship of guitar-making that we have filmed at the famous workshops

Musicwood is an ecological investigation, a cultural history and an adventurous journey to the heart of a primeval forest. It is a hopeful story of CEOs becoming activists, a story about music that may build a bridge across a centuries old divide, and help protect the largest coastal temperate rain forest in the world.

Although the forest destruction is an important topic, we wouldn't have made the film if we didn't have Famous Guitar CEOs fighting to save it. We made a film about forest destruction multilayered and exciting, full of characters because trees can't speak for themselves.

For an example of a good synopsis check out the HBO documentary website and read about any of their documentary films. The synopsis will really tell you what you will see, not the history of the story or the issue that is the undercurrent of the whole premise of the film. I have seen too many treatments that are just a history of what happened and why the story exists. Not what is the story we are going to see on screen.

Preparing a synopsis or treatment will help you define your story and will eventually have multiple uses for raising funds, applying to festivals and as marketing material. Maybe save it on Google docs, keep revising and revising until the film is what you want it to be.

Many filmmakers prepare shooting scripts. It is reported that Jessica Yu, who makes both fiction and non-fiction, brings her scripted sensibility to her documentaries and pre-scripts her films, as do Stan Neumann and Patricio Guzman. Guzman states that having a plan allows you to surrender to what you encounter. I know this rings true for me personally: if I script or more often with my features make a beat sheet, I know I have the major plot points and shots covered in that scene, and then if something better comes along when I'm in the field then I can analyze the strength of replacing shooting that scene for this new and possible stronger and more exciting dialogue and shots. Essentially giving me the confidence to drop some shots or locations for this new and better action.

With short documentaries, I help my students prepare a shooting script. Imagining what people will be telling you in scenes, what vérité you may capture that will reveal a plot point is all supremely useful. Not only for the story arch but when planning schedules for shoot days. The scripts I prepare for clients have two columns, on one side you will have the video column and on the other the audio column. This video column allows you to imagine what the best action or location could be for certain dialogue. It will help then to start building a shot list to capture those moments. And the audio column will enable you to think of the questions you might be asking your characters to enable you to capture a response that is similar. You can then start preparing shot lists and interview questions as separate documents. Ask yourself: What questions can I ask to reveal that answer, to hit that story beat or plot point? See the production chapter on questions etc. (Chapter 5).

Take a look at this pre-production shooting script for a short documentary "Trumps Against Trump" which appears on YouTube (www.youtube.com/watch?v=cfsbSoRkmxQ).

Video	Audio
GFX title card reads Trumps Against Trump	Music comes in
Maxine to camera, Maxine shows birth certificate	*Maxine*: "My name is Maxine Trump, here's my birth certificate to prove it, in case somebody would argue otherwise."
Maxine EXT outside Trump building with name of building in shot	"It used to be ok seeing my name everywhere, when Donald Trump was just a TV celebrity, but now it's just embarrassing."
Someone walks into frame asks Maxine a question	*Person on street*: "If you're a Trump you must be voting Trump?"
Maxine	*Maxine*: "Nope."
INT Maxine to camera in office	"And his campaign team assume I'm voting Trump."
Turn camera around to crew in shot	"So with the help of my crew I'm going to see if other Trumps have the same problem."
Crew saying hello	*Crew*: "Hello"
Close up of computer search of Facebook names	*Maxine:* "All the Trumps in New York seem related to Donald Trump."
Maxine in MS phone call to Fred Trump	"Is Fred there?" *Fred*: "Nope...you can contact his son Donald Trump."
Wide shot Maxine picks up her cat while at computer	*Maxine*: "He can't grab my pussy."
Maxine looking at Facebook, on screen reads Rebecca Trump (no relation)	"So here's one...that even has 'no relation' in her Facebook title."
EXT UNION SQUARE meeting other Trumps. Maxine walks in, camera follows to reveal other Trumps.	"Hi, I'm Maxine Trump."

(Continued)

14 Pre-production

(Continued)

Video	Audio
Other Trump	*Rebecca*: "Hi I'm Rebecca Trump."
Maxine	*Maxine*: "Why did you have to put 'no relation' against your name on social media?"
Rebecca Trump (younger woman)	*Rebecca*: "Because I couldn't escape from the people contacting me because of my name."
Maxine to Fred Trump	"So how is it to be called Fred Trump?"
Fred Trump (older white man)	*Fred*: "I had to change me telephone number and go ex-directory…"
Maxine to Rebecca and Fred	*Maxine*: "In the UK to Trump means to fart."
All Trumps gathered with placards	Everyone makes fart noises
Maxine asking other Trumps that have arrived	*Maxine*: "Are you voting Trump?"
Other Trump	*Trumps*: "Nope"
Maxine writing sticker	*Maxine*: "Want to wear a sticker?"
Other Trump	*Other Trump*: "I'm worried about even wearing the name."
Maxine sitting with placards at their feet, with general public looking at them	*Maxine*: "A friend suggested people would love a 'punch a Trump' booth."
Fred holds sign that reads "punch a Trump"	atmos
Other Trump	*Other Trump*: "I don't think that's a good idea."
All Trumps walk streets of New York with their placards. Arrive at Blair Trump's office, talk black guy, he meets them.	*Blair*: "Hi I'm Blair Trump"
Maxine to Blair Trump at his office	*Maxine*: "You know there's only 100 Trumps in New York State, it's a really rare name, so we're probably related."

(Continued)

Video	Audio
Blair Trump response	*Blair*: "Yep that's what's worries me."
All trumps gathered with signage	*All Trumps*: "We're all Trumps but this election day WE'RE NOT voting Trump. Join Us. Trumps Against Trump."

If you have watched the short documentary on youtube you will notice how different the film became *after* production and in the edit, but the tone and much of the script remained the same. Even when filming under stressful circumstances with protesters surrounding the crew, I felt calm knowing I was getting everything I had imagined this film to be.

Another reason I prepare scripts is for clients for my short form work. Of course capturing hours and hours of vérité would be wonderful but you may not have the luxury of time to do that with all of your characters or for the budget the client has given you. Either you have budget restraints or your character can't give you that access—see earlier regarding CEOs etc.

You may find this too onerous a process to script all your feature scenes and it may make you feel too constricted. I definitely didn't script all my scenes for my feature, absolutely not, but I would often note plot points of what I hope to get from the scene, if interviews these plot points often became the questions. Your script will not be the one you shoot due to circumstances when out in the field, or edit, but it is a plan, a great outline to know you have a story. Sam Pollard (editor, director and producer) talks about the production of three films: the one you conceive, the one you shoot, the one you edit.

So after your research you might now know who your characters are in your film, the protagonist or antagonist, but how can you express that to the audience on camera? How can they come alive?

It was very hard to not tell *Musicwood* from a biologists POV, that a valuable and unique old growth forest was being destroyed. But would an audience come to that film? Would they see a surprising story that they hadn't heard before? Tonally we did know that we wanted the film to be part drama, part adventure film. We wanted it to feature BBC-wildlife-style beauty shots of the gorgeous landscape. These were the major elements of the story that we identified before production that we felt were dramatic and unique:

1. GUITARS CEOs—The disappearance of guitar trees available for guitars in the Tongass forest in less than 10 years; all guitars are made from Spruce from that one area. SHOCK The guitar company CEOs banded together, dropped competitive differences, to travel together to convince loggers to practice sustainable logging. UNIQUE ACCESS Guitars are still made in North America.
2. THE TONGASS FOREST—Primeval forest, some of the largest trees left in the world. Last supply of guitar wood in the USA. No doc ever made on Tongass forest, beautiful incredible landscape that very few people have seen. FOREST NEVER SEEN BEFORE ON CAMERA
3. MUSIC EMOTION—Film intimate performances, the music makes us care, accessible, music builds bridges. EMPATHY
4. NATIVE TRIBES—Complicated cultural values. A tribe is not a corporation; they use corporations and not reservations in Alaska. They have over-logged their supplies too quickly and too soon, the corporation has not protected the land. AFFECT CHANGE—Vital now to find a solution before huge old-growth trees are lost forever. Raise consumer awareness for sustainable purchasing of wood.
5. SHOCKING AND UNEXPECTED that Native Americans could allow this to happen. How and why? CONFLICT between members.

If we were going to do our job properly the need to affect change would be subtle and only expressed by what our characters were doing. We did not want to use narration; we wanted to make the film as cinematic as possible by using vérité or the characters in situ interviews telling us the story. Narration can make the film less cinematic because you have someone telling you information as opposed to seeing it play out on screen.

It was also important that we didn't express only one point of view that it wouldn't come across as propaganda and turn off an audience. Shades of grey and unclear heroes and villains makes an audience want to figure out the story for themselves. It is immersive viewing; audiences will then watch actively as opposed to passively. Making the film much more enjoyable.

We decided in our initial pre-production discussions that we wanted to make a difference with this film, we actually hoped relationships were building. But we knew this would be fraught with conflict and be a delicate balance and could break apart at any time.

Having music performances was integral in trying to craft a film that had music at its heart. Hearing the voice of the guitar would bring moments of reflection in pacing, and we hoped this eco thriller would have many moments of beauty that were visual and aural.

My mantra was the audience will come to the film caring about the guitars but they will leave caring about a forest. Just show them; don't tell them how to feel. I think we eventually managed this—see what you think when you watch the film. So yes creating change was important, but more important to us was to get people to watch the film and get amazing reviews to encourage more people to watch the film.

Sheila Curran Bernard draws attention to tips from the screenwriters David Howard and Ed Mabley in her book *Documentary Storytelling*. I gave the tips an acronym (WEEED) to make it easier for my students (and myself) to remember when interrogating whether a story is worth telling—and, yes, it does have three Es

David and Ed's tips are that the film:

- ▶ should be about someone, or something, for which we have some **Empathy**.

- ▶ shows that somebody **Wants** something badly

- ▶ is something **Difficult** otherwise there is no tension

- ▶ is told for maximum **Emotional** impact

- ▶ tells a story that must come to a satisfactory ending, with our characters **Evolving** in some way.

How many characters should be in your film? Too many characters and the audience will lose track; too little and who is your protagonist rallying against? Which characters have the potential to evolve or transform in some way? Who are starting with the most extreme views and may have the most distinct narrative arcs and possibly transformation, in that they have changed position or altered in some way by the end of the film?

If a universal theme (that all audiences can connect with) is central to your film, for example hero's hubris, or sibling rivalry or maybe the corrupting force of power, it can make the film reach a bigger audience. How can you offer your own unique twist to these themes? They are central to the culture we live in, and have existed for centuries, from Shakespeare's plays to Greek mythologies, and they still work today.

Your protagonist may have a goal of saving a forest but you're also examining the power of the Western influence of capitalism on native tribes. Cowboys against Indians, bringing the age-old story of the white men against Native Americans to the present day with a surprising twist to that story. I never thought I would be making a film where you can feel like you're routing for white male CEOs against Native Americans.

Where does your story begin? What makes your character want to go on a journey, what has happened to motivate them to act. Or rather the inciting incidence of your film, what began our journey—was Greenpeace getting CEOs on a boat together. The train, or action, of the film was saving the forest (and can it be saved). The theme, or thesis was how corporations have infiltrated Native American culture.

By being very sure of the train of your film, the action that moves the film forward will help you to keep your film focused. And helps you analyze whether your protagonist has obstacles that get in the way of their goal and pressures the character into action. You have a sense of the stakes, an escalating sense of urgency, discovery and relevance. Good stuff. All strong story elements that will let you know you have a story that can be dramatic and hold an audience's attention. If there isn't a hard goal to achieve, then where is the drama? *Musicwood* was a character-led story.

As the documentary professor and author Michael Rabiger states: "Documentaries are stories that organize events that pressure characters towards a revelatory purpose." I couldn't say it better myself; that statement is going up on the wall in my office.

EQUIPMENT

What cameras are you going to use? Small cameras with great lenses like Kristen Johnson (*Camera Person* DP) who doesn't own her own camera? These days camera equipment changes so quickly, so check in with your camera operator or cinematographer about which camera they prefer to use or have experience of. The Canon C300 (which Matt Heineman used on *Cartel Land*) is a more robust camera, larger and more stable, and possibly offered Matt some protection filming in such dangerous situations.

Smaller DSLRs will give you the opportunity to get more intimate access to your characters, because they can easily forget a camera is there and the more agile your camera operator, or yourself, can be. But they are less stable and micing up subjects with lavs, at the time of writing, is not synched with the camera. Thankfully the editing software, premiere, can handle the plural-eyes sound synching process well. But consider all of this in pre-production, especially if you are shooting yourself.

Sound—are you going to put a lav on your main character at all times, and then make sure you stay close to the action, within 3 feet or so, so the on-camera mic can pick up conversations? (Jesse Moss shot the wonderful *The Overnighters* film in this way.) Or will you always have a shooter and sound person?

All of these considerations could change what you see and hear on screen so think about them carefully.

3

How to Choose Documentary Genres

In pre-production you've taken time to consider not only your point of view about the film you are making but how best to tell your story which may govern what genre of film you want to make. Let's consider the creative approach of different films here.

In fiction films it can be easier to determine the genre of film you make because, as the author Neil Gaiman states, fiction genres have certain things that have to happen. A western has to have horses; a gangster film, crime; sci-fi, spaceships. But this isn't always so easy to define in non-fiction filmmaking. Do we even need to categorize? I think at times it's helpful, helpful to search for and analyze successful films like your own that can only make your film better.

The audience and film reviewers tend to like to classify a story to understand the Director's subject and approach and find films we enjoy. As Documentarians we can still be making the fiction genre type of film—i.e. a buddy film, crime drama or coming of age story—but we can go further and apply genre terms that can help us analyze our own process. How do we make our film? What style of filmmaking will we utilize? What will be the best method and approach? Are we going to be in our own films. Will it be narrated? These questions makes us consider the best way to tell our story.

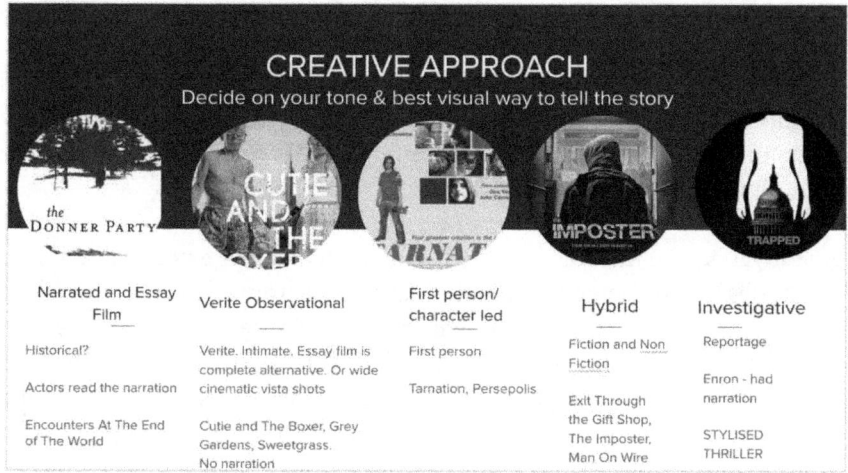

FIGURE 3.1 Creative approaches

Genre terms are guides, a classification of types to help rather than hinder your creativity. There are no real absolutes and genres can be merged and adapted. Often the best documentaries are hybrids of a few. So don't feel you have to make your film fit neatly into any one. Don't put up those false walls around your creativity. There are other boundaries or rules worth exploring, but not these.

There is a huge breadth of genres of documentary. The American film critic and theoretician Bill Nichols believes there are six genres and gives definitive terms to the types of films I have shown in Figure 3.1. This list isn't exhaustive, and my students and I often discuss types that don't fit neatly into these categories as shown in Figure 3.1—hybrid, for example, or could there be another genre called reflective, as opposed to reflexive? But would reflective films sit in the Essay film genre? Yes, if they're narrated. There could definitely be more examination and theoretical discussion about documentary genres; there could be a whole book on the subject (maybe my next one?), and the landscape moves so swiftly and is so exciting that you should make sure you look out for blog articles and essays on the subject. Look at the great blogs and magazines such as *IndieWire*, *No Film School* and *Film Independent*.

As there is so little written on the Essay genre, and (in my opinion) as it can be the hardest type of film to make entertaining, here we will examine this genre in depth. However, we will discuss a number of genres to help define our films.

Participatory films which are often character led. These often include interviews and first-person story telling accounts. The films of Errol Morris, Amir Bar-Lev, Marshall Curry and Laura Poitras are good examples. The film critic Richard Brody believes "All Documentaries Are Participatory Documentaries" (*The New Yorker*, February 27, 2015) and I would argue that most films fall under this category.

Investigative documentaries or as Nichols calls them, **Performative** documentaries are character driven films that emerge from the wants or needs of the characters. Similar to **Participatory** films but these are subjective (you could argue most films are subjective) but it is the truth as seen through the lens of the documentary maker and can be autobiographical in nature. The personal experience of the filmmaker provides the entry point with the filmmaker often addressing the spectator and audience directly. *Catfish, Gasland, Stories We Tell, Sherman's March* and *Tarnation* are all good examples. Laura Poitras's film *Risk* ended up including herself in the film, via narration only, but it then became a more personal account of Julian Assange's lead up to and asylum in the Ecuadorian Embassy (in the UK) as witnessed by the filmmaker.

By its name this film genre suggests that there maybe a performance aspect to the film, not as typical "acting" but the personal experience of the filmmaker as a participant and protagonist in their own film. The prolific Nick Broomfield and Louis Theroux straddle genres as they immerse themselves as characters in their films that *aren't* personal in nature. Not all films can be easily aligned within one genre; many use a mix of a number of stylistic choices. Michael Moore often isn't the protagonist in his own films generally so it isn't necessarily performative in nature. He is usually representing other groups of people and questioning how events happen to them and their struggles. But as Michael Moore often constructs scenes or makes events happen he sits between the **Participatory** and **Performative** genres. And many of his characters would probably say he does become the protagonist because he is their hero, fighting for their injustices.

In **Observational**—otherwise known as **Vérité** —films, the director films scenes whilst trying to *not* exert influence on the action. Drew Associates or most of Frederick Wiseman films, The Maysles, Richard Leacock and D. A. Pennebaker are lauded **Vérité** filmmakers, but you often see the characters of *Grey Gardens* (Mayles bothers) reacting to the brothers in scenes which suggests the characters also have a performative nature to the film. The secret is how to get these characters to forget the camera is even there.

There are **Reflexive** films often associated with experimental films, because the films can be as much about how they are constructed as to the film itself. I would sit **hybrid documentaries** within this category. These films can challenge the assumptions and expectations about the form itself and are rare and hard to do but when done well can be exceptional. *This Is Spinal Tap, Exit Through The Giftshop, Kate Plays Christine* and *The Imposter* are good examples of these. They often use fictionalized recreations with actors and interviews. As Nichols argues reflexive films often question the principles that underlie traditional filmmaking and social representation.

Poetic films, Nichols would say, often aren't a window onto the world but a construction or a representation of it, using tone, rhythm and juxtaposition. Godfrey Reggio's *Qatsi Trilogy*, and Ron Fricke's breathtaking *Samsara* and *Baraka* are good examples of this. Films that have no interviews, few people, few clips of any spoken language and may seem to have no defined narrative structure as we know them to be. In these examples shots of vast vistas are edited together poetically and dramatically, both in conflict and contrast, to create emotion.

Expository films use the voice of God (third person) narration and are often heavily researched with a specific argument or point of view. Historical films by Ken Burns, social commentary films by Adam Curtis, wildlife documentaries such as *March of the Penguins*, or such films as *Enron* or *The Corporation* (see the selected filmography in the Appendix) are good examples. **Expository films** often are also called **Essay films** as they aim to explain things—events, issues, ways of life, worlds and exotic settings—we know little about.

I believe Essay films and Expository films need to be known as two distinct categories, and I'll explain why. I would describe the fantastic last Al Maysles' film *In Transit* as a great Essay film, no narration or voice of God, often with interviews so not an observational documentary; it doesn't fit neatly into a category.

And what about plot-driven films, where characters are secondary to the events, i.e. events happen to the characters where they often have no control? Fictional thrillers fall into this camp—think of all the Jason Bourne films—but so do documentaries, *The Thin Blue Line* by Errol Morris, possibly *Client 9* by Alex Gibney, or *If a Tree Falls* by Marshall Curry. And what about *The Hunting Ground* by Kirby Dick, or even *Edward Snowden* by Laura Poitras? You could argue that Edward Snowden *caused* the events to happen because he leaked confidential government information. But then events pressurized him, which he had very little control. It was a feat of filmmaking to shoot Edward Snowden in captivity at an airport.

Sometimes it isn't easy to characterize a film by its genre. Participatory films will often have elements of expository and observational filmmaking but the filmmaker is an investigator—that's why I prefer to call them Investigatory; it helps me easily categorize. I feel most films fall into this category, whether the filmmaker is on screen or not.

So what type of film do you want to make? With *Musicwood* we were lucky enough to follow a story that was unfolding largely in real time. In essence, it was an investigatory/participatory film; someone called it a thriller. I prefer that definition; thriller sounds cool. It's then a known commodity, or a definition that people can understand and connects well with potential audiences. I try to use terms that can be applied to both fiction and non-fiction as we're all making "feature" films and audiences understand this terminology. We ended up calling it an adventure film, an eco-thriller with music at its heart.

Yes, it was a social issue film. You will hear this term used to refer to documentaries a lot, often used to describe films that want to create change, whether through policy, community support or awareness. With our film this was true. We especially wanted to give a minority group a voice. But we didn't want it to appear educational with any third-party narration lecturing to you. We're making films, we're making entertainment, we wanted to make a film that someone working on forestry issues every day on the front lines would come home and find enjoyable. Even the BBC has now dropped the word "education" from its mission statement.

We worked hard to eliminate all narration, to let the characters really speak for themselves so it wouldn't feel like a one-sided argument and propaganda. This is a much more cinematic form of storytelling, as it avoids the sense of a narrator espousing a particular POV. The audience then can feel an authentic reaction to what they see on screen and less like they are being manipulated by the filmmakers.

The characters' own words are leading the audience to make their own conclusions as to who are the protagonists and antagonists of the story. If done well, most of the time the film's POV is sitting in a grey area, undulating from side to side, creating empathy for one side then the other. With this structure the audience has the impression they are solving the mysteries for themselves and uncovering their own truth, and this is very satisfying.

So depending on the exact story you want to tell, you will have various options as to how to tell your story. The theme, the thesis, the questions you want to answer—all will drive you to consider the best way to tell your story.

THE ESSAY FILM

I was asked by a student to teach a class on the Essay film, as it can be the hardest type of film to edit into a dramatic structure. As with this genre of film you are not following a character on a journey with a story that unfolds.

Essay films are films that explore a theme or an issue, events, or ways of life and aren't necessarily dependent on scenes of action unfolding. But this definition is deceptively simple. As we look deeper into the Essay film, we will reveal how difficult it can be to define an Essay film or make a film in this category engaging, entertaining and cinematic. This is my essay on Essay films.

Often hour-long television documentaries (non-digital streaming films) are made as Essay films, especially in Europe where there are more outlets for these one-off documentaries. In the US, think Discovery ID shows, ESPN, Frontline and National Geographic. They have to be made quickly, can be very formulaic and may not be leading to a satisfying climax in a three-act structure unless they use investigatory reporting techniques to undercover a mystery or reach a conclusion. These TV documentaries are often made in a five-act structure to allow for advertising breaks. This structure is a very different proposition from a feature documentary. 52–54 minutes makes the TV hour and it will often have a host, investigator or narrator. You could argue that Louis Theroux makes great Essay films but they are investigatory by nature, as he inserts himself on camera, and his personality and sense of humor gives a very strong POV to his films. So again he straddles two genres and by using investigatory methods makes his film more engaging.

These should not be confused with **Non-Fiction Series**—such as *O.J.: Made in America* and *The Staircase*—which are TV series, not Essay films but more akin to true-crime dramas. You could argue **Biopics** like Al Maysles' *Iris* or all of Ken Burns' films are essay-type films. I list my favorite documentaries by genre and subject in the Appendix; it might be worth just taking a look at this list while reading this chapter to familiarize yourself with titles in different categories.

You could pick up a camera right now and begin making an Essay film on any subject you want. But how do you make a good Essay film? It isn't always easy to make a dramatic documentary if little action is happening. There is a reason a presenter or host is often used in these TV shows.

Often, a documentary will focus on one particular issue, and explore different aspects of it in depth. So are all Issue films essays, or Essay films based on issues?

Fantastic Issue Films have been made by the amazing director Kirby Dick. *The Hunting Ground* and *The Invisible War* are incredible films that indeed have an impact and bring about political change. Dick uses **character** stories to drive the **issue** to take his audience back to events that unfold in the past. One could argue these are Historical Investigatory films. Dick directs his characters to recount their stories in present tense, to make them feel very current, as these issues still exist today. Rape in the military, rape on campus, are just some hot topic issues that Dick explores.

Hearing first-person stories about horrific events injects emotion to an issue in a way that we all strive to find. Emotion drives an audience to care, and is hard to do without compelling characters. As an audience, we engage with these stories and the brave women that recount them. Dick makes you give a damn about his issues, often not expressing a counter-viewpoint. I would argue that in this case the film doesn't need to, but I also would not consider Dick's films as Essay films. They are examinations of an issue but with a very strong POV that we feel from the characters' stories.

The film critic Scott Tobias calls these films "a powerful, damning record of institutional crime. Cinema makes these stories stronger because there's drama in the telling, even when the form is simple to a fault." I've been told many times by interview subjects that they haven't talked about their story before, or "I haven't told this to anyone." We will talk later about ethics of filmmaking, but this is often how you get drama into a film that has no active-scenes. Recreation has been a solution that some directors turn to, but this is hard to do well. (see any of James Marsh documentaries for exceptional recreation). The camera picks up on human emotions in the retelling that makes these stories stronger than reading them on a page.

So what do you do if it seems like you don't have characters, because your film is about a topic, like health-care? What if your characters are more like pundit interviewees, as opposed to people we build relationships with, or whose story we are following over months or years?

When this is this case, many directors will insert themselves into the films, to make the film more dramatic. They will use their own conflict with their subject to drive the story forward. A First-Person Essay film, if you will.

Think Nick Broomfield, Michael Moore, Louis Theroux, Lisa Ling and Josh Fox. All masters of their trade. I am a big fan of these first-person documentarians but are these Essay films or investigative reportage? To me, these are fantastic exposé films that a talented investigative reporter/host/character uncovers in a Performative or Participatory film.

Morgan Spurlock wanted to examine whether fast food corporations should be deemed responsible for our bad diets. When he made *Supersize Me*, he was smart enough to add a competition structure to the film, setting up a test to see if he could maintain a healthy body while eating nothing but McDonald's food for 30 days. Who doesn't enjoy watching a competition? It brings in obstacles, challenges and struggles that wouldn't be in the story otherwise. Think of *Spellbound* or *Racing Dreams* or *Kings of Pastry* for great competition films.

Moore, Theroux and Broomfield all use different exposé techniques to make very successful films that reach a broad audience. But not all of us have the type of personality where we can easily insert ourselves into the film. Not all of us want to be in front of the camera, or maybe our subject isn't right for that genre of storytelling.

So what about the Essay films that don't use this mechanism for drama? The head of my teaching department tells students that if you find a character that is passionate about a subject, you will also often find conflict. And if you find a conflict you will find a character. Some students pick passion projects with inanimate themes, such as water, religion, or pollution, and we still strongly suggest they find compelling characters that can talk on behalf of these themes.

Ava Duvernay, Robert Kenner, Mark Achbar and Jennifer Abbott are great documentarians that make issue films. While exploring a given theme—mass incarceration, food, corporations, etc.—they will find people that are most affected by the issue and cast them as interviewees. Authors and experts are interviewed, and a point of view is very obviously represented. The phenomenal documentary *13th*, by Ava Duvernay, is the latest from these exceptional thematic issue documentarians and I argue are, Essay films.

The films made by these directors—*13th*, *Food Inc*, *The Corporation*—are structured elegantly, typically using graphics and illuminating interviews. These are thematic documentaries, and are often narrated. There is a central question to explore and an extremely strong POV in all of them. But let's consider how they are made, and the stylistic choices that make these films so successful, how do they resolve, and what are the climaxes of the films?

These films represent a very well-constructed argument and sometimes the counter-POV won't be given a strong voice, or voice at all. You could argue the work then runs the risk of being seen as one-sided, propaganda, or fighting for a cause. However, with the subjects covered and the surprising information and statistics that are delivered (and we wouldn't have heard otherwise) whether they are propaganda or not, these films have the potential to create change. So does it matter?

Scott Tobias gives a word of warning in his article for the A.V. Club concerning the Issue film *A Place at the Table*:

> [A]ll the human-interest elements in the film exist entirely to reinforce them. It's pure propaganda—well-meaning propaganda, and at times crudely effective propaganda, but nonetheless a form of cinematic activism where art is of secondary concern. For the makers of *A Place at the Table*, that may not matter.

He warns us to "avoid the stereotype of the documentary as a hearty gruel of talking heads and archival footage, spooned out as artlessly as the school lunches *A Place at the Table* criticizes."

Geoff Andrew, a senior programmer at the British Film Institute—who also helped curate the landmark 2014 Essay Film Season at the Southbank Centre in London—talks about this in depth. He thinks part of the issue is that some filmmakers try to provide an objective POV when it is just not possible. "There's always somebody manipulating footage and manipulating reality to present some sort of message," Andrew says.

The documentary producer Adam Curtis doesn't shoot any original footage, and instead uses archive footage from the BBC library to construct his films. Although no new images are shot for his films, his documentary work is known around the world. His own unique commentary, alongside the edit of these images, provides a spectacular punch and has an effect on us as viewers. Adam Curtis is usually way ahead of his time in his cultural commentary; it takes time for other media outlets to catch up with his ideology and philosophy on culture. A very definitive Expository film, he is the character of his film. Different in style from the Essay films I have listed.

Yes, the style of narration for *The Corporation* was designed to sound like a monotonal corporate voice, as if the corporation were speaking to you as a person. This is a great sound design decision. If you have seen any of the films I have been writing about so far, you may have noticed that the sound and cinematic vision for Essay films is an important framework on which to hang the rest of the film's argument and make the film effective. I am a huge proponent of sound being a very strong "voice" in a film and these films use this method of storytelling competently.

Let's take a moment to discuss wildlife films. Why wildlife films? It may sound obvious, but animals can't speak for themselves. The animals in *March of the Penguins*, *Winged Migration* and *Blackfish* had people speak for them, either through narration or a proxy, like a trainer speaking for a whale. You couldn't have a David Attenborough film without his narration.

Or what about a film that focuses on an inanimate object? A text font in *Helvetica*, or a continent like Antarctica in *Encounters at the End of the World*? As opposed to films like *13th* or *Food Inc*, the documentaries *Helvetica* and *Encounters at the End of the World* are both heavily narrated but they don't have a strong POV, choosing instead to simply dive into their subjects. What makes them good, or worth watching? The charisma of Werner Hertzog is one reason, but think more on the artistry of these films, in *Helvetica* shots were heavily designed with great art production. I was a fine art major and this background has really helped me to examine the creative approach to my films.

OK, so you don't want to make an Issue film with a one-sided POV, or use only archive or heavy narration. Can we split the Expository and Essay film into two here? The Expository has a strong POV and the Essay film may not.

Have you thought of the film you do want to make? Is it a question you want to examine? Maybe you just love sushi making in the same way Gary Hustwit must have loved Helvetica, or at least its ubiquitous use as a font. You want to find a unique entry point into this world. You wonder what keeps a sushi chef working for decades, using the same repetitive sushi-making processes? Doesn't sound exciting, but...

You start out researching sushi chefs. You find the best sushi-maker in the world, you get him to trust you enough to film in his tiny restaurant for a few weeks, follow his son and shoot some amazing scenes of craft-making of the very fine food dish of sushi.

Doesn't sound too hard? Ok, we know no film is easy but this should inspire young or new filmmakers.

The director David Gelb says his film *Jiro Dreams of Sushi* really came from his deep love of sushi. "I was watching the BBC documentary *Planet Earth* and I got to thinking that somebody should make a 'Planet Sushi' using really cool cinematography to film sushi in an artistic way."

Let's think back to *March of the Penguins*, the repetition in the penguins' behavior, how far they had to waddle to find food, how often we were gripped by that waddling. It was wonderful. We're all animals, all part of nature, and we have our patterns too.

Gelb was anticipating filming a number of sushi chefs, making a true Essay film with many characters speaking on the same theme. But when he started filming, he found he had a fantastic character, Jiro, the star of the film, who has been refining the same sushi processes for 60 years. Jiro believes it took him that long to perfect the balance of the rice and fish and a Michelin star for his restaurant. But even after 60 years, and with the best accolades in his business, he still thinks he can improve.

Now you're going to argue with me and say *Jiro Dreams of Sushi* is not an Essay film. And I'm going to say this: the more we look deeply into films, the more we will find that films rarely fit into neat categorizations. Yes, *Jiro*

Dreams of Sushi is character-led, examining the craft of sushi through the lens of a father-and-son relationship. It has a universal theme—that of a father passing on his business to his son and trying to retire his life's work. It further examines the fact that this obsession has also caused Jiro to be an absent father. It's philosophical, familial and doesn't have a huge character arc; the audience only feels a small transformation in Jiro's character by the end of the film.

When Jiro finally comes out from behind the counter of his restaurant, and takes off his chef's whites, Jiro's countenance changes and you see a physical transformation when he laughs and smiles and becomes human. But I think you're also intrigued as to what keeps this person so engaged with his work, so meditative in repeating the same process again and again and again.

The term *Shokunin* is used by Jiro. According to one Japanese dictionary, it means worker, mechanic, artisan craftsman. Jiro expands on this term in the film, saying it is the repetition of processes that never change, that bring you to a higher level of craftsmanship, or mastery. One who is more concerned with perfection of his or her craft than with money. David Gelb did a great job to make these scenes of process transcend their actions, and not feel like weak and repetitive scenes in the film. Not easy to do.

In a society where all information is at our fingertips and technological change is running at a speed that we have never known before, a return to an interest in mastering old-world skills and craftsmanship seems to be on the rise. There is no surprise that "slow TV"—programs that unfold in real time, spending 6 hours following a train journey or 12 hours following a boat arrive at a harbor—has become a fashionable form of non-fiction TV.

Gelb was introduced to Jiro Ono and spent some time building a relationship and his trust to be allowed to shoot in the tiny ten-seat restaurant (the filmmaker is also 6 feet tall). "The first few days I didn't even bring a camera with me. I just went to the restaurant to observe. I stayed out of the way as much as possible." The film was shot in several weeks, and took ten months for the edit. "I shot for the month of January in 2010, and came back to do the editing. I went back to Japan in August with a much more focused and targeted shoot to get everything else I needed."

Gelb reveals what inspired him, and not just wildlife photography but the Errol Morris film *The Fog of War*:

> [Morris's film] is mostly archive footage, but then they have all this great metaphorical B-roll footage. And the slow-motion photography and the Philip Glass music was a major inspiration for me.
>
> The editor and I began to realize that the driving, repetitive nature of Glass's music is a perfect metaphor for Jiro's work ethic. The music repeats but escalates and builds. Jiro repeats the same process every day but is always looking for that baby step forward.
>
> (PBS Blog 2012)

Gelb was moved by the personal story and Jiro's philosophy: "Here's a story about a person living in his father's shadow while his father is in a relentless pursuit of perfection" (*IndieWire* interview, March 2012).

The film started out as an examination of sushi-making but it became an intimate movie about family, legacy and the philosophy of hard work. Gelb told *Filmmaker Magazine*, "It was only in the editorial stages that I realized how much it was going to be about his family and his own personal history."

Let's now turn our attention to an Essay film that doesn't have central characters. Like Gelb's film it mirrors David Attenborough's Wildlife documentaries as an anthropological study of a region that we rarely get to see. A documentary that is an examination of the human condition choosing to spend time with and interviewing a small community of people who reside at the end of the earth.

Unlike many of his other films, director Werner Herzog doesn't "include" himself in the footage of *Encounters at the End of the World*, though we do hear his voice in the narration (it wouldn't be a Hertzog film without it). His conversational tone makes you consider the uniqueness of where he is taking you. Hertzog fills the film with his own reflections and philosophies. It's no surprise that his online master class for filmmakers sets obscure Icelandic poetry and mythology books as required reading. He has found his own extremely unique voice that is full of statements about the human condition, that works very successfully.

He provides us with a visual and aural feast all the way down at the end of the world. The whale and dolphin noises raise the soundtrack to provide us with an experiential journey. He makes you feel what it's like to be there and live among those surroundings. You hear it, you can see it, you can almost smell it, touch and taste it.

Both Gelb's and Herzog's films give a special emphasis to audio, whether soundtrack or location sound. I often play the clip of the underwater noises from *Encounters at the End of the World* to my students and it makes them intrigued to know more.

Students often ask how they can make a story in the short time they have in class. Especially if they don't feel that they have a story unfolding for a character, or a really strong POV, or an issue they want to fight for. It's a valid question, as most of the films on my best-of list took years to make. On the one hand, they're feature documentaries, long films with major narrative arcs. On the other hand, there are films by directors such as Errol Morris and David Gelb who have shot their feature documentaries in a matter of weeks. See also the film *The Work* by Jairus McLeary and Gethin Aldous, who follow three men during four days of intensive group therapy with serving convicts in a rare and powerful look into rehabilitation.

So what if my students tell me they want to make a pure Essay film that isn't examining an issue, doesn't have a strong point of view, or have a story unfolding? I would simply ask them: what is their story? Think on that for a minute. What is your story?

The next film I want to examine was shot in a small number of train trips across the USA and I would argue really is the perfect example of an Essay film.

After many months of negotiating permission with Amtrak, Albert Maysles' crew was given full access to film on the Empire Builder, Amtrak's busiest long-distance train route. The result was the fantastic documentary *In Transit*, which I would describe as a journey into the human condition.

Sometimes the characters you film may never have considered some of the themes your interview questions raise. It may give them room for the first time to analyze something that is painful to consider. They may open up in a way they haven't before because no one may have ever asked or listened to what they have to say on the matter. What a great job we have, and what an honor to be allowed into these people's lives for a short period of time. Also, what a responsibility.

In Transit allows us to enter this personal world and experience the universal themes through testimonial interviews and conversations on a three-day train trip. Train journeys often allow us the time and inclination to speak to people we may never have spoken to otherwise. I know I have had some amazing conversations on trains that I can still remember to this day.

The filmmakers had a crew that included a Story Producer and an Associate Producer. These two people would go onto the train first and begin meeting passengers and getting a sense of who might be interesting on camera, or at least willing to participate, finding their subjects spontaneously. The four to five cinematographers would then film these passengers. Talking to AFI Docs in 2015: "Sometimes we'd be able to record several hours of someone's story and sometimes we'd only have captured several minutes of footage before the passenger had to disembark at their stop," says Lynn True, the film's Producer and Editor. The film is a beautiful examination of the multitude of choices people have made in their lives, or situations that they have been thrown into, and how they've survived.

So will your film be an art film, a spiritual film, experimental or anthropological, what theme do you want to explore? You may not have a strong POV, or a character's story unfolding, but is there a literal journey being taken? There is the literal "train" in *In Transit* and the shepherd's journey in *Sweetgrass* which takes us into a world we also rarely visit, or never would have access to otherwise.

In an interview by *Gawker*'s Rich Juzwiak, Lucien Castaing-Taylor, co-director of the fantastic **vérité** film *Sweetgrass* says:

> I hate most documentaries. The moment I feel like I'm being told what to think about something, I feel that I want to resist the authority of the documentarian. We're more interested in making films that are more open-ended, that ask the spectators to make their own conclusions. We're always implicitly, if not explicitly, fighting against how bad documentary is. Documentary claims to have this privileged purchase on a truthful version of reality—it's not fiction, this is the real—but most documentaries' representation of the real is so attenuated and so discourse-based and language-based. We lie and we mystify ourselves with words. Words can only take us so far.

So many interesting points Castaing-Taylor raises here—he is not a fan of narration at all which is a primary feature on an Essay film.

It's no surprise to me that when you research Essay films, articles often mention films from the first half of the twentieth century. In 2013, the British

Film Institute retrospective of Essay films played in London's South Bank cinema, and at the Whitechapel Art Gallery. The exhibition featured works by the French artist Chris Marker, who also often narrates his films. In a BFI article, the French film critic Andre Bazin dubbed Marker's method a "horizontal" montage, "as opposed to traditional montage that plays with the sense of duration through the relationship of shot to shot…a given image doesn't refer to the one that preceded it or the one that will follow, but rather it refers laterally, in some way, to what is said." Thus the very thing which makes it "extraordinary," is also what makes it "not-cinema" according to Bazin. Marker is often called an audio-visual poet. Interesting that poetry is becoming a dominant form in this Essay film chapter, thinking back to Hertzog's reading list and own methods.

In 2014 The Whitechapel Gallery held the first UK retrospective of Chris Marker's work, describing his vivid film-essays as lacing realism with science-fiction and lyricism with politics. His influence extends across art, experimental film and mainstream cinema: his 1962 masterpiece *La Jetée* was the basis of Terry Gilliam's 1995 *Twelve Monkeys*.

But, as Bazin suggests, it would be difficult to find outlets that could distribute these films today outside of a gallery setting. I won't start a discussion here on what categorizes film as cinema or art, except to say only great blockbuster directors such as Christopher Nolan or Peter Jackson and possibly Errol Morris can encourage a movie house to show anything nearing 3 hours in length, let alone longer.

Film academic Michael Rabiger commits just three pages to the Essay film genre in his 550-page tome *Directing The Documentary*. There is no surprise that both the BFI exhibition, and Rabiger's chapter, mention films where sound is often non-synchronous, or non-diagetic, i.e. not from the images. Rabiger believes that "the unsync shooting, coupled with brilliant writing, composing and editing, can raise a screen essay to the level of a major requiem in meaning and emotion. Today the possibilities of this technique are little used." He then brings up 1931's *Night Mail*, a UK government film about a mail train. Another train Essay film, did the makers of *In Transit* know about this film, I wonder?

At the time the UK General Post Office (GPO) had a film unit made up of young artists. The composer Benjamin Britten was just 22 when he wrote the music for *Night Mail* and the poet W. H. Auden wrote original poetry for the film. John Grierson—a filmmaker rumored to have coined the term "documentary"—headed up the Unit, and commissioned work from these artists as part of an extensive rebranding exercise for the GPO.

Poets being used again and it's interesting that one of the very first documentaries that Grierson commissioned was about communication. Grierson would go on to make a major impact on the British and Canadian film industry and he helped found the National Film Board of Canada (the NFB). Its mandate was to help Canadians across the country understand the ways of life and problems of their fellow citizens.

Why watch and study other film genres? How will you know what works to move you and why? You may borrow from them all or you may, as Gelb's did, stay focused on *Shokunin*—the process that just keeps reaching for one small step of transformation. The fact that the film succeeds as well as it does should encourage us as filmmakers. Just keep doing, working, making, exploring the processes.

In the same way that Hertzog is influenced by poetry what are some of your influences other than film? Where do you go to be creatively inspired? Remember how imaginative Hustwit is, watch out for the new films *360 Hollywood* and *Memories of a Penitent Heart*. All of these films were inventive in their approach to the form.

The creative director Brett Morgen always approaches his films from his protagonist's POV. He has his characters read letters; he has animation, archive and interviews. All of his films are character-led Participatory films but he utilizes many fantastic artistic influences and cites Errol Morris as a major influence, as does Gelb.

Although I haven't yet made a pure vérité film (some filmmakers have argued that pure cinema isn't even truly possible) some of my favorite influences have been from vérité films—I've mentioned the film *Sweetgrass* earlier in the chapter—otherwise called an Observational film, not an Essay film. It does follow a group of characters over a journey. We pick up snippets of language, of the everyday shepherds on horseback, as they sit around the campfire cooking their meals. But it is also a sublime example of wonderful imagery and pacing, and long stretches of sinking into vast vistas. It should definitely be marked on your list to watch with its deep reading of the shepherd culture, a world we rarely see explored, it will come as no surprise that Lucien Castaing-Taylor is also an anthropologist.

I always go to galleries for my inspiration. The visual artist Christian Marclay explores connections between sound, noise, photography and film in his incredible piece "Clocks," using archive clips of films to show the passage of time. No connected commentary is offered; it is simply an edit of clips with sound bites, and the only connective imagery that we see on screen is time, clocks, watches, sundials. A character might mention the time, or write it in a journal as text to read or we see it on the wall for e.g. each moment the "time" is mentioned or shown it hits exactly at the same time of day the viewer is watching the film. The piece lasts 24 hours and then loops. Maybe one day The Criterion Collection could show it in its entirety on TV. The Museum of Modern Art called it a cinematic tour dé force. We can't make films that last 24 hours, unless we are considering some kind of immersive experience, or Virtual Reality (VR) or exhibition—these are all other forms of story telling that are worth exploring. At the Sundance Film Festival in 2018 for the first time, VR scored the kind of film-festival deal usually accorded to conventional movies. It's an interesting landscape for filmmakers, as is the landscape featured in the piece that got acquired called *Spheres*, set in space. As *Wired* magazine stated, for a medium that's never sold at Sundance, it's a very big deal, one that demonstrates VR filmmaking has the clout and buzz of its traditional film predecessors.

I trained as a visual artist, and my final thesis project explored identity. It was an installation, a room people would walk into where motion sensors would activate videos and projectors. These would play film and TV clips that varied dependent on the choices people made as to how they moved throughout the room. If done today, this could be done in a VR environment. No narration was involved and all was dependent on the viewer's POV. A type of Essay film, possibly, an immersive environment, definitely, entertainment…sure.

There are a lot of filmmakers working with new technology to see how it can be harnessed in the world of storytelling. Keep an eye on the cutting-edge, check it out, be inspired by the old and the new, and remember *Shokunin*.

4
Budget

While you're planning and researching your film, you should begin to put together a projected budget. It goes without saying that it will be helpful to know how much the film will cost you, but it's also an essential document for pitching and fund-raising.

We've been told an average budget for a feature documentary is around US$500K–600K, and that isn't deemed expensive. Our film cost a third of that, but read on.

FILMMAKERS' COSTS

We were also given some interesting budgeting advice from a panel of seasoned filmmakers. If a Director gets paid US$100K, the Producer fee should be US$25K, as they can typically be doing about a quarter of the work. If you are bringing an experienced Producer on board, their fee can be 2.5% of budget. But there are a number of types of Producer: they could be the Executive Financier, or others could be working hard on production aspects every day working on logistics, booking locations, etc., as they would on a TV program or commercial. So the Producer fee could be significant and will vary, and may over the length of production, become closer to the Director fee after all.

From the same filmmaker panel we were told, as a Director, never budget your own fee at more than US$200K and don't bank on it being less than a year and half of work for a feature.

PRODUCTION INSURANCE AND LEGAL

Make sure you budget for (and get) production insurance. On one shoot in Alaska, the Cameraman's bag was left behind when we left a location. (We didn't have a budget for a PA; the Producer had to produce, drive the cars, etc. Be careful of over-stretching your staff.) The bag was filled with expensive and vintage lenses, and when we went back to the location, it was gone. The equipment was worth US$90K, but we only had to pay the US$5K deductible. That was a huge relief.

You also never want to put yourself at risk while making your film. Production Insurance covers equipment and bodily risk, but what about the financial risk? The best way to avoid this is to start a production company to make the film, or what's known as an LLC. We actually already had one because we had our own small TV production company. This makes sure that if anything goes wrong with the film, or you get sued, you don't lose all your personal assets, they can't take your house or car away! If you don't have an LLC, put a line item in the budget to make one, or hire someone to make one for you. If you want to read more about personal risk as filmmakers, look at the issues and costs Joe Berlinger incurred because Chevron tried to sue him and he had to defend himself in court. The court costs alone were over US$1 million.

FINISHING COSTS

Seasoned producers often mention that finishing costs are the thing that gets forgotten by new filmmakers because they think they can raise more money later on in the filmmaking process. But this should be considered and accounted for in the full detailed budget. When you're looking at your finishing costs, remember to consider:

- ▶ whether you will be composing or licensing music
- ▶ commissioning graphics, maps, graphic lower third id's
- ▶ how you will do credits

- whether you need a 5.1 sound mix as well as stereo
- color correction.

There are a few items that will come in after the film's completion that you also shouldn't forget:

- A marketing budget for P&A (prints and advertisements). Prints used to mean film prints but think of it now as your screening copies, digital DCP, Blu-ray, etc. Advertisements means just that, money to run ads.
- Legal fees.
- Errors and Omissions insurance.
- Hiring at least one, if not two, PR firms for your premiere on whatever platform.
- Film festival submissions.
- Will you be spending time on outreach and who will do that.

EXAMPLE BUDGETS

As well as the *Musicwood* feature documentary budget I have included an example budget for a branded content documentary short. This budget was at the US$60K range and it included travel outside of New York, paying for travel costs for the crew, the Director of Photography, myself as the Director, etc. It was a branded—i.e. a sponsored 1-minute documentary that would run in a programming block on national television. The documentary also had a number of versions that were tagged at the end in voice over promoting certain show times with date and time.

It was a one-day shoot but we had a location scout which included pre-lighting the location, so we could bring in all the lights and leave them overnight for the shoot the next day. Post-production costs included color correct, sound mix and making versions of the documentary with different end tags/voice over for the different show times hence having a higher post production cost to a stand-alone commercial documentary.

Note production insurance costs, extra luggage costs when traveling, travel, accommodation, car rental, taxis and hotel internet. Per diems are a payment to crews who are away from home and production companies pay for their meals even when you have craft services on set (these are often given in cash and the crew sign a receipt). And don't forget to budget for art, set dressing, office supplies and so on.

If you are a production company then you also add, at minimum, an 8% production fee. This covers overages or can be your profit margin. A weather contingency day for bad weather would need to be discussed with the client, if you are shooting exteriors. We were shooting exteriors for half the day but it was in an area of the US where the weather was warm and fairly consistent. Georgia and Louisiana are areas of the US that at the time of writing have a great local film community, so local hires of some staff can mean a significant saving regarding travel, hotels and per diems, etc.

Note the first budget is for estimated costs. You will often be using a budgeting system called Showbiz budgeting software, but this isn't a free software system so in the interim familiarize yourself with Excel.

My Line Producer would often prepare the *actuals* (the actual money you spend and receipts that came in) in column J, so they would appear next to the *estimated costs* so you can see if you went over budget or under budget very easily. You wouldn't submit the actuals to the client; they only want to make sure you have budgeted correctly and reasonably with the estimated budget.

The Musicwood Budget

Have more than one budget for your feature documentary. Have at least one where you're not cutting corners, i.e. like your mum putting up the film crew so you don't have to pay for a hotel (yes we did that). The reason to include everything, even your own estimated costs, is to make sure that you have one budget that is realistic (even if it is a "high-ball" budget), that encompasses all of the real costs it would take to make the film, your best-case scenario. Funders will want to see that you know how to realistically budget. They want to know that you really can deliver on everything you have stated in the films description.

What equipment will you need? Are they employing a camera operator (so they may not be able to light scenes) or are they Directors of Photography? Are they documentary shooters used to running and gunning and don't need

	A	B	C	D	E	F	G	H	I
1		Hitman Productions Cost Estimate -							
2	A	PREPRO				Day	Person	ESTIMATE	tax
3		Producer	$600.00	day	x	6	1	$3,600.00	
4		Director	$750.00			2	1	$1,500.00	
5		Line Producer	$600.00						
6		1st AD	$350.00			1	1	$350.00	
7		DP half day	$700.00			0.5	1	$350.00	
8		Legal	$1,000.00			1	1	$1,000.00	
9		PA	$150.00	day		2	1	$300.00	
10		office supplies						$0.00	
11									
12	B	PRODUCTION CREW (costed for 10 hour)							
13		Director	$1,300.00	day	x	1	1	$1,300.00	
14		Producer	$700.00			1	1	$700.00	
15		DP	$700.00			1	1	$700.00	
16		2nd camera/camera assist	$500.00			1	1	$500.00	
17		1st AD	$350.00			1	1	$350.00	
18		PA (local hire)	$200.00			1	1	$200.00	
19		Sound (include equipment)	$600.00			1	1	$600.00	
20		Gaffer	$775.00			1	1	$775.00	
21		Key Grip/Best Boy	$750.00			1	1	$750.00	
22		Grip	$750.00			1	1	$750.00	
23		extra Camera PA	$0.00			1.	1.	$0.00	
24									
25	C	LOCATION EXPENSES							
26		Director pre light	$700.00			1		$700.00	
27		Producer pre light	$450.00			1		$450.00	
28		DP location pre light	$700.00			1		$700.00	
29		Camera B pre light	$0.00			1		$0.00	
30		Sound pre light/scout	$275.00			1		$275.00	
31		1st AD pre light	$200.00			1		$200.00	
32		Gaffer pre light	$500.00			1		$500.00	
33		Grip pre light	$500.00			1		$500.00	
34		permits	$250.00			1	1	$250.00	
35		insurance	$1,000.00	flat		2	1	$2,000.00	
36		parking (crew & grip truck)	$40.00	per day	x	2	2	$160.00	
37		parking (talent, parents, TNT, clients)	$10.00	per day		2	15	$300.00	
38		gratuities, expenses, dressing set	$70.00			1	1	$70.00	
39		phone	$20.00	flat		1	1	$20.00	
40		per diem - DP + sound	$80.00			2	2	$320.00	
41		per diem - producer + director	$80.00			2	2	$320.00	
42		per diem - 1st AD	$80.00			2	1	$160.00	
43		per diem - PA	$80.00			2	1	$160.00	
44		hotel valet	$25.00			1	3	$75.00	
45		TNT exec/Talent meals evening	$250.00			2	1.	$500.00	
46		crew lunch prelight	$50.00			1	1.	$50.00	
47		craft services, breakfast and lunch	$200.00	day		1		$200.00	
48		misc costs (flowers for talent, venue clean up)	$50.00			1		$50.00	
49		Fuji polaroid film for releases	$90.00			1		$90.00	
50									
51	D	TRAVEL							
52		Travel day rate Producer	$325.00	day	x	2	1	$650.00	
53		Travel day rate Director	$600.00	day	x	2	1	$1,200.00	
54		Travel day rate DP	$500.00	day		2	1	$1,000.00	
55		Travel day rate Camera assist	$275.00	day		2	1	$550.00	
56		Travel day rate 1st AD	$250.00			2	1	$500.00	
57		flights DP and Camera Assist	$300.00			2	1	$600.00	$42.00
58		flights Producer & director	$300.00			2	1	$600.00	$42.00
59		hotel Producer and Director	$180.00	night	x	3	1	$540.00	$37.80
60		hotel DP and CamB	$180.00	night	x	3	1	$540.00	$37.80
61		flight 1st AD	$300.00			1	1	$300.00	$21.00
62		hotel 1st AD	$180.00	night	x	3	1	$540.00	$37.80
63		travel meals/per diem - producer & director	$50.00	day	x	2	2	$200.00	
64		travel meals/per diem - DP, assist	$50.00	day	x	2	2	$200.00	
65		travel meals/per diem - 1st AD	$50.00	day	x	2	1	$100.00	
66		rental cars	$150.00	day	x	4	1	$600.00	
67		gas	$50.00			2	1	$100.00	
68		crew baggage expenses	$200.00			2	1	$400.00	
69		taxis	$70.00			6	1	$420.00	
70		hotel internet	$15.00			3	1	$45.00	
71									
72	E	EQUIPMENT HIRE							
73		lighting include monitors, walkie talkies	$3,500.00	flat	x	2		$7,000.00	$490.00
74		camera and tripod	$500.00	day		2		$1,000.00	$70.00
75									
76	F	POST for 4 x film executions							
77		Line producer	$600.00			1		$600.00	
78		Offline days (Preditor and room)	$900.00	day	x	13		$11,700.00	
79		Producer online	$600.00	day		5		$3,000.00	
80		Online editor includes versioning	$250.00	hour	x	16		$4,000.00	$280.00
81		color correct	$250.00	hour	x	12		$3,000.00	$210.00
82		mix	$250.00	hour	x	16		$4,000.00	$280.00
83		Misc (lunch)	$25.00			2		$50.00	
84		transcription	$55.00			1		$55.00	
85									
86								$65,265.00	
87							tax		$1,548.40
88		GRAND TOTAL							$66,813.40

FIGURE 4.1 Branded Content Documentary Shoot estimated budget

assistants? These should be conversations you had in pre-production and will all affect the budget.

Don't leave anything out and make a robust high-ball budget. We were turned down by one grant because our budget was too low for music, so include *everything*, even if you know many of the costs will be deferred or donated. One funder told us: "If you're not told a quarter of the time that your budget is too high, then you've done it wrong, you've budgeted too low." I wish we'd had that as a mantra posted on our wall from Day One.

Then make your "low-ball" budget, which will end up being your more realistic budget. Some of the ways we cut corners to save money is doubling up on roles. I did that with my Producer. I directed, co-produced and was an Assistant Editor; my Producer was also the Editor. But make sure to line item for each role in your high-ball budget (even if one person does both); it's a way to be paid what you should actually be paid. And do remember, doubling up on roles is hard work.

With *Musicwood*, we had two and even three budgets at any one time, dependent on who we were pitching to:

- ▶ our most probable budget where we were realistic, but deferred as many costs as possible (i.e. there would be no line item costs for Director, Producer, Editor and so on)

- ▶ a production and post-production budget with In-Kind (or donated) services, as well as deferred salaries taken out; we then put in a very small amount for marketing and festivals (this was our low-ball budget, displayed in Figure 4.2)

- ▶ our high-ball budget, as detailed earlier, which included *all* costs, nothing deferred, no savings listed, expressing exactly what it would cost to make this film if all fees were reasonably paid.

Look at our low-ball budget. You can see we concentrated most of our money on production, post and finishing, as most filmmakers do, but really neglected marketing. We scrambled together US$7.5K to hire a PR team way after post was completed. This only paid for a very basic service and we should have had more for P&A. Bear in mind, some studio feature films spend more on marketing than the whole production itself.

44 Budget

LOW BALL BUDGET
Hitman Productions Cost Estimate - 05/14/09
Musicwood documentary
1 x 60/90 minute Film and TV proposal
Please note that this budget is estimated for 1 further location shoot and interviews
Three shoots have taken place, NAMM x 2, Alaska (and DC)
We will also interview 2 artist performances and interviews. This does not include pilot pre production

							SELF DEFERRED	TOTAL DONATION
PREPRODUCTION								
preproduction	$450.00	day	x	40	days		DEFERRED	$18,000.00
PRODUCTION 2 day shoot	local sound							
producer/director	$700.00	day	x	2	days	$1,400.00		
Line Producer	$450.00	day	x	2	days	$900.00		
cameraman + pkg	$650.00	day	x	2	days	$1,300.00		
sound + pkg (full sound pkg)	$500.00	day	x	2	days	$1,000.00	local hire	
travel days - cam	$350.00	day	x	2	days	$700.00		
travel day Producer/AP	$350.00	day		2	days	$700.00		
travel day Director	$350.00	day		2	days	$700.00		
hotel - producer/LP	$300.00	night	x	3	nights	$900.00		
hotel - camerman	$300.00	night	x	3	nights	$900.00		
car	$100.00	day	x	4	days	$400.00		
meals/per diem 4 crew x 3 days	$80.00	day	x	8	days	$640.00		
baggage expenses & taxis						$300.00		
car hire						$300.00		
flights	$500.00	pp	x	3	ppl	$1,500.00		
lighting	$200.00			2		$400.00		
						$11,640.00		
4 x 2 day shoots							$46,560.00	one camera hire paid with guitar donation
Plus three shoots								Three shoots self funded $14,000.00
Filmed Music Performance - two performances in one day								
Studio and shoot costs	$15,000.00			1	flat	$15,000.00		
talent	$5,000.00			2		$10,000.00		
							$25,000.00	
POST PRODUCTION								
Stock footage	$5,000.00			1		$5,000.00		
digitize days	$350.00	day	x	6	days		DEFERRED	$2,100.00
edit	$700.00	day	x	50	days		DEFERRED 2 months	$35,000.00
audio mix	$225.00	hour	x	20	hours		DONATED	$4,500.00
graphic elements and open	$25,000.00	flat	x	1	flat	$25,000.00		
Music library and composing	$2,500.00			1		$2,500.00		
online	$1,800.00			4	days	$7,200.00		
dubbing tapes	$1,000.00			1		$1,000.00		
color correct	$5,000.00			1	flat	$5,000.00		
						$45,700.00		
TALENT								
VO 60 minute script	$5,000.00			1		$5,000.00	$5,000.00	
DISTRIBUTION								
PR representation						$5,000		
Travel - 2 festivals						$2,000.00		
Film festival entrance						$500.00		
Press material						$1,000.00		
Web site design						$2,000.00		
Lawyer						$3,000.00		
						$13,500.00		
TOTAL minus donations						$135,760.00	DEFERRRED/self	$73,600.00
							Deferred	$69,100
							donated	$4,500
TOTAL DONATIONS						$73,600.00		
TOTAL BUDGET						$209,360.00		
Still to secure Post productio						$50,700.00		
Still to secure Production						$85,060.00		
						$209,360.00		

FIGURE 4.2 Our low-ball budget for *Musicwood*

Our budget doesn't reflect at all what we actually paid per line item but we were weren't far off with what we spent overall, at US$151K. I am amazed we didn't spend more and I think we really cut corners because of this low budget. Our edit time was *way* underestimated probably due to our cable TV editing experience which doesn't give you time to edit for nuance and subtleties. Often editors can spend a year editing a feature documentary.

This was a budget for an hour-long documentary which then became theatrical length so costs were accrued because of that. Our shooting time was longer and lawyer fees higher. We used our production company's insurance, but we forgot E&O insurance as many filmmakers do. This is a great training exercise for the future: try and keep notes of expenditure all along the way—that's why you have the LLC, so you can really know what you are spending, and hopefully raising money for those expenses as you proceed.

5

Production

So you have delivered your synopsis to your crew. Have you had a conversation about tone, style, equipment, shooting days, weather, talked to the crew about the characters themselves, story beats etc.? And when do you actually pick up the camera? For us it was the first meeting of guitar company CEOs, once they agreed to let us film.

The filmmaker Steve James shows up with his camera from the beginning, at his very first meetings with characters so that he doesn't go through a lot of meetings beforehand. Matt Heineman becomes great friends with his subjects; he builds a lot of trust. For us it was hard to plan who of our characters would be most transformed by the story, who would have the most significant narrative arch and be changed in some way when the film was completed.

We followed the three guitar maker CEOs, the Native corporation (both the white loggers and CEOs) and Scott Paul from Greenpeace. Then the dissenting voices from other tribal members to add layers, texture and meaning to the story. Our protagonist was Scott Paul from Greenpeace. We hoped his work would have an effect on the Guitar Guys, motivate them into action to help transform the Native Corporation logging practices. We hoped by the end that every character would be transformed in some way.

The pressure then was on Scott Paul to achieve his goal. And the Guitar Guys and Corporation could be antagonists or protagonists along the way. We would never be sure if they would remain antagonists.

Trying to get initial footage for fundraising can be hard for this type of film. You'll want to make a teaser for your film as soon as you can so plan to film at least one or two of your major characters, and generally three or four initial scenes that can suggest what will happen in the film. A cut of roughly 10 to 15 minutes in length is a good aim.

RELEASES

It's obvious to say but you need a written record (in some instances these can be on camera agreements) that people have agreed to be in your film. These are called releases. Remember to get signed releases from everyone who appears on-camera. (There are a couple of examples in the Appendix at the end of this book.) You'll need individual releases and minor releases for those under the age of 18 (standard boilerplate releases can be found online, but be sure to have a lawyer look them over for your project if you have any concerns). Also, if you want exclusivity to the story, get a line added to that effect on the individual release form.

Get the releases signed *before* the shoot begins, never after the shooting has happened as you'll set yourself up for a ton of work if you do that, and you run the risk of never getting them!

We had a very hair-raising situation when we were sitting in the Seattle airport on the way to Alaska to film, and the Native Corporation were refusing to sign a release, even though our lawyers had gone back and forth making their changes. We had to make sure we got those releases before filming and arriving in Alaska. We would never risk the cost or the emotional time and energy spent on production, only to *not* have the release signed and then all of the footage deemed unusable later.

THE LOOK OF THE PRODUCTION

Some filmmakers actually create sets for their interviews. See *Jane* by Brett Morgen, or *A Brief History of Time* or *My Name Is Lenny* by Errol Morris. Matthew Heineman talks about how difficult it is to express danger in a featureless hotel room, when his characters are in hiding in his film *City of Ghosts*.

Brett Morgen cites the films of Errol Morris as a major influence, and he feels Morris has a different adventure stylistically with every film he makes. When talking together on a DOC NYC festival panel they discussed their shot lists; they both hate the term "B roll" as it's all "A roll" to them. Think of every shot as moving the story forward in some way; for example, what is that cutaway to the picture on the wall telling you?

Brett Morgen prefers the term "ephemera" and it can all have emotional warmth, whether a photo, animation of a newspaper article Xeroxed a thousand times. Take a look at *Montage of Heck* as an example of the amazing ephemera he collected.

Morgen, before shooting, will think of his subjects and write down all of the adjectives that describe them, and that becomes the tone of his films. He loves the use of asynchronous sound (non-diagetic). He talked at a DOC NYC panel about how much it saddens him when the films he makes for theaters have to be stripped of some of these subtle sound effect elements for broadcast TV. In his film *Jane*, Morgen even used lighting and different times of the day to ask certain question when interviewing Jane Goodall to symbolically represent different stages of the story.

CREW

Some filmmakers use local Directors of Photography that can get access to characters. This was true of the film *Final Year* (about President Obama's last year in office), which used a well-known Whitehouse cinematographer.

I have definitely booked female cinematographers for certain films, and a male cinematographer when I've filmed a vasectomy surgery, to make sure my characters feel more at ease.

If you can, use the same camera and cinematographer/DP for your film, it will keep the look of the film consistent. You're going to have enough issues with consistency getting the archival footage to work and look good, especially if you screen in theaters. So keeping the photography consistent really helps.

We had a great wildlife cinematographer (who we had worked with before) that shot all the Alaska scenes in *Musicwood*, and you can tell it was the same person. All of the music performances and musician interviews were shot by different people and you can see that too. They don't look as consistent.

A lot of equipment can help or hinder you. For example, people could play up and possibly perform to a larger camera that is very present and noticeable, but it could also mean you are taken more seriously as a filmmaker. I know certain camera people will build out a DSLR rig with extra equipment just to make certain significant characters take the filming seriously. Yet this small size of camera can be incredibly useful when filming intimate situations with people as we have already discussed.

I think filmmakers often are gifted with a lot of emotional intelligence and can read rooms well, and reactions of their subjects. Laura Poitras talked at a DOC NYC panel about feeling like an actress in one of her films when her voice is used as voice over. I can relate to this; at times I feel filmmakers are chameleons and I would play up certain parts of my personality in different situations as called for to make characters feel at ease, relaxed or unthreatened.

Remember to look after your crew and communicate well. DPs aren't mind readers and they will have great ideas too. I generate a shot list and schedule and prepare my interview questions but always pad time in the schedule to ask the DP what shots they would like to get in that location. They are your visionaries too, they may have some other great shot ideas or a question to ask.

FILMING

Getting that footage that's hard to access will make your film stand out, in whatever quality. The best story, the most emotional incredible story with fantastic and unbelievable access, even shot on mini DV, will trump a beautiful boring film. I can't believe I'm saying this as a director—I love beautiful cinematography!—but it's true.

Take a look at the film *Garbage Dreams*. I didn't think I'd be able to watch it as the opening shots were shot on mini DV, but the film was so compelling that it transcended any visual quality issues. It was absolutely incredible. I can't wait to see the documentaries that are being shot on iPhones because of the intimate access to characters it will provide. The film *Tangerine* started out as a documentary filmed on an iPhone. Take a look at how it feels.

With *Musicwood*, because of over-logging it was very hard to find the huge Spruce trees that were under threat in Alaska to film (a comparable size to the Redwoods in California). From watching our early edits of the film, we knew that this was footage we desperately needed. After our fourth trip to Alaska, and taking a small canoe into the interior of a remote island with all of our equipment, we eventually found our needle in the haystack and the footage of those trees provides some of the most incredible moments in the film.

BTS

It's really hard to even remember this with everything else going on, but make sure you have someone take some behind-the-scenes photos while you're filming. I add it to my shot list to make sure I remember to ask someone—even if it's the producer—to take some stills. Get shots of the actual production with equipment in shot—the more exciting the better. These will come in handy when it's time to fundraise (they make great Kickstarter updates) and for all of your social media platforms and for your release of the film.

INTERVIEWS

We did phone pre-interviews which were super useful, but to generate a sincere emotional response on camera (a la Robert Durst in *The Jinx*), avoid asking *that* question until the camera is running. Your subject may reveal more on the phone when not being filmed, which can be great for research for your interview questions but you want to be sure to get those great emotional moments on camera. Needless to say, type up your notes from every phone call.

Don't list too many questions. Memorize your most important ones—the more relaxed, casual and conversation-like you can keep your interview, the more likely your character will reveal things to you that they otherwise wouldn't. Maintaining eye contact, listening and responding to what they say, not just moving on to the next question, can work wonders. Also don't 'umm' and 'ahh' as they answer. In other words, don't make agreeing sounds over their answer; nod your head and smile, but don't ruin the audio. I've seen this happen a lot surprisingly.

How can you relay character? Through shooting scenes of action, interaction, reactions. I always make sure to have a list of shots that include these:

1. Extreme wide shot of scene with and without characters.

2. Interaction, pan or two shot. Often mid shots.

3. Reaction character 1, listening and talking, and emotion. Tight shots for emotion.

4. Reaction character 2 (generally HS head shot, a tighter shot so we can see emotion).

5. Transition shot, in or out of the scene.

6. Coverage of vérité action in pans, wide, mid, tight shots.

7. Cutaways that detail the dwelling place of the character, even if that's a hospital surgery, that could include patients waiting in the corridors, etc. These can be single shots *and* traveling shots. Do both.

So this is very approximately about ten shots per scene, although you might get a number of movements on cutaways, etc. And think of moves down or around your character for reveals: who or what are they sitting beside, or looking at, etc. Are there holes in their clothes, are they wearing meaningful jewellery, have they torn their coffee cup to shreds in nervous anticipation? Anything that says more about their character?

Once you capture all those reaction shots. It can be hard moving between characters talking, so think if that will be using a hand-held rig, a shoulder mount, etc. And make sure you stay aware of how long you have asked your camera operator to shoot. Are they tired? (Hand-held is more difficult to shoot than being on sticks—tripod.)

Some interviewees will want to see questions first. Avoid this at all costs, as the prepared interview often comes across as very rehearsed. Securing some of the interviews you need will be tough, but don't give up; your gut instinct is right, and the hardest interview to secure is probably the one you most need.

With *Musicwood*, we were trying to secure musician interviews and film their performances. We would go to performances and then meet the artists afterwards and literally put a clip of the film in their hands. We did this with lots of bands, from Mumford and Sons to Bonnie Prince Billy to Lambchop. We didn't give up, didn't stop trying, and through this method we eventually managed to secure Kurt Wagner of Lambchop—what a great guy—and had an amazing line up of artists in the film. It actually made us feel like we were making two films at one point—the Tongass forest film, and a music performance film—but we knew that having musicians was integral to the film—at least that was my vision as the director.

TRACKING THE DETAILS

We set up a production spreadsheet that was shareable with the team on Google Drive. The spreadsheet included details on all the interviews, each shoot location, resources for research, details on archival sources (books, libraries, archival footage) and whether we had to credit a person or institution. Everything about the film could be put in this one place. Especially as some of your interview subjects will provide you with material, make sure you get all the credits needed. For example, with a photo, were they the photographer of the photo? Or are they in it? Do they know the photographer, etc.? Do they have their contact info for you?

This then morphed into more detailed individual spreadsheets as the film progressed, to include outreach, foundations we had applied to, TV pitches, etc. It was a one-stop shop that every member of our team could access. We love Google Drive.

EDITING WHILE FILMING

We started our edit before finishing principal photography. This helped us analyze the film, and list all the footage (in a Google Drive spreadsheet) that we still needed to fill the big gaps in the story and helped planning for further shoots.

With *Musicwood*, we had 15 periods of shooting with individual call sheets for each location. We would spend weeks at a time in Alaska. We would piggyback on other productions (if we were doing commercial work), or try to arrange a large period of shooting where we could capture a number of scenes at one time. For one shoot, we spent a week with our crew, traveling to the Adirondacks in New York for an interview, down to Martin Guitars in Eastern Pennsylvania, over to DC for a shoot with Greenpeace and then

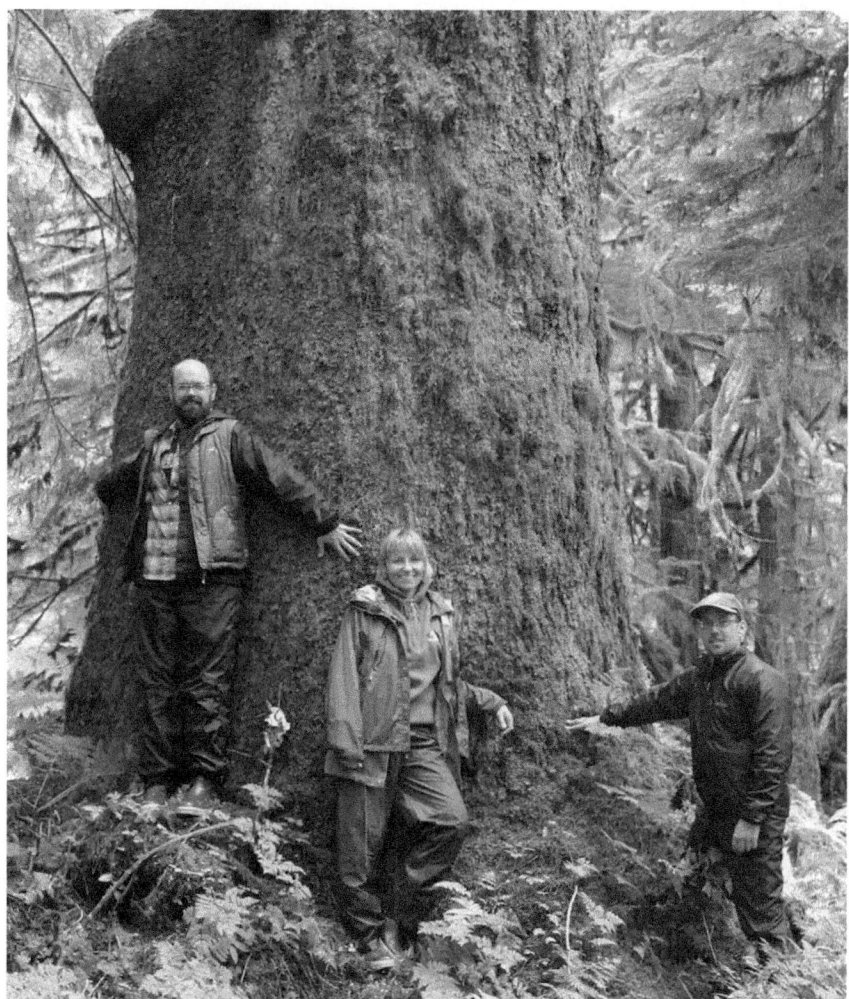

FIGURE 5.1 *Musicwood* **crew at the base of a Sitka Spruce tree**

back up to New York to film a music performance. It was an exhausting tour, but we captured so much footage, and it made it much more affordable.

Some of our major characters, because they were incredibly busy CEOs, couldn't give us as much time as we would have liked, although Bob Taylor was amazing. So we struggled to find time to shoot coverage for scenes and meant we had a number of talking head interviews. I'm not a big fan of those.

If we had had a better understanding of feature filmmaking as opposed to the hour-long documentaries, we would have interviewed fewer characters for our film. We ended up dropping a number of interviews (some with forest ecologists, activists and so on). We came to learn that it's more satisfying for the audience to really get to know characters, spending time with them, caring about them, following their individual story arc, rather than listening to even more talking heads that aren't active participants in the story. We would have saved some real filming costs if we hadn't done some of those interviews. In the end, they proved useful for research and outreach, if not for the bank balance.

One other thing we would consider looking into next time is considering whether there is further life for scenes elsewhere. Can our film expand its reach in a different way—through interacting with the story and absorbing and engaging with content with a more connected audience online? There are a number of trans-media funds out there and the National Film Board of Canada has developed this style of storytelling really well. With more fundraising could we provide interactive elements and build out the website in this engaging way. Or can the feature be the start of a web series. Or should the feature actually be a series? Hertzog, Gibney, Warrior Poets and other documentary filmmakers have all expanded their work in this way. There are lots of opportunities for series, and you may even get a bigger audience this way.

6
Funding

It is hard to place this chapter about funding after production because of course it will go side by side. For new filmmakers you are often shooting a few scenes to make a short 10-minute pitch reel possibly before you have raised any funding. You will probably be looking to fundraise after you've shot a few scenes, so that you can make a trailer for your grant applications and pitching purposes or even crowdfunding (Kickstarter, etc.) to help raise money.

Unless you're a seasoned filmmaker and have been able to raise money from a treatment alone, you will probably be raising money as you go along. Perhaps you've raised some funds before you go into production, but this is very difficult for first-time filmmakers.

Here are eight ways you can raise money for your film:

1. In kind, or donation of services (editing, graphics, camera equipment, etc.).

2. Self-deferred salaries.

3. Foundations including film funds (5% of applications are successful).

4. Individuals (through crowdfunding, bricks-and-mortar fundraisers and more).

5. Corporate sponsorship.

6. Individual investors.

7. Non-profits.

8. TV pre-sales.

1 IN KIND

This is a lovely term given to services that you get for free. Here it's pretty much up to you to use your own contacts, who do you know or who knows someone who knows someone? We approached a local businessman who we knew would be very keen on our film's subject. He owned a sound studio and we approached him initially just for advice.

He was the very first person we pitched the film to. He ended up offering us a huge amount of in-kind services that were totally free. From graphics for our opening titles, to sound design, music composition and the sound mix. All of our music, apart from one track, was composed by his company, and people always compliment us on the soundtrack. What a score, literally.

There's a great saying that if you want money ask for advice, if you want advice ask for money.

2 DEFERRED

We not only deferred our salaries but we self-funded the production initially with our own US$35K investment from our production company.

We were very lucky as we work in TV and we had a big freelance contract at that time that took us all over the country. We would try and piggyback on these shoots whenever we could to film for *Musicwood*. The profit that we made on all of our TV work for those five years didn't have to go to pay business overheads (we work out of our home office so overheads are low) or vacations, it all went to *Musicwood*. But now we can successfully say that we have made back that investment from our international sales and have covered all costs, except all of the deferred salaries, we were able to pay ourselves a small amount for our time as we haven't made any profit.

3 FOUNDATIONS AND FILM FUNDS

Foundation funding can come in the form of donations, or through the awarding of grants. Generally you will need a fiscal sponsor to accept any funding from foundations, as it will need to be tax-exempt. Fiscal sponsors usually take 8% in administration fees but may offer other services as well, and there are many groups out there that offer this service: for example, IFP, WMM and Fractured Atlas. More information on film funds can be found in the case study section on Funders, Festivals, Distributors, TV (see Chapters 13 and 14).

Our Producer actually set us up our own tax-exempt non-profit: Helpman Productions. This involved a lot of paperwork but we saw this new organization as being worth the investment. Making social issue documentaries, we hope, will be a significant part of our business moving forward.

The Foundation Center Library is a searchable online (and bricks-and-mortar) grants database, where you can search by the issues grants fund. Some do not fund media or documentaries but they may fund outreach for your documentary, again more on this later in the book. This is a fantastic library resource, we spent many an hour in their head offices, researching potential grants.

You'll write a lot about your film, especially when you pitch for funding. Your grant application could begin the preparation of a treatment or synopsis which will help you focus the film, communicate to your Director of Photography and be a great start for your press kit for marketing purposes (yes you will need a press kit—and sooner than you think).

Synopses are shorter and requested by all granting bodies; treatments are longer and requested by TV networks and may also be used in the second level of the application process for grants. Budgets are very important at this stage (refer back to Chapter 4); remember, a funder is looking to reduce as many risks as possible so wants to believe you can raise the money but also that the film will, or can get made (refer to Chapter 13).

Since we first applied for funding for *Musicwood*, the Documentary Core Application has been developed, which is great news for filmmakers. It's a collaborative effort by grantors who regularly fund documentary projects to standardize application requirements which can be found on the IDA (International Documentary Association) website:

> The Sundance Institute and the IDA joined forces to create and disseminate a common funding application to the field. With the Documentary Core Application Project, a small but growing group of documentary funders have made a commitment to a more filmmaker friendly way of grantmaking…with the aim of fostering greater access and a more equitable and sustainable documentary field.

These are the current funds that accept this core application:

- SFFILM
- Sundance Institute
- BRITDOC
- Catapult Film Fund
- The Chicago Media Project
- Chicken and Egg Pictures
- Fork Films
- ITVS
- LEF Foundation Moving Image Fund
- The Miller/Packan Film Fund
- The Redford Center
- Tribeca Film Institute

Applications can vary with requests so to have a formalization of application is so useful. Some grants ask for more than just a letter of inquiry (LOI), and other foundations might want details of your campaign goals if you're submitting a social issue documentary. Ours changed many times, and increased in ambition and size dependent on the grant.

If you are successful and get funding, keep your funder up to date throughout the whole production process, as they may even want to provide more funding later in the process! Someone once said your best funders are those that have already funded you. One filmmaker felt that developing your project for funding prepares you well to fight for your distribution pitches later in your filmmaking journey.

These were the grants we concentrated on at the time. Some of these have merged—for example, Tribeca and Gucci—but all the others are still very active:

- ▶ Chicken and Egg provides grants for approximately 14 films out of 600 applications. They now have an accelerator program.

- ▶ Tribeca Film Institute Documentary Fund—6 to 10 films; they no longer fund social issue documentaries but they do fund character-driven documentaries. They often fund portraits and eccentric pieces like *Marwencol* or the films of documentarian Doug Block.

- ▶ Gucci Documentary Fund—grants for 6 to 10 films a year; they fund social issues but not outright advocacy.

- ▶ Tribeca All Access—5 narrative and doc grants for filmmakers from underrepresented communities.

- ▶ Cinereach—fund fiction and non-fiction films.

- ▶ Fledging Fund—fund after the production phase.

- ▶ Patagonia Environmental Grants—fund campaigns; your film would have to be an addendum to that campaign.

- ▶ Wilberforce as above.

- ▶ Creative Capital offers non-monetary support as they very much want to invest in you as an artist, as a long-term business, and they will help leverage your project to get other support. They receive 3,700 applications for 46 awards. Creative Capital can come in very early to the project, and they can incentivize backers if the project is deemed controversial.

With *Musicwood*, we got very close with a number of grants and made it to the final round with Chicken and Egg, and Fledging Fund. We eventually raised US$75K from foundations. We love Patagonia!

4 INDIVIDUALS/CROWDFUNDING/FUNDRAISERS

We held an initial, bricks-and-mortar fundraiser in Washington, DC (where we had most of our contacts at the time) with our 10-minute early pilot of the film. We reached out to a ton of businesses in DC, managed to get sponsors that provided beer and held the fundraiser in a swanky screening theatre at the Goethe Institute, so it felt like a really special night for everyone who came along. We raised nearly US$10K and Bob Taylor (of Taylor Guitars) just happened to be in town, so he stopped by and it was a great event for us.

The only downside was that it took a heck of a lot of organization and money to make the fundraiser happen, spending money to make money—we had to hire the venue, dress the venue, get volunteers to help, etc., so that's when we first looked into crowdfunding, and Kickstarter.

At a great DOC NYC festival panel the well-known producer Marilyn Hess talked about how she strategizes her bricks-and-mortar house party fundraisers. "At house parties you should show something," she says. Hess has screened clips and at times slideshows. She will also invite people to come earlier to see her previous film.

At the event her team present the near term ask for: "We're trying to raise $200K; we have already raised [x amount] and we're trying to raise $25K tonight." One thing they do every time is share how they would reach that goal and the months they have put into planning it.

She makes pledge cards for house parties, and makes sure she has a square facility. She also hands out folders with cards with SAEs to return, and a box set for her funders to share. If appropriate she also asks contacts from her film to send out letters to their own network.

Hess makes sure she stays in touch with funders four times a year with an email update. Not always asking for money but a general update of where her work is now. When she's at the finish of the edit she will often share a clip of the new film. "People want to be part of something not just as an ask for money."

I love her advice that "no" sometimes means "maybe," which means no contact is a waste of time. So keep in touch with the nos, although it can be hard to know where to best expend your energies. She references the book *Fundraising Houseparty: How to Party with a Purpose and Raise Money for Your Cause* by Morrie Warshawski.

We could devote a whole book to fundraising. I do go on and devote the whole of Chapter 8 to crowdfunding, especially because I have now raised funding for two films from Kickstarter, the second in 2017 for my new film *To Kid Or Not To Kid*.

My best advice is to have a team—some great interns, your producer, etc.—all on board working together. Don't forget, Kickstarter takes a cut of the money so budget for that. Take some time to decide how much you will try to raise, research projects like yours that had successful campaigns and see what you can learn from them. However, to make a decent amount it really is a full-time job, but there are a ton of benefits to running a campaign so don't be disheartened with the hard work.

This is how you will connect with people on Kickstarter (the crowdfunding platform we used), and if you do this right, they will become your audience for the film in the future:

- person
- cause or idea
- rewards
- community, yours and your backers'
- non-profit.

Look at all possible intersections for an audience. Where do they hang out? Go and find them.

I will use *Musicwood* as a quick example here but jump to Chapter 8 (the crowdfunding chapter) for much more detail—especially as crowdfunding may be your first funding that you will raise for your film.

Person

If you've chatted to anyone about crowdfunding, you know you need to do alot of planning before the launch.

Tell everyone you know that you're running a campaign. Face-to-face if possible, or if not, "individual" emails are the most productive way to get help. A friend thanked everyone by name on his Facebook page, with a witty and complimentary note about each person, and it gave me a nice warm glow when I read what he had to say about me. It totally worked and made me want to give more.

So don't be shy. Look how crazy our website was for the duration of the run.

Rewards

A very famous filmmaker gave great advice on a panel at a festival. He said a film is hard to reward as there is no physical property—so get a designer on board to mock up the DVD artwork. Also, on your crowdfunding page, don't give away all your best clips; have something, sure, but hold back for when your film is completed for your big press launch.

Think hard about your rewards. Our film was heavily based around music, so we approached music venues in NYC, which were fantastic at offering tickets as a reward. But because the rewards weren't band-specific and they were local to NYC it didn't have a specific core to connect with, and didn't necessarily create the buzz we expected. But it made us *love* these venues.

Non-Profits and Other Communities

Crowdfunding is an amazing way to start your outreach for the film. We contacted 130 relevant organizations about our campaign, from "green" non-profit groups, guitar blogs, enviro news blogs, outdoor magazines, to Native American museums and more. Some of that worked in our favor in a big way: 22 organizations posted about our campaign, and posts by guitar blogs seemed to get us the most return in donations.

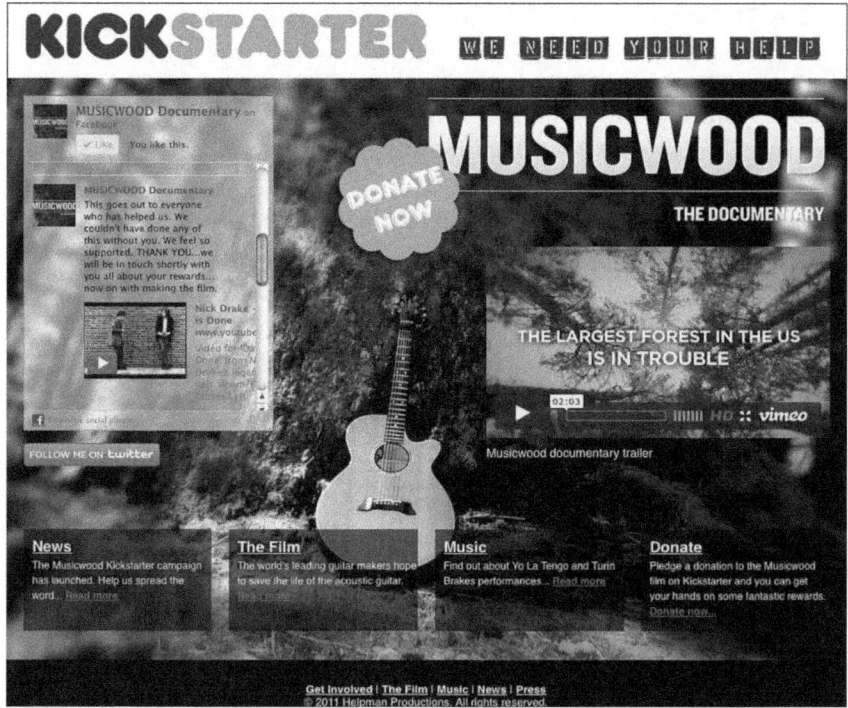

FIGURE 6.1 *Musicwood* website for Kickstarter campaign

If your film isn't focused very specifically on a goal that fits a non-profit's remit then you might not get as much support. So really research relevant organizations.

What would I do differently? Sometimes we would email organizations only once and never again. So we'd take more of a quality over quantity approach next time and chase up on emails.

However, we did get some great press from national magazines and blogs. We got great articles in *Acoustic Guitar* magazine and *Wend Magazine* and, in *IndieWire*, we were a Kickstarter "Project to Watch."

OUR GOAL

With *Musicwood*, we reached our goal of US$25K and actually ended up raising US$27.5K, which was 15% of our total production budget. Other films average about the same amount: 10–15%.

5 & 6 SPONSORS AND INDIVIDUAL INVESTORS

There are a number of ways to approach sponsors and investors, from corporate sponsors, who would not necessarily have any input on the film, to Executive Producers, who either invest their own funds or bring in investors.

The film director Roger Nygard, writing in *Documentary Magazine*, talks about the simple one page proposal: "People with money don't like to read. In fact, if your pitch doesn't grab them in the first three sentences, your chances decline with each line of explanation." I give the same writing advice as Roger to my students: remember to write with exciting, bold and colorful descriptions. "Propose some of the questions you will ask and some of the answers you expect." Roger Nygard will write the toughest questions and test them out on friends. Your take on subjects needs to stand out and break new ground and that needs to be obvious in the proposal.

If you approach an Executive Producer or individual investor, ask them what they want in return. Don't offer an EP credit for US$2K in your Kickstarter rewards; you're selling your film for too low a price. You need to have a legal contract stating how the money will flow and what editorial control an EP would have. Try to make the contract one that accepts their investment without onerous conditions. We didn't use an Executive Producer because thankfully we raised enough money through self-funding, grants and in kind services, but it is another option.

The group Impact Partners work with documentary makers to get funding. They work on eight films a year and they look to make a return. They work with investor-type philanthropists, and review 400–500 applications a year, choosing about 12 films to show their investors. IP only look at projects in production or post-production. Impact is the final money, to get everything to finish the film. They're essentially getting you personal introductions to that donor who has money.

We did however try to got sponsors when we toured with *Musicwood*, taking the film to music festivals and community screenings. You can send letters with DVDs to potential sponsors but you have to ask directly for what you need—there is nothing like a face-to-face meeting, or a phone call and being upfront about your request. We actually did have meetings with potential sponsors and got very close to some commitments. On a few occasions, once they watched the film, it was deemed too controversial for them to sponsor, and although we never locked in a sponsor we would definitely try this again. You can approach corporations to invest in the production too but then you won't be able to air on the TV networks PBS or BBC, so bear this in mind. This is true for non-profits aswell.

7 NON-PROFITS

If your film is in line with the goals of non-profit groups, you could contact them to provide funding. This can be a tricky line to walk; if it seems that you are just preaching a non-profit's messages, then your film could be deemed an advocacy film instead of a non-biased documentary. We didn't have any non-profit investments, although various NGOs donated their time to attend Q&As at screenings or, in the case of Greenpeace, their archive videos.

8 TV PRE-SALES

Pre-sales are rare for docs. When you're thinking of your budget it's good to remember that Submarine, a very successful sales agent (a company that sells films to networks), advises that US$500–600K might be all you can get from US rights to the film. Often budgets that are presented to them are US$1 to 2 million, which is very high. They say that if the film is budgeted at US$700–800K it's a better proposal for them to sell the film.

You can certainly approach sales agents—who will represent you at film festivals, etc.—but normally only when you have been invited to festivals and have a finished film. Submarine apparently saw *Catfish* too early to represent it, and *Catfish* was a great doc that has now become a TV series.

Do bear in mind if you're lucky enough to get a sale on your sizzle reel (rare for first-time filmmakers) and get a TV deal before your festival run, that makes it difficult for sales agents to come on board, as broadcast TV rights are a big part of their income package.

Pitching can be hard for unknown filmmakers that don't have an experienced member of staff on board. The makers of *Weiner* were first time filmmakers. They had incredible access to an amazing character and they took the sizzle reel to Motto Pictures. Bringing on board a great producer can help sell your film at pitch meetings. You can apply to pitch at forums such as IFC in the US which can be instrumental for first time filmmakers but be aware that funders often want to see that someone on the team has experience. There are numbers of festivals that offer these pitching forums but some of the best are the Hot Docs Forum in Canada and Sheffield pitch fest in the UK, among others.

7

Social Media and Print Assets

At a recent panel I attended one filmmaking consultant talked about how marketing is the area that we should be concentrating on most. I've written this book in a chronological fashion, taking you through the exact steps of how we made *Musicwood*, so if you've followed the same route you will already have generated written information about your film. Crowdfunding should come after you have worked on your social media presence. Making your presence felt on social media as a filmmaker or an expert on the issue your film is about will help your film find its audience; it is an integral part of that process.

You will probably have written a number of different length descriptions about your film now (500 words, 75 words, two sentence loglines, etc.) for your grant proposals and treatments. Obviously you'll want to change the language to something less formal for your social media platforms.

We saved all of these descriptions in a Google Drive document and would make sure all of the production team had knowledge of how we talked about the film. If you have a team helping you with your social media make sure you talk about tone, that they read all of your written information about the film, and have seen your 10–15 minute sizzle video, which showcases major scenes of the film. This way all of your team can talk about your film knowledgeably and be on message.

Again think of your goal for your film. If it's to make money then maybe you want to really drive people to all of the merchandise on your website. So your website will be more important to you than Facebook. For us our goal was getting great reviews for our film, which would encourage others to watch. This then shaped our social media outreach. For some it's to raise awareness of the issue through educational and speaking engagements, so making educational screening packs became part of the key art, etc.

SOCIAL MEDIA

There are many platforms that you can use: Facebook posts, Instagram, LinkedIn groups, Twitter, Reddit, YouTube. As this is a constantly morphing landscape, do your own research at the time of making your film as new apps are appearing all the time. Facebook and Snapchat stories may become part of the deliverables as you run your campaign, etc. You will need a team to help you with your social media outreach as this can be a full-time job and a continuous one for the life of your film.

Just remember, one size does not fit all. Each platform, you will interact with differently.

At the time of writing here are some general suggestions from our own experience and research.

Needless to say you really boost your audience by interacting with groups interested in your subject, engaging meaningfully with them and not just pushing out the occasional tweet with an ask. We made sure to have a "news" section on our website as well so it would act like a blog. Building your audience before your crowdfunding campaign will be tremendously beneficial. But having a website that also asks for an email address is helpful.

Facebook

To keep the presence of the film foremost in people's minds post at least daily. Videos and links get the best reach, then photos, then text. Make sure to add a sentence or pull quote from you. If posting a link, share from the original source as otherwise it diminishes reach.

Twitter

When you see your film's themes being talked about, engage with those people in a meaningful way, and then invite them to your pages or website (don't go for the hard sell straight away). They will come if you have had a meaningful conversation with them.

It's more beneficial to reach out to users privately before reaching out to them in public posts. DM (direct message), or email them if they have posted their address in their about section.

Then tag people's Twitter handles when you do share their work.

Interact and add to the conversation on related topics. Hashtag the topic so people can find your conversation. Make and share a list of hashtag topics so your team can use them too; add them to the Google doc. Start populating your timeline with material about the film—ideally between two and five posts a day.

There is conflicting advice about Twitter. Someone once told us that unless you're a celebrity or journalist, or selling something, don't worry too much about using Twitter. But to some extent you are selling your film, so filmmaker Gary Hustwit (*Helvetica, Urbanized*) takes a different tack: people are investing in *you* as a person, so he believes your Twitter handle should be *your* name, as opposed to the name of your film. That way you can take the audience with you after every film, building a community around your work. We eventually changed @MusicwoodDoc to @MaxineTrump but referenced my current film name.

With *Musicwood*, we tweeted celebrities we knew were environmentalists, or celebrities who had an interest in trees, or guitars—Edward Norton, Daryl Hannah, Richard Gere, Cameron Diaz, George Lucas—to very little success. We tried to send DVDs to their agents and they were all returned unopened.

In the end we did get some wonderful celebrity endorsement. Taylor Swift "liked" our Facebook page, and Wilco shared and tweeted about their love of the film (see Figure 7.1), as did David Crosby and the band Guster—all people who are "actively" engaged in the issue and care. That makes all the difference.

70 Social Media and Print Assets

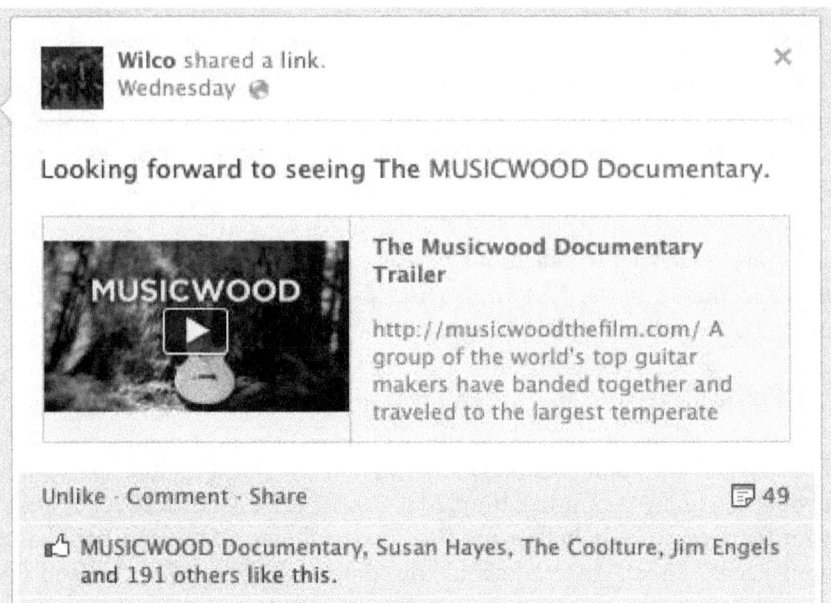

FIGURE 7.1 Wilco's Facebook posting

Stay on top of what is happening on these platforms when you start making your film. For us Reddit, LinkedIn, Instagram and YouTube were all useful platforms too. We used Snapchat and Pinterest less so, but Pinterest could be useful to you.

Join Reddit conversations, and post high quality pictures to Instagram two or three times week. (Remember, the largest Instagram following are outside of the States—good to note as this is not the best platform for outreach if you are opening a film in a certain city or town for example.)

I mention Snapchat because you can do your own short documentary series. Pinterest has a high engagement of older women. Are they your audience?

As this is a morphing landscape I am keeping this chapter short. You can read the most up-to-date blog posts about the best platforms to use when you begin your own journey. But be engaged, be active, interact—this is how you will build a presence for your film and an audience.

KEY ART

Websites, posters, postcards, photos, thumbnails, etc. If you're smart about your artwork now, it could save you money in the long run. It may be hard to come up with the artwork before the film is finished, so don't worry if you don't get it right on the first pass. We changed our website's design a number of times (but the domain name *never* changed *nor* the title of the film).

Things you will need: include a professional-looking photo of yourself (you'll need it for all of those festivals you'll get into) as well as the major crew members and behind-the-scene photos. Use your behind-the-scenes content on your social media; people enjoy seeing how the production happened. Start designing postcards and leave a blank space for labels that can be printed out with relevant screening details or addresses. You can also use these as business cards while you're raising money for the film; it's always useful to have a handful with you at all times.

You'll need artwork that can work in landscape and portrait format — landscape for Facebook banners and website header, and portrait for your film posters.

To save on costs, start thinking about iTunes now too. Will your postcard image be useful for your poster and still readable as a small thumbnail on iTunes? Our poster image for *Musicwood* is a little abstract, although it works at poster size, and we love it and others do too. So for iTunes we had to create a more legible and easy-to-read thumbnail-sized image. In the end we created three different artworks with designers. I would have liked to have just designed one or two—it would have saved time and money.

WEBSITE

You can use a WordPress or a Squarespace template; they make it reasonably simple to make a website these days. Buy your domain and make your site as soon as you start filming; it makes the film more of a reality and easier to fundraise. It gives the audience somewhere to go to find out more, but make sure what's on your site doesn't affect your film when you're still in production. You don't want your characters withdrawing their consent after visiting the website and seeing how you're telling your story.

Remember to include:

- ▶ a donate button

- ▶ an email sign-up section (and fundraising trailer when you launch)

- ▶ details about the film

- ▶ email contact info

- ▶ eventually a screenings tab for the theaters and film festivals you'll get into!

TRAILER

As a word of warning DON'T launch your "real" trailer yet. Save it until you have your festival premiere. This will create buzz and press. You don't want to release it too early; save it to make a big splash when the public can see the film.

8

Crowdfunding

Just hours after we ran the Kickstarter, our home internet went down. We had scheduled a Facebook Live and Kickstarter Live interview when our campaign came to an end to celebrate with everyone. (We streamed them in tandem; there is a slight delay on Facebook Live if you do this, but more on that later.) It would have been tragic if that had happened before the campaign ended. We had just enough time to go live and thank everyone.

Our Kickstarter was full of amazing synchronicities like that. We got just what we needed when we needed it. As you run your campaign, be sure to hold onto these moments to encourage you. It'll help you keep going. Hearing from funders as to why they love your film; people that "need" your film; I was even told that people "loved" me for making the film. All such wonderful feedback. This truly is one reason to run a crowdfunding campaign, to not feel alone in the production process.

THINK OF YOUR STRATEGY AND WHAT CROWDFUNDING CAN DO FOR YOU

So what are you raising funds for? Be specific in your ask, and convey urgency and importance—for example, *to raise $X in funding to cover the remaining expenses to complete the film.*

You are creating a network and community for the film, to be used not only for fundraising but also for promoting the film in the future. Do bear that in mind throughout your campaign and beyond.

LEAD TIME

I was once told if you could get 1,000 people to fund your campaign then should be able to fund your movie. If you've chatted to anyone about Kickstarter, you know you need to do a ton of planning before the launch. Start prep 6 months before, if you can. For my second campaign, I started two years before, making authentic connections with people.

1. Build up your social media presence. Who do you know who has interest in your film?

2. List everyone you know—go through emails, Facebook, Twitter, Snapchat, Instagram, etc. List them as P. A. (Personal, Acquaintance) or D (Do Not Contact). Use MailChimp or another service to collate emails.

3. List the contacts that you can reach out to and ask to fund on your very first day.

4. Ask people to be your ambassadors or patrons who will email others. Someone's grandma was the best ambassador for them. For my second film—which is about making the decision to live child-free—I had an advisory board, made up of leaders in the child-free community. More on that later.

5. List all the outlets (blogs, press and so on) that might cover your campaign and find email addresses for these people. I started saving every article written on the subject as a bookmark in my search engine, so by the time I ran my campaign I had a list of blogs and reporters. Often reporters will have their email addresses in their Twitter profile, which is really useful.

OUTREACH/REACHING PEOPLE

As mentioned already in the funding chapter (Chapter 6) there five main areas in which you will connect people with your crowdfunding campaign:

1. Person (you as the filmmaker).

2. Through the cause or idea.

3. Rewards or perks.

4. Community, yours and your backers'.

5. Non-profit or for-profit organizations, fan groups, etc.

With these areas in mind, what avenues should you take to reach people?

There are seven points of contact when communicating your campaign (and later for PR to promote your film).

1. A friend referral.

2. An article.

3. T-shirt/poster/PR materials.

4. Tweets.

5. Emails.

6. Texts.

7. Phone calls. Often overlooked, and very important.

Tell everyone you know that you're running a campaign—face-to-face if possible, or if not, individual emails are the most productive way to get help. I am also a member of six local groups with hundreds of followers that meet in person weekly and monthly, and these very real relationships really did come through for me. So what groups are you part of?

MAKING STRANGERS YOUR FUNDERS AND YOUR AUDIENCE

The hardest part of fundraising is engaging strangers to fund your film. How do you do this? If you haven't spent time thinking of your audience for the film, stop and do that now. Make an audience map (see ours below—Figure 8.1). Think of your first passionate audience and then a second related audience. Who can be extrapolated from those groups to become a third audience? Brainstorm, so you can cover the obvious and the unlikely and think leftfield.

The first audience for our film *Musicwood* was tree huggers/forest lovers, which led to another audience of outdoor enthusiasts/hikers and then fishing and hunting groups. Hunting groups…really.

Look at all possible intersections for an audience. Where do they hang out? Go and find them.

My mantra was: "It's important that your audience hears from you because it's so important to hear from them." So how are you going to "talk" to them? Think of it as a conversation—not as continual requests to fund your film. Of course, every piece of content you post on any social media platform will have a link to your crowdfunding campaign. Web link shorteners (bit.ly, etc.) will become your best friends.

Remember, you are building a consistent and ongoing relationships with this audience. You want to keep them until, and after, your film is made, so you can take them with you to the next film. Effective engagement is built on solid relationships.

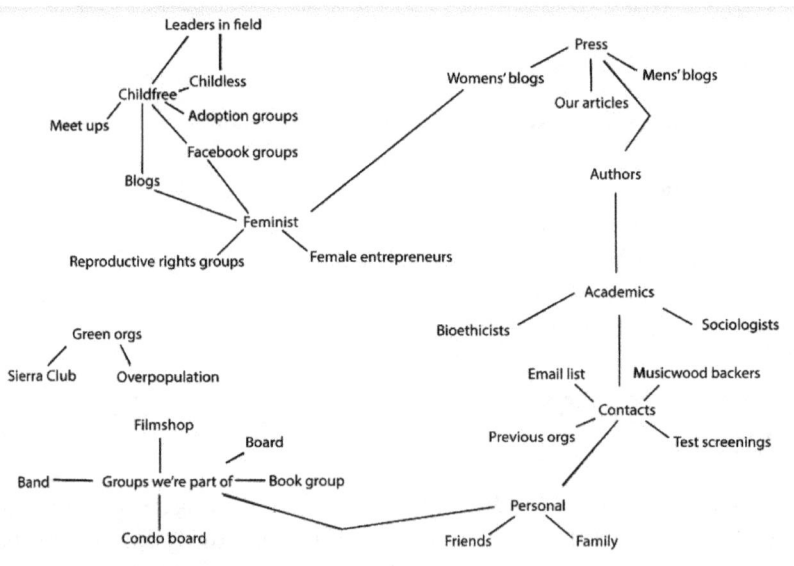

FIGURE 8.1 My audience map

THEN AND NOW

I had a different strategy for my second campaign. I wanted to reach more strangers who were passionate about my film's issue and get significant blog posts to help me reach those strangers.

Organizations are effective and innovative partners that can come on board and connect their dedicated audiences to your film for you. It's harder to reach those organizations now than it was when Kickstarter was younger in 2011, so start early and build a strategy to involve them in a win-win relationship. I started building relationships for two years before I ran my next Kickstarter for my new film *To Kid or Not to Kid*.

PRE-LAUNCH

Team

You have to have a team. Along with the audience, this is perhaps the most important part of your strategy. You will need support and encouragement from your team, but remember you have to incentivize them too.

Some famous directors train, physically train, before they direct their feature films. I feel that you want to prepare mentally too for crowdfunding. It's a campaign, and it's no surprise that we've coopted military procedure terminology. Be prepared to work from when you wake up until you fall asleep. Be prepared for your sleep to be interrupted, as ideas will come to you at all times of the day and night. The notes app on your phone will be full, and so will the notepad by your bed. Don't be like me and write on the backs of envelopes that take precious time to find. Try and keep your notes in one or two places, so you don't waste time trying to find that scrap of paper. This may seem obvious, but you may be surprised at how frequently the ideas will be flowing.

From my research, the size of the team exponentially relates to how much funding you raise. This is so important!

For my 2017 campaign, I brought on a team of three interns. One dropped out just before the Kickstarter started, so I was forced to quickly replace her. This knocked back a significant piece of content in the schedule, so it affected fundraising, which was damaging to the campaign. I have worked with over a dozen interns, and only a few have ended up not being passionate about the project or not meeting deadlines. I can't speak highly enough of interns. Just make sure you interview them in-depth, they are really valuable, look at examples of their work. Invest that time upfront to find passionate staff.

In any interview be very clear about what the internship involves. Make sure they understand that an internship is not on-the-job training every single day of the week. For a part-time internship of two days a week, over three months, I give two days of one-on-one training programmed around the needs of the job. Make it clear and be sure you do not over-promise. I also try to live by the motto that unless we're on a shoot, I'll buy my own coffee and no one picks up dry-cleaning for me.

If you are recruiting for an outreach or social media intern, ask them to give you examples of previous work. If they're completely new to social media, don't recruit them for that role. Outreach can be trained, but social media is time consuming and they need to be actively engaged on those platforms. You can always give a sample email to send out to organizations for outreach, but in my experience social media is not an area that everyone is interested in so be very clear of expectations at all times.

I believe you have to have an inherent interest in social media to be enthusiastic and as active as those platforms require. I learned that just because an intern worked in marketing doesn't mean they will come up with great ideas for social media or even be really engaged in social media. Social media is a big part of any crowdfunding campaign, so for that role I would be very, very clear about what the role requires.

I try to give interns full ownership for their responsibilities and ask for their ideas. They may have great creative solutions. Enjoy your time working together. On their first day, ask them again what they want to get out the internship and be clear and honest about what they can expect. I offer short placements with the hope of a paid position at the end if the internship is successful or credits for their academic studies or interviews or references for jobs with my film and TV contacts.

We celebrated the launch the crowdfunding campaign with a Happy Hour, and a team-bonding lunch. If your team doesn't come up with ideas or seem engaged after a probationary month, then maybe you need someone new. After all, they will have to be your support as well. Look for at least one person on your team that might stay involved in the project after their three-month internship as a paid Production Assistant. Mention that to them. Bring them on board two months before the campaign so they can get acclimated to your project, and begin to have a sense of ownership and "buy-in" before the campaign starts.

Playing to their interests will get a better result. Have group meetings together. Let them know what you're doing, share Google docs, etc. And find out where their interests lie—see how you can weave in some training in that area but be realistic, they are helping you, and will get a reference, a credit and possible paid PA position at the end. Some interns have very high expectations and then are frustrated and may not have absorbed the advertisement in detail. So being supremely clear on Day One, this is important.

We created a document of responsibilities for each week, with a lot of room for creating new content if the need arose. Do this for the lead time before, as well as during, the crowdfunding campaign. Google docs can avoid repetition. You don't want everyone reaching out to the same Facebook group multiple times for example (see Figure 8.1). Can you think of goals, competitions or incentives that your interns could reach that are fun for them and keep them motivated.

Motivate Yourself As Well As Your Team

You will be trying to keep your team engaged and motivated, but who will support you? I made sure to chat and meet with other people who had also run successful campaigns, which really helped in motivating me. One conversation really encouraged me to be bolder about my asks, another helped emphasize that my campaign was doing really well. These conversations are so important to help you keep going.

I did give myself a few hours off over the four weekends of the month-long Kickstarter (just to give you an idea of how hard you will work). I went to an art gallery with friends, and they came up with a great idea for a shoot that I made into an awesome GIF for the campaign. Surround yourself with supportive people while you're running the campaign, so they can help re-energize you.

If you have already built an advisory board for your film, this is the perfect time to bring them in. I had "fairy godmother" child-free doyennes who were bloggers who reached out to their fans on my behalf. I also think of my past Kickstarter supporters as my patrons.

Why Kickstarter Over Other Platforms?

Here are some notes about the major crowdfunding platforms:

> **Kickstarter**—If you don't hit target, you don't get funded.
>
> **Seed&Spark**—Can keep 80% of what you've raised.
>
> **Indiegogo**—You keep whatever amount you raise.

These three are based in NYC. You can reach out for help, but you must have a relevant question to get noticed. They do all have blogs for any questions—for example: indiegogo.com/blog/tips.

For me, I like a goal. I like having that level to reach with Kickstarter. I think it makes me raise my game. So having that all-or-nothing goal works for me. With Seed&Spark you make the goal if you reach 80% but it is a platform only for filmmakers, although they're doing some interesting initiatives with the Duplass brothers for example and now have a distribution platform.

I like that Kickstarter isn't for just one creative field. I like browsing Kickstarter for products and music too. And vice versa, other creatives making music will browse films. That's how the lead singer of the Spin Doctors came to be one of the funders in our 2017 campaign which was fun.

Liking other fundraisers and donating a small amount to them will also bring them to you too. You may not be making money doing this, but you're engaging strangers and a new audience.

Press

I thought with my second film I had hit such a zeitgeist topic that the blogs would love covering it. But what I've noticed is that crowdfunding has now become somewhat de rigueur, so it's harder to get press for a film that isn't made yet. I actually found it harder to get press during my 2017 campaign than in 2011.

From the very early days of production I would bookmark every article that appeared on the subject. I collected over 100 articles, and then in the build up to the campaign the interns divided the content and researched pull quotes. After that, we collected these as content to post and made sure to tag the Twitter handles of the reporters. It may not have got them to write about the film, but it did give us a pool of great content to share. And a large list of press contacts for when the film is released.

Write your two-line pitch to theses reporters. This should be your logline on all your social media outlets anyway, so you probably have this. Then write press releases of three short paragraphs. Make it easy for press to lift your words and use them directly if need be. Don't send this as an attachment; put the text right in the body of the email. No one wants to click on an attachment. Make it easy for them.

You're not going to get the big outlets—*New York Times*, etc.—and nor should you until the film is available to the public. My hope/wish was to get at least one big feminist blog to cover the film. Set yourself and your team targets to hit.

Unsurprisingly, press really helps reach strangers. The benefit of that, beyond the donations you can receive for your crowdfunding campaign, is that it also gets the word out about your film.

Just remember you're doing two things: you're raising money, but you're also doing outreach for when the film is released. My second goal was to have NowThis, Mic or Upworthy share my video. I scored on the first and at least got interest from the second.

Utilize all the connections you have. It's surprising the people you know. In the end, most of the press for *To Kid or Not to Kid*, my 2017 campaign, came from people I knew. I often put out asks to certain friends to see if they had contacts, and it really worked. I did use a PR person, but in the end my own contacts, and their contacts, got me the great press.

I had another significant blog, that I already had a relationship with, ready to post an interview with me the day after the launch of my Kickstarter.

I also asked people to write articles for me. My sister and husband are both writers. I released my husband's article a few weeks into the campaign to promote a particular reward. As my film is about the decision to not have children, we had a vasectomy procedure donated. The promotion fit in perfectly with the film's subject matter, and was audacious and noteworthy (note that you can't, however, offer surgery as a Kickstarter reward; we didn't list it as a reward but promoted the free voucher).

For my first Kickstarter I pitched an article to my local hometown press, and that worked well. This time I wanted to try to reach more national and international outlets. But if this is your first campaign reaching local press is a great idea.

Key Art: Postcards/Video/Crowdfunding Page

These are all the assets you will need to make for your crowdfunding campaign:

- A kick ass video.

- Great rewards.

- Fresh content to deliver throughout the campaign (images, text, video, etc.).

- Postcards or business cards.

- Emails to potential donors over the course of the fundraising period. (Idea: think of stories you can email; the campaign itself could tell a story and have an arc…)

Crowdfunding Homepage

How are you going to design your crowdfunding page? Find pages you like. Some don't need graphic design, but I know I back more projects when they look really professional. I know the film will be made or the product will launch when the page looks stylized and time has been spent designing it. Once you've picked your favorite sites, study what they do. They may have lots of photos (Kickstarter likes behind-the-scenes photos).

What will you include in the text description about the film and your story? Why should YOU make this film now. Why your team? What's your bio?, etc.

Video

Don't give away all your best clips. Have something for the start of your fundraiser, but hold back the best stuff for the press launch when your film is finished. You can also test out your marketing ideas with running certain content in your Kickstarter campaign.

Find the videos you like, then analyze if they might be possible for you. How can you make your video not just a talking-head request for money? Can you shoot anything that looks like the film and have that teased in as well? Kickstarter now has great how-to guides all along the way. Watch them, even if they seem obvious. I got something worthwhile from each video.

With my 2017 campaign my goal was to make a video that people would share, that felt original and this worked. It worked well.

Rewards And Funding Level

Think of the amount you want to raise and be realistic. A friend raised US$60K with six people full-time, or rather 11 people part-time. *Musicwood* raised US$27K with four people—two almost full time, two part-time. Another friend working alone raised US$10K.

It does feel like the amount of people you have supporting you directly correlates with amount raised. To make a significant amount, it really is a full-time job with a team. For my second campaign I raised US$35K after all the donations came in with one full-time and four part-time staff, one of the team was purely making content.

Most crowdfunding platforms take a cut of the money. Take some time to decide how much you will need to raise. Research projects like yours that had successful campaigns. Investigate what they did to be successful, I was inspired by an acquaintance's campaign video.

Get a designer on board to mock up the poster, t-shirt, etc., and other rewards.

With my second campaign, I thought I'd get a lot of traction with really fun rewards. Vasectomy anyone? I felt it would encourage people to share the Kickstarter page, and it really did help. People told me how much fun it was seeing the condom reward with the slogan "I Will Not Be Your Father" (a take on the Darth Vader line to Luke Skywalker, in a fun *Star Wars* font design). Having rewards for people to talk about also engages people with the campaign. Kickstarter has a list of the kinds of rewards you can offer.

Plan for the costs of fulfilling your rewards, and remember to include postage in your estimates. Thank goodness for the digital film download reward! Think hard on these rewards, really evaluate them strenuously. In retrospect, for *To Kid or Not to Kid* I put one reward in at too low of a pledge level. Make a spreadsheet of costs, and think about the time-costs of all the envelope stuffing.

Have a spread of levels too. A friend gave me advice to offer a lower level of US$10 as that will help you reach more people.

How might you incentivize people with special promotions throughout the campaign? I kept back single rewards—like a free day-pass to an event, a spa day or Patagonia backpacks (thank you again, Patagonia). These were rewards I could release weekly, over and above the rewards I posted at the start of the campaign. I also ran a competition for a slogan for a tote bag. It gave me content to write about. I carried postcards for the film wherever I went.

The reward that worked really well was having a very popular *New York Times* bestselling book on the subject, signed by the author. It worked so well that the author, Meghan Daum, kindly gave me another batch. I have seen other sites with very little merchandise as giveaways so again look at a type of film that would mirror your own.

I had a lot of very generous people who chose no reward, and it was good advice to make sure there is a very low thank you level too, as those people might come back if they see the project doing well.

Metrics

So as you think of the level of funding you want to raise, it's useful to be mindful of the metrics. We used Kickstarter for our campaigns, and they seem to have the most transparency. I couldn't find the same kind of analytics on Indiegogo or Seed&Spark.

Kickstarter statistics are updated daily. Six months into 2017, out of 350,000 projects 35% were successful.

Of those 120,000 projects, 56% of the successfully funded projects raise less than US$10K, 13.5% between US$20K and 100K, 14% raise under US$420K, 3% under 1 million, and 0.002% over 1 million.

Content to Share

You're going to have to constantly brainstorm ideas to offer new and great content throughout the campaign. This avoids the awkward job of continually asking for money with nothing new to say.

You have a great video created for the launch, then some clips that are ready to be rolled out during the campaign—that's got to be it for videos, right? Well, that used to be the case, but for my 2017 campaign I also ran a lot of Kickstarter Live videos. I had a new video to release in the fourth week. One intern created a photo series of each of the teams' child-free heroes. We tried to think of interactive ideas. We asked our Facebook followers about their child-free heroes and made the same series for them to share on Facebook. Getting people to share the campaign afterall is a way to reach strangers.

Some of these ideas you will continue to brainstorm as your campaign progresses, but try to have as many as you can ready in time for launch. Think of at least three to four pieces per week, GIFs or photos, not just text (text doesn't perform as well as images on Facebook). See the chapter on social media (Chapter 7) about posting on different platforms. But do your own research, platforms change constantly.

Facebook Groups

Some of our most successful funding came from Facebook pages and groups. Before you start your campaign, be sure to "like" pages, and ask to join relevant groups (so you can post on their group page). It seems obvious, but if you're a fan they're more likely to share your campaign. Search for groups using search terms, but also look carefully at the pages that Facebook recommends on the sidebar. This was extremely useful to me. I contacted these groups months before, and when they accepted me, I would interact on their page and then months later I posted about the Kickstarter. One of those posts resulted in a US$1,000 donation, so that was really useful. These groups may never have turned up through researching directly online.

The difference between six years ago and now (2018) is that organizations, non-profits, and other groups aren't always responsive. We've seen a huge rise in documentaries on social issues. It can be tough to ask these groups for funds when they have to constantly fundraise for themselves. Keep this in mind, and perhaps they don't have to give you money (or ask their subscribers for money), but can post on their Facebook with a link to your Kickstarter.

Also look at groups they follow, which can lead to groups that you wouldn't otherwise find in your research.

LAUNCH

Avoid holidays. As I mentioned, I had some unforeseeable delays, so I pushed back my launch, meaning my campaign ran into Spring break/Easter vacation. People were traveling, vacationing, spending time with family, and I was worried that they wouldn't want to think about funding a film, so not ideal. Avoid this at all costs. I often think February might be a good time, when everyone is usually hunkered down inside, at their computers. Or maybe right after tax time, maybe people will get a really nice tax return and want to fund your film.

I've already mentioned having your list of 100 people that can back you on your very first day. I lined up a lot of people that I knew would give; it was a fantastic resource and enabled the whole campaign to start strongly. Earmark the people you think will become evangelists for you, who will share your campaign, who will support you, thank them and lean on them, you will need them.

Going Live

…and I don't just mean when you launch your campaign!

I mentioned Kickstarter Live earlier when talking about the videos you will be creating for your campaign. At the time of writing, Kickstarter Live was fairly new. The service is essentially a way to broadcast a live video stream through your Kickstarter (and/or Facebook) page and talk about your campaign. People tuning in can engage directly with you in a chat-box, and make pledges with one click of the mouse.

Once the Kickstarter Live stream is done, it then is archived on your project page, where people can replay it to watch later. As with everything on

Kickstarter, you can access the analytics on how many plays a video gets, and from whom, and where.

If you're going to run a Kickstarter Live, be sure check your sound and that of any guests. Do a test run before you broadcast. This will save the potential embarrassment of a live stream with technical mishaps—something that could send the wrong message to your audience. Kickstarter has a lot of tips on their website, read them thoroughly.

You may decide Facebook Live is your preferable way to do this instead, so work out what is working best currently and try anything new.

One of the best pieces of advice we had was from a fellow filmmaker. They mentioned that even though you may only have 20 people watching you live, these live videos show how hard you are working to raise funds. They can help your audience really care as to whether you make your goal and invest in you. You'll hear over and over again that people are coming to Kickstarter to invest in you as a filmmaker as much as the project. Broadcasting a live stream is a very real way that people can engage with "you."

We ran a number of Kickstarter Live sessions, and finally managed to get the simultaneous Facebook Live stream for our last, "passing the finish line" recording, which was great.

I think if I did it again I would change some of the content of the Kickstarter Live streams. I'm a doc maker. I interview—that's what I'm programmed to do. However, your audience want to hear about you, the film, etc. Our best-performing video was when my interns interviewed me, so make it about you and the film as well as your characters in your film.

FIRST WEEK SHARES

In my first week I was hoping the launch video would be shared widely within my community. This worked so well for my second campaign the video became content people wanted to share. In the first week, most of my donations came from Facebook shares and my top 100 contacts list. Gradually I finished writing all of those emails to those 100 people in the first week, I had contacted about a third before the launch. So I didn't have to do much further outreach in the first week to reach my first week goal.

Week 1—This is the MOST CRUCIAL time for your campaign! Spend the first three days working to get to 25% of your overall funding goal. Analytics show that this directly increases the chances of a successful campaign.

During the Campaign

I thought I could possibly have a big funder or two that might want to back my work again from my last campaign. I reached out to ten of them and three came through again, thank you lovely backers.

I planned my list of contacts accordingly, how to reach out to who and when. I planned a tiered approach throughout the month. My personal list of 100 people came first, then I had my contact list for a conference I attended and reached out to each individual person by name. The first week we sent out a general launch email to all of our email list (we have collected emails of people interested in our work over the years), then every week a more detailed update (making sure to include people's first name in MailChimp). Then previous Kickstarter backers (which I kept until the third week). In my last week I contacted people on Facebook.

Emails

Mailing list software like MailChimp will be your best friend. This way you can keep track of exactly who you have emailed, and when, and with what. You can tailor emails, and be sure to exclude those who have already donated from future email requests.

I was really lucky that I didn't have to reach out to everyone I knew until the last week of my campaign. I saved those for last in my strategy, and I didn't mind Facebook-messaging people even if they were on my MailChimp email list. It certainly helped that we have an email list on MailChimp of nearly 3.5K emails which we collected from working on *Musicwood*.

Email addresses are your biggest funding asset. Make sure people are easily able to subscribe to your mailing list on your website and through Facebook. Don't be annoying with your MailChimp emails. You want to make sure they're personalized. We tried hard to have first names in our MailChimp database, to ensure an email didn't just start with "Dear friend."

We sent an email newsletter out about six months before Kickstarter as a general update. Then we emailed at launch, in our second week, just before our last week, and on our penultimate day. We emailed each time with different news. For example, when we'd received great press, etc. Always make sure that you're sending news that is unique and with fresh content. Kickstarter recommends sending one email update per week to fans and supporters throughout the campaign.

Test Screenings

What other events can you plan? In 2010, before Kickstarter was a known platform, we had a bricks-and-mortar fundraiser. Although we raised a decent amount of money, it was a lot of work. The idea of doing it in the middle of a crowdfunding campaign is daunting, to say the least. If someone can plan this for you, and plan it well (with giveaways already set up, etc.), then consider doing it. Otherwise, it can take a lot of time to plan and take you away from your crowdfunding campaign.

I had planned three test screenings during my campaign. We showed test screenings of the film, in its work-in-progress stage, with the hope the audiences at those screenings would become ambassadors for the film and campaign. Would I do this again? I'm not sure it really brought people on board as the film was a rough cut; maybe showing clips is a better option and not the full film. It was also a lot to process mentally regarding feedback about what was working in the film. What seemed to work better was a having a screening of my previous film *Musicwood* to a group. Showing that film before I launched gave me more credibility and served as proof of my filmmaking capabilities. Next time I would show great scenes alongside the fundraising trailer.

Crowdfunding Platform Updates

Your updates are a great way to promote new rewards and ask people to share your campaign. Don't do this more than every other day and only when you really have something to say—i.e., for new rewards, announcements, good news. We have heard that campaigns which send 11 or more updates raise 137% more money than those that don't.

But also think about how you can make it really easy for your backers to share the campaign. Write a 140-character (or 280-character now) tweet (including your shortened bit.ly link) for your friends to make it easy for them to copy and paste. You can even write email copy for them. We actually had friends thank us for doing this.

Social Media

I had built my Facebook page to 1,500 followers before I launched my 2017 campaign. It was hard to measure analytics, as Kickstarter doesn't track whether it's from other groups or your own page. If you make a Facebook group (as opposed to a page), you're able to message each follower directly. So that might have worked better. But you have to approve each person that wants to join the group—there isn't any way to automate access. And groups really are for people who are part of a specific group, as opposed to a page which gives details about a specific project. Think about which would work best for you.

All of your social media platforms should have the crowdfunding link on your profile when you launch. Twitter, Instagram, Facebook (your personal page as well as film page, and any other pages you have), your website, LinkedIn, etc.

Have your shortened link (through a site like bit.ly, etc.) in a shared document for your team with your list of hash tags to use. Refer to the chapter about social media (Chapter 7) but do your own research to see what is currently working well.

Your Twitter Influencers

Some of the organizations I had worked with in the past were Oxfam, Greenpeace, etc. Huge orgs may not be able to solicit money for your campaign or share on their organization's Facebook page, but they may be happy to send out a tweet on your behalf.

Not a lot of money comes from Twitter, but I had individuals and influential filmmakers, festival programmers. editors of blogs and podcasters who were happy to tweet about my campaign. After the campaign ended, our surveys revealed that we definitely got one or two funders from Twitter. Don't be afraid of hashtags. Tag people and organizations in appropriate posts.

Further Rewards

Go back to the rewards you held back and offer incentives for the first backer on a certain day. For example, weekends tend to be slow, so maybe add a reward for a weekend pledge. Have something special available for your 100th backer, for example. These can all drive traffic to your campaign.

Cross-Promoting Content

So you want to embed any new video content straight into Facebook, but you can also cross-promote this exact same video with other pages. You want to do this as it harnesses more views in the Facebook algorithm. It gives the content more gravitas and more views if it looks like original content for a Facebook page. A social media filmmaker gave us this great tip as it brought a huge audience to his short viral videos.

Use this function the first time you post the video; you can't add this later. Also be sure to tag relevant people involved in the film. Who helped you with your launch video? Crew and cast—tag them all.

Thanks

Thank everyone as soon as they donate. Don't wait. I think this is incredibly important, and my other filmmaker crowdfunder compatriots agree. Write the copy for your thank-yous in a Google doc so that anyone on your team can take the lead on thanking for any particular day. That way all they have to do is paste.

A funny or personalized thanks on Facebook works a treat for those people you know (otherwise you won't be able to link to their name). A friend thanked everyone by name on his Facebook page, with a witty and complimentary note about each person, and it gave me a nice warm glow when I read what he had to say about me. I copied that because I loved it.

We also incentivized people by tweeting a thank-you GIF personalized with their name (GIFs don't work well on Facebook, so it has to be Twitter). Making each GIF was a lot of work, so make sure the recipient has a twitter account before you create it. The hope is that they will then retweet the GIF, with a link to the campaign of course.

Stretch Goals—Third Week

We hit our goal in the third week (for both of our campaigns), which was fabulous. Every film hits a different audience but would I raise my goal further next time? I think so. However, it's the hardest decision to make, deciding on the level of your goal.

I had created a great GIF that launched the stretch goal and people loved it, which incentivized them to keep sharing even though we had reached our goal. That is the hard part. Make sure to explain what the extra money is going towards and make sure that is different from what you quoted as your initial expenses.

In the end we raised US$35K. Our initial goal was US$23K.

Last Few Days

I am thrilled that we had a email list of 3.5K people, mainly from using sign-up sheets during our film festival screenings and events for *Musicwood*. I went through this list in the last few days of the campaign and pulled out people to specifically target with individual, personal emails.

This should also help to harness your previous funders. I know for a fact that the MailChimp emails reached people and we had funders, but then backing this up with individual personalized emails in the last few days also really helped.

RESULTS

Of the 500 film projects on Kickstarter, we stayed in the top 20 videos throughout the whole of our campaign. They also picked us as a "Project We Love." This may have been helped by the amount of Kickstarter Live videos we made.

In 2017, the *To Kid or Not to Kid* campaign made our goal with 400 backers, as opposed to the 180 we had in 2011 for *Musicwood*. We managed to reach more strangers in 2017 than in the previous campaign. Of the 400, we have 110 people that we didn't know. We got a ton of great press and most of the strangers seemed to come from one of three ways—we asked them when we sent follow-up thanks in Kickstarter:

1. Through Facebook groups that we reached out to.

2. By browsing Kickstarter projects, or being recommended through Kickstarter.

3. From individuals that referred the campaign to them.

We seem to only have one or two backers from Reddit or Twitter, which would fit with research findings.

Take a look at a project's Kickstarter page and where you find Updates and FAQ tabs you will also find a Community tab. It's really interesting seeing which country your backers have come from. We had 336 from the US. Kickstarter is definitely better known in the States. And 137 backers had never backed a Kickstarter project before.

From 2011 to 2017 I almost tripled my backers from the UK and the US. I didn't have to lean so heavily on my friends and family for support for my campaign in 2017. That was its own reward, for me personally not to have to lean on those familial relationships again.

What Would I Have Done Differently?

If I could have paid a team of staff to help, that would be amazing. Often the crowdfunding campaigns you see doing so well have been run by for-profit production companies, so don't feel deflated if you don't raise as much as they do.

I would have had the interns come into the office and not work as remotely as often as they did. The teamwork can be fun. Remember to incentivize them (see team notes earlier in this chapter). I couldn't have raised what I did without them.

I tried to find a funder that would match funds for a day to drive and incentivize funders. A lot of people have said that helped.

I hadn't built out my Instagram account, and my Twitter following is just under 1,000 people. I worked hard to get my Facebook page to 1,500 followers before I launched. I think I could have run competitions on Twitter, and built out my YouTube page as well. In the end, I had two interns creating content, when I needed one really devoted to driving Twitter outreach (make sure one of your team is really interested in social media).

In 2011, we flyered music venues and handed out flyers at concerts, thinking the music audience would be sure to back *Musicwood*. That didn't work at all.

There are apps or services that can help you raise money but get references from other filmmakers as they change constantly, some went out of business between our two campaigns so I won't list them here, we didn't use them.

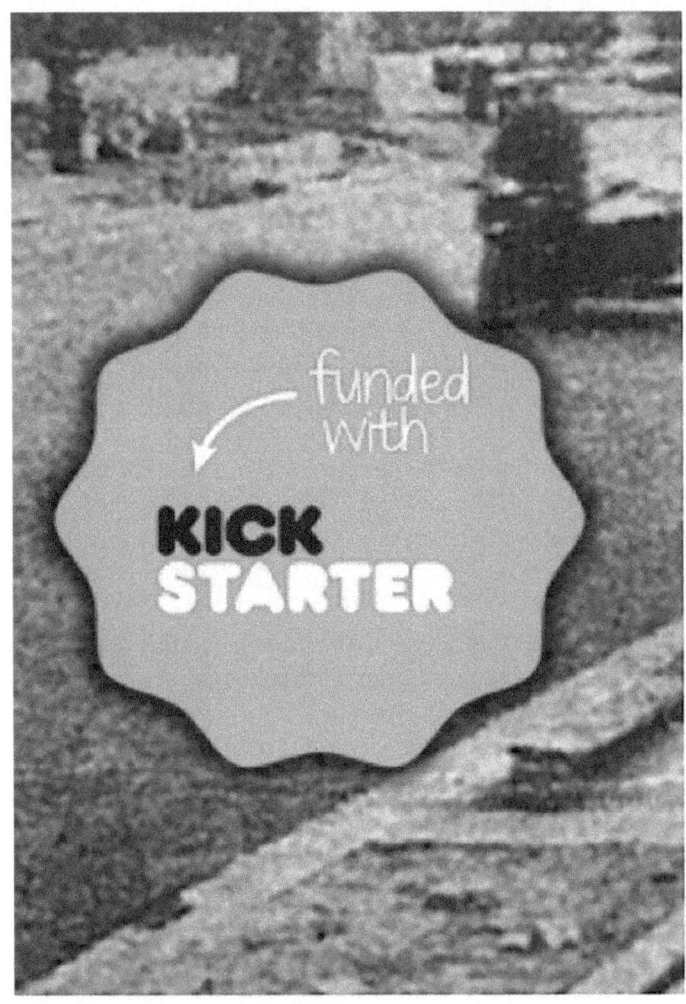

FIGURE 8.2 "Funded with Kickstarter"

Think Outside the Green Blob

As I was looking through other projects, I found people that did some questionable promotion, like copying the Kickstarter "Project of the Day" badge. This totally worked on me: I thought it was indeed a Project of the Day. It's a little cheeky, but Kickstarter didn't ask them to take it down.

We didn't do anything like this, but we did emblazon the opening video graphic with the fact I am a *New York Times* Critics' Pick director and my last film got 100% on Rotten Tomatoes. Be sure to clearly state your accolades, or anything that helps people have confidence in you.

Well Done!

Congrats, you finished your campaign! Send an update to your backers to let them know that you made your goal, thank everyone then and there on the day. EVERYONE. Then take a breather and celebrate. A week or two later start sending out your reward surveys. Send an update via your crowdfunding platform a month after your campaign ends, thanking everyone again and telling them you are gathering their details for their rewards.

Don't forget you are building authentic relationships with your core audience. Remember I mentioned we sent out a newsletter months before we launched? Now keep a regular newsletter going to your backers or as a Kickstarter update, keep them engaged, every quarter is reasonable. This way you are staying in touch with everyone who expressed an interest in your film. This will help to bring your crowdfunding audience with you as the film moves forward, and who doesn't like to be thanked?

9
The Edit

When you're deciding on the length of your film, bear in mind these durations:

- international broadcast TV is typically 52 minutes

- US broadcast TV is 54 minutes

- theatrical release is over 80 minutes if you want a distributor

- theatrical release self-distributed can be any length

- mid-form is now becoming more popular, now that Netflix has opened up barriers to duration, and Vox and Vice are also producing at this length.

Of course the film should be as long as it takes for the story to be properly told. But it's good to have duration information in mind for later distribution meetings.

Documentaries are really made in the edit: you'll hear that often said and for so many documentaries this is true. It really is the second chance to direct.

As mentioned already, we analyzed a number of documentaries that we loved (*If a Tree Falls*, *The Pat Tillman Story*, *Daughter from Danang*), breaking them down by scene, music, sequence, act, etc. We loaded the film into editing software, and then manually put in cuts where the scenes change, adding color-coded media slugs to show where music falls, or when voice over comes in. You will end up with a timeline that shows a rough idea of how the film works, and seeing patterns in the cuts or music is extremely helpful.

Many editors work in different ways but many filmmakers study the film structure of documentaries that they feel are similar to their own. There may be an assistant editor who has logged all of the rushes of your footage, made sub clips or selected sequences. You will undoubtedly have everything transcribed, whether vérité or interview scenes. The assistant editor may have set up your project for you with listed bins—for graphics, music, original footage, third party material, sound effects, etc.

If editors have time they will watch all of their rushes to make notes for emotion, active scenes, reaction shots. Anything a transcriber or logger (or assistant editor) may have overlooked.

We had all interviews transcribed; this is critically important and these days not too expensive. We then went through each transcript and put the various SOTs (Sound On Tape) into a Master Script grouped by category, or theme. We did this after every interview and ended up with a giant document of all the relevant bites by theme. Remember you are doing this for your vérité action scenes too, not just interviews. This sounds obvious but watching vérité can be much more powerful than listening to an interview.

Matthew Heineman working with Matt Hamachek combed through hundreds of hours of vérité footage that the characters provided themselves in *City of Ghosts*. It can be hard working with vérité that you haven't filmed, as the footage might be limited in shots of emotion, close ups, etc. Heineman said it was hard to establish character from this footage but they mined this trove of material and once again Heineman was shortlisted for an Oscar with his film *City of Ghosts*.

With *Musicwood*, once we felt we had finished almost all of the principal photography, we edited this Master Script into a sequence in a timeline, 7 hours long. We called this the Radio Cut, as it was all dialogue, all audio, no b-roll (coverage footage). If we had new interviews after we made the initial

Radio Cut, we would mark them in red on the Master Script, which would help us find where to place the new information in the edit. Once that material was added to the edit, we changed the bites from red to black.

Our next step was to tighten all superfluous information in the Radio Cut. We realized very quickly that we didn't need three people saying the same thing—just one person was all that we needed to hammer a point home, especially if you drop the music out to highlight an important fact, statement or conversation.

Using the Master Script, we broke down the structure into plot points and story beats, and this helped us to keep refining the story. We put each story beat on a notecard so that we could easily move them around and experiment with structure. Sometimes we felt the forest was really the most significant character, and its fate, its literal rise or fall, was making us care and gave us the drama. Saving the forest after all was our protagonist's goal.

We edited from a script, but you should be sure to watch the footage/the rushes to make sure you have logged all of those reactions. Your transcriber won't log a facial expression and won't have the tone of delivery of the bite. So annotate your transcripts with those notes. This is important because you want to make sure you have logged the most emotional moments in the film.

Other editors will only cut from their selects and make a string-out from that which allows you to build a tighter duration of cut. This makes sure you have the best footage in your film, with the most emotion or hints of conflict that may not come through from reading your transcripts. I feel that there are real benefits to this, and now working on my next film this is the process I will be taking. I have already started editing scenes from selects and then placing that dialogue into a script.

Whichever method you use, you will be writing your documentary. But what does that mean if you have no narrator—i.e. no narration has been written and recorded?

Editing is the second chance to direct and directors often have written something down before they shoot—either a script, shot list, synopsis about their film or treatment. But you are "writing" your documentary with the literal arrangement of scenes and how you construct dialogue and build the structure of your film.

With *Musicwood* we had decided early on not to use a narrator, so that the various voices in the film could tell the story. This worked well, especially once we realized we could use graphic cards (of text) to move the story along if factual information was lacking, where interviews didn't convey facts succinctly. This made for more cinematic solutions, with no voice of God telling you *how* to feel; the audience is *feeling* the story by watching the scenes.

However, we did have too many sections where an interview would run under footage and act as voice over. Let the footage tell the story too, and definitely don't see and say with your voice over—i.e. telling us exactly what we're seeing on camera.

After this process we had a 4-hour string-out. We then broke down every scene into beginning, middle and end, to see how each story beat moved the story forward. We placed these into a beat sheet (more writing!). We looked at the length of time we spent on each scene and rated it in importance. That really helped us focus, and helped us do a very quick cut to 90 minutes.

I even went through and watched *all* of the footage twice, because we had relied heavily on the transcripts and I felt a nervousness that we could be missing vital reveals of subtle emotion. Also because we now had the very definite story beats, and we logged at first without this in mind. I went through the interviews, scenes of action and b-roll—to see if we were missing any opportunities to sharpen the conflict. This was hard work, but it made sure that we made the best film we could make with the footage we had. EMOTION and CONFLICT are some of the most important storytelling devices.

While watching it all again, I listed the best SOTs and made a separate string-out of all the best footage to make sure we had it easily accessible. To this day I wish we had included a line from Bob Taylor where he says, "We only got in the room because we were guitar makers; we'd never be there if we'd made 4x4s." But even now I think we made the film a little long at 82 minutes, so it was very hard to add anything. After all your film shouldn't be packed with dialogue, there needs to be pacing breaks for moments of reflection and for the audience to really be able to hear what is important in the story.

STORY BEATS AND STRUCTURE

The most fundamental building block of a narrative is the beat. A string of beats make a scene. A string of scenes make a sequence. A string of sequences make an act. A string of acts? That makes your film.

Filmmaker Marshall Curry (*Street Fight, If a Tree Falls, Point and Shoot*) analyzes his beats and scenes, to make sure that every two minutes the audience is learning something new or is surprised, or wants to know what happens next.

Matt Hamachek (*Gideon's Army*, etc.) has talked of making "rules" for every film he edits. While editing *If a Tree Falls*, he would introduce each new character with three shots in their own environment, and then when coming back to the same a character later in the film, he would only use one establishing shot, as the audience has already gotten to "know" that character and recognize their surroundings.

Hamachek tells a great analogy about editing: he talks about going to a party and the very first person you meet doesn't usually tell you their whole backstory, the story of their life, what they ate that day. You don't know them yet so why should you care? If that does happen at a party you usually try to move on from that conversation because often you're bored senseless (my words, not Hamachek's). You have no sense of who that person is so you're not interested...yet. So don't front load a film with facts, give people what they need when they need it. This can't be stated more strongly.

I was thinking on that theme, maybe you're in line for food at this party and someone ahead of you declines a drink, because they're telling their friend that their mother is arriving early the next day to visit NYC for the very first time. Their Mum is a member of a Native American Tribe, you overhear that some tribal members don't drink due to religious reasons. The mother has never been to NYC before, she lives out West and cities make her nervous. OK, so I made that conversation up, but I know if I heard that story I would want to join that conversation. If we know later that it was a big battle with the family for the daughter to leave and study in NYC, we care that their mom has a great visit. Maybe the friend is making sure the daughter doesn't stay out late, but you notice that the daughter is still there at midnight and still drinking. It might even drive you to action, to check in on how she's doing.

Michael Rabiger advises you to scatter clues about your character in your film: too much exposition before action can weaken the tension; explanations can be better after the action. Maybe the protagonist realizes they have lost the goal and so that signals the need for a new phase of action. The daughter in the story stayed out late, got drunk and had to call a car to collect their mother from the airport. How will that scene end, I want to know, don't you?

Filmmaker Amir Bar-Lev, in the DVD extras for his film *The Pat Tillman Story*, talks of using a four-leaf clover structure in the film. He uses the main character's memorial as an entry point to the story and the central movement that the narrative bounces away from to explore a new story beat or scene, before circling back to the funeral once more. Film historians would call the death the inciting incidence to begin that journey.

As mentioned in the production section, think of your inciting incidence—the moment that starts the whole train moving forward for your story. This needs to come very early in the film, as this is what motivates your whole story to move forward.

Here are some of the quick reminders, the most helpful tips, that were given to us or that I heard at panels, to help structure our film during the edit:

- ▶ Simplify. Less info is more powerful.

- ▶ Natural sounds tell a story, and are more cinematic.

- ▶ Show, don't tell.

- ▶ Don't see and say—i.e. don't see footage and hear the description of that exact same footage in VO under it.

- ▶ Where you place music is very important, if you cover a whole interview you may not absorb what is being said, but it works well over montages and VO.

- ▶ Each scene needs to pick up the story and move it along: variety is as important as storytelling.

- ▶ Every scene should have beginning, middle and end, you should go into a scene thinking about one thing and come out thinking another,

- Think of each of your characters separately, making sure they have their own personal journey and three-act structure.

- Jumping around in your storyline is good, as this keeps the audience guessing about what happens next. Then when you come back and reveal the answer it can be very satisfying for the audience.

- As the story moves towards a conclusion, the scenes should get shorter, tighter and the stakes higher.

We also had mantras posted around the office on notecards: "Make them want the next scene," "No audience likes stories made too easy," "Never be afraid to make them wait."

"Make them want the next scene" was especially critical to us as a way to evaluate whether each individual scene was working. With each scene's end, we interrogated it deeply. Did it make us *need* to know what was coming next?

Also when we want events resolved, it motivates us to demand what happens next. Audiences also like guessing what happens, so by delaying these expectations can increase viewer involvement and makes an audience more engaged in the story.

We learned so much along the way in our editing process. Although we had worked in TV, we had to learn the language of feature documentary filmmaking, which is quite a different format or style of storytelling. Coming from TV, we made it very talky with a ton of interviews, numerous characters and quick cuts. Big mistake for a cinematic film where you should get to know characters: the characters were so important to the film. We had so many characters at one point it was hard to know who to invest in as an audience member. We had to hone the story and drop interviews; we referred to it as self-imposed film school.

Don't be disheartened if you don't use all of these interviews. Sometimes you have to go through those steps to get you to that next person or to reveal a better part of the story. What's the saying: "The best shots always end up on the cutting room floor"? So try not to fall in love too much with any particular scene. I remember arguing at length about the necessity of some scenes with our Editor, only for them to be dropped, and I can honestly say I don't remember now what they were.

A sophisticated edit with wonderful pacing that has kept the audience engaged every two minutes (Marshall Curry!) and at the edge of their seats can take months, a year plus. There can be other editors who will work for 4–6 months (see *Tickled*) but that is rare. I know of one director and editor who just watched the rushes every day for 8 weeks before they even started the edit.

You will undoubtedly hit creative blocks in the edit. Our great editing consultant and now friend, Matt Hamachek, knew an editor who watched his cut in a mirror to give them creative solutions by watching the film from literally a totally different perspective. Steven Soderberg talks about watching *Raiders of the Lost Ark* in black and white, with no sound, so the stimulus is really about looking at the shots and the edit; he was closing off the other stimulus that his senses would otherwise pick up.

Think about it; I also try to look at film techniques when watching a film for the first time, but when the film is good I always get lost in the story and that's the sign of a good film—it pulls you in even when you don't intend it. But that's why you go back again and again to look at the structure.

There is a fantastic series called *Every Frame a Painting* made by director/editor Tony Zhou and animator/editor Taylor Ramos that unfortunately at the time of writing has just come to an end. Many of Zhou and Ramos's video essays about film making exist on their YouTube channel that they started in 2014. The one entitled *F Is For Fake* gives a great tip on film editing structure. They discuss "the therefore or but" principle rather than "and then and then"—meaning, don't give us a literal or chronological list of what happens in your film; give us the cause and effect. At the end of every scene if you continually ask yourself, or apply to your script the question "therefore?", or "but…" to your character's journey, it's a great method to interrogate whether you are making an engaging film.

VOICE OVER

Laura Poitras makes sure to stay as close to her protagonist as possible when filming. In her film *Risk* she eventually found she had to break the fourth wall, i.e. inserting herself into the film as voice over. In *Risk* she brought her own production notes as voice over in the film to answer audiences' questions if the story was unclear.

I could write a whole chapter on voice over alone. We generally attempt not to use it for cinematic films, but you may find you need elements of voice over, as did Poitras. Maybe your main character is the best person to narrate. But it does take some skill being able to direct your characters reading narration. That's why so many actors are the narrators of films like *March of the Penguins* or *Enron* as they can give you great dramatic intonation to the read, and be directed. Brett Morgen got Jane Goodall to read her own diaries for the film *Jane*, which can fill those contextual gaps that narration is often used for, and this worked really well. It also worked really well in the fantastic film *The Donner Party* by Ric Burns, where he used actors to read incredibly emotional letters that had been archived.

There can be different types of narration in tonal quality: the naive inquisitor (aka Nick Broomfield), the character from the film with insider knowledge, the letter reader, or the voice of God that has nothing to do with the film at all—i.e. Morgan Freeman's voice in *March of The Penguins* or Peter Coyte in the film *Enron*.

So remember, as you write and direct voice over, whose point of view are you using. Then stick with that voice. Are you using the first person voice over (I) or third person voice of God (he, she, them) narration? And remember text cards and graphics may be able to do this just as well as voice over.

Narration or voice over should be adding information to the picture, not just describing what we see on screen. There is a reason why Werner Hertzog has poetry books on his reading list in his film classes.

You may be using voice over:

- ▶ because there is confusion—the characters aren't quite saying what you need them to say to hit the important story beat
- ▶ to make a transition work between scenes
- ▶ to write into a character that sets the stage.

So a few things to note when you write narration to picture: make sure it hits at the exact spot intended; and be economical with word use—let the visuals speak for themselves where they can. The audience can lose track if there is too much information.

Narration will constantly be rewritten; that's why they call it a scratch track when you use your own voice as a placeholder for timing. Avoid tongue twisters, question marks, irony and conjunctions like *shouldn't* which can be misheard as *should*.

GOOD NARRATION

Good narration:

- avoids cliché
- uses a direct active voice language of speech
- uses the simplest words
- avoids jargon
- avoids condescending humor
- doesn't talk over sound effects or good natural sound.

Say It Less, Say It Better, Say It In the Best Possible Way to Advance Your Story.

MUSIC AND SOUND

Think carefully about your sound—your soundtrack, atmospheric noises, tonal drones, sections of quiet and music. I tell my students there are five ways to absorb a film through your senses:

1. Watching footage.

2. Reading graphic information or text cards.

3. Hearing dialogue, or narration.

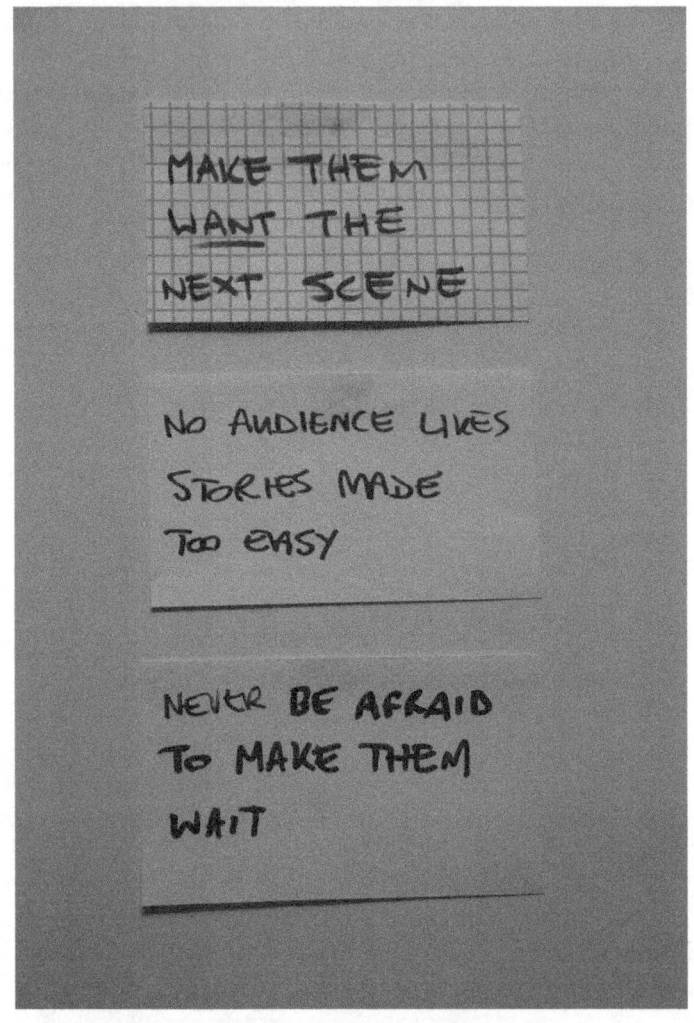

FIGURE 9.1 Editing mantras posted around the office

4. Hearing music.

5. Hearing sound effects, natural or otherwise.

From images and graphics (including text cards), to dialogue, sound effects and music. Three out of five ways to get information from a film is through sound. There are so many purposes for sound in film.

These can be all diagetic sounds—that is, literally linked to the image you see on screen—often called Sound On Tape (SOT) or synch sound. This can be dialogue linked to the scene or interview, or natural wild sound from the area or room, often called atmospheric (ATMOS) sound or room tone.

Or you can use non-diagetic sound—for example, music (other than music that might be playing on a radio in the scene, for example). So non-diagetic sound is added sound or commentative sound. It could be narration, as well as music and sound effects. I love the term "commentative," as that really is what this sound is doing; it's the filmmaker's POV as to what sound they add. There are some lovely films about Foleying sound on YouTube. My first job for the BBC was working in radio where they use Foley sounds all the time, to find sounds that will work as effects—for example, people walking in boots in mud (not easy to find in the center of London where I worked). Often sound mixers have their own libraries of SFX (sound effects) that they have already created; you can buy these effects at sound libraries too.

Non-diagetic sound can be used very effectively as a symbolic sting for each character to clearly make you feel a certain way every time you see that person on screen. A different tone of music will change how the viewer feels about the images you present. The lack of sound or dropping the music out to emphasize something, or just using natural sounds, can be really effective too. Music can also reference an ending of a scene or sequences and take you through the transition into the next scene. Natural sounds can be used as grammar in the film, adding punctuation points, telegraphing to your audience when a scene ends.

It can help with the continuity of the edit, so remember to get your sound person to record room tone from your interview. When you make a cut in the edit, the room tone can be layered underneath on other tracks as an L cut and can make the edit sound much smoother. I often get my students to close their eyes and listen to all the sound you can hear in a room; they all have unique reverberations, or heating elements, or air conditioning, or traffic noises outside, or sound from the neighbors, or me typing right now and my cat snoring in a chair (think of all the sound a room can hold). If you are editing an interview that was recorded in that room and you have pacing breaks that you have added in the edit, the film will lack that ambient sound. If you have recorded the room tone clean (without dialogue), at the end of the interview, having asked everyone in the room to be quiet while you record it. Make sure you say the words out loud "room tone" as soon as you turn on the mic. That way you won't think it's just random silence that you can ignore when logging in the edit room. The camera could also be pointing at the boom mic and recording. In the edit you can then add the room tone on Tracks 3 and 4, underneath the interview dialogue to smooth the audio.

You want to make sure you lay your tracks in your edit in a particular way so that if music is changed you can easily isolate that audio track. Often you'll lay your SOT (including dialogue) on Tracks 1 and 2. Tracks 3 and 4 room tone if you need it. Tracks 5 and 6 sound effects, non-diagetic. Tracks 7 and 8 music. Then if you use narration you will add extra tracks…

If you work with a Composer, a temporary music track will be really useful for them, and you. When you edit after your score is composed, the beat of the music shouldn't be as hard then to match with the edit of the image. But if it's tonally a completely different piece of music, that's a major job. Work with temp music that will sound the way you want your final music to sound. Don't rely on the emotional power of a known piece of music or song unless you know you can license it for your film. Licensing music can be extremely expensive depending on who wrote and recorded or performed it. That is why so often filmmakers use a composer or music libraries, which are less expensive.

You can use a Music Supervisor who can help articulate your ideas to a composer. They are really helpful but of course come at a cost. We used a Music Supervisor because our film was also about music, and although our Editor is musical, I'm not, so my musical vocabulary is limited. Our Music Supervisor was able to translate what I wanted to the composer really easily and made this process much smoother.

We used library music for our temp tracks and considered sticking with those tracks to keep the costs down (those libraries introduce better tracks all the time) until we realized how important music was to our film, and thankfully our music composition was donated, so it was free! And people compliment us on the score all the time. Thank you Clean Cuts.

FINISHING AND ASSEMBLY

We had a lot of different footage formats in our cut, of widely varying quality. Some SD, mini-DV, archival footage, news reports downloaded from YouTube, etc. That lower resolution can fall apart in a high-resolution film, especially when you project to theatrical screen sizes.

We wanted to get the best out of our footage, so we went to a well-known post-production house in NYC, to use their Digital Intermediate process to help improve this footage, and they worked some magic. But it wasn't cheap, and while you're making your film you should review how important each piece of archive footage is, and how important theatrical distribution is to your film. And whether it is Fair Use (i.e. free to use), which we cover in Chapter 11.

This is what you will also need to prepare for finishing your edit (refer also to Chapter 11):

- ▶ script with timecode

- ▶ credits

- ▶ music cue sheet (timecodes of when the music appears, its title, artist, length of track used, etc.)

- ▶ clearance footage log for lawyers (the entire film broken down shot by shot with timecode, clearly identifying the origin of *all* footage, so your lawyer can see what can be deemed fair use and what footage you need to license)

- ▶ releases

- ▶ Errors and Omissions (E&O) insurance.

10
Case Study: *Cartel Land* Edit

Often a documentary's story really comes together in the edit. Think of it in terms of writing fiction. The "writing" of a documentary happens in the edit and that's why often you see an Editor also getting a writing credit on the film. It expresses the amount of work that she/he has committed to the film's final story. I know, and have heard, many Directors and Editors say their films were saved in the edit, or the filmmakers bought them a cut of a very different film and it's now transformed.

We've already talked a little about story beats— beats making scenes, scenes making sequences, etc. Whether you have a vérité, essay, hybrid or investigative documentary you will analyze story beats in exactly the same way: what do they do to serve the purpose of your film or story arc? How does your film progress? How do your characters develop, grow and transform in some way?

I talked earlier about analyzing films, and I do this in a very basic way in a spreadsheet—see Figure 10.1. When I analyze films, I look at the underlying purpose of each scene. Where are the turning points, raising tensions, heightened emotions, surprises? I plot each dominant emotion as being the resonant tone of the scene.

Case Study: *Cartel Land* Edit

CARTEL LAND		PLOT POINT	FULL SCENE DETAIL
		Matt Heinmeman is a shooter, director and shot on C300	
		Matt Hamacheck is a friend and amazing editor - uses puntuation to end a scene, often sound	
OPEN		Cartels making meth	Sets up promise, access to cartels. Nothing like this
			Not easy enemies
			Bit of a cheat as doesn't appear elsewhere
			Here it feels like inciting incidence
			We tried 4 or 5 opens.
SEQUENCE	SCENE 1	ACTION	Arizona Vigilantes - makes it accessible to US
			Newsfeed explains who they are
			ACTION Infrared, TENSE search, **ends scene on spit 1:32**
	SCENE 2	OBSTACLES - NO GOV HERE	Back story "wild wild west" as no law here
	SCENE 3	CARTELS HORRIFIC	MEXICO devastated family funeral EMOTIONAL
		NO GOV	Innocent workers killed because of boss, Gov doesn't do anything
	SCENE 4	COMPARISON	Mexican Character protecting himself
			Intensify horror, heads cut off
SEQUENCE	SCENE 5	START OF GROUP/1ST ATTACK	
		HOPEFUL	1ST attack took three weeks to clear town
			town meeting getting recruits
huge 20 m	SCENE 6 & 7	HUGE ACTION SCENE AUTODEFENSA FIGHTING CARTEL	
		hope to disarming, to hope	Army arrives to disarm
			TENSE woman screaming at army
			weapons given back
			end scene army tells head of autodefensa "it's on your head"
END OF ACT 1?		AT PINNACLE STORY A MOVE TO B	Jose Manuel Mireles gives victory speech
24 MINS	SCENE 8	REVEAL DRUG ADDICT (24 MINS)	US vigilante news "anti gov patriot groups all time high"
			back story of character meth addict, lost job illegals got them all
			but only care now about drug cartels
	SCENE 9	ACTION VGILANTE GROUP MEETING	US gov in with cartels
	SCENE 10	MEXICO BACK STORY CHARACTER	JOSE MANUEL MIRELES
:33 MINS	SCENE 11	CARTEL STORY	Character tells terrible story and
			covered by fire and time lapse shots
	SCENE 12	YOU WANT TO SEE NEXT SCENE THE AUTODEFENSA ATTACK	

FIGURE 10.1 Excel spreadsheet of beats

Scenes and sequences are a big part of how you change the rhythm of the film. If there is no change of tone, mood or pace the film gets tedious. Sheila Curran Bernard describes this well:

> So there is likely to be a turning point at the end of a scene and even bigger one at end of sequence. Each scene creates a shift or reversal, each sequence minor change, each act major change. This turning point acts to release you into a new environment and motivates you to want further scenes.

There is one film that I have chosen here as a case study that I now know very well. I ask my students to watch the film before a class and we analyze it together in-depth. Focusing on Mexican drug cartels and the citizens and agencies that battle against them, the film is *Cartel Land* (2015). This documentary feature performed very well around the world, was nominated for an Oscar and won many awards. It was directed and shot by Matt Heineman and the lead Editor was Matt Hamachek (who I mentioned in Chapter 9 for

112 Case Study: *Cartel Land* Edit

his editing on 2011's *If a Tree Falls*) but also edited by Heineman, Bradley Ross and Pax Wasserman.

Have a look at my spreadsheet breakdown in Figure 10.1. You can see the ebb and flow and undulations of the story beats.

I also break my own work down this way. It's a tremendously effective way of working through the film, especially when an Editor is blocked, when you can't see the wood for the trees, so to speak. I also help students apply this to their own work, and I can physically see the light bulb moments when they realize they have broken through the block. They pick up their drooped defeated shoulders and their whole countenance changes. I go one step further with my own films and break down each scene into the beginning, middle and end. To make sure every few minutes you are being given new surprising information or feeling an emotion. This 2-minute analysis is a great tool borrowed from the filmmaker Marshall Curry (*Street Fight, If a Tree Falls, Point and Shoot*).

Using these tools I can make sure I don't have scenes with the same plot points one after the other, so my film won't start to drag. No one can absorb scene after scene of unrelenting action, action, action. A film needs scenes with moments of reflection, or revelation, or struggle or conflict, or hope, rising tension or humor. Humor is so often forgotten in documentaries.

Back to the film we're about to analyze. The Director Matt Heineman is a cinematographer and shot most of this film by himself on a Canon C300. He readily admits that he doesn't know much about lighting, which is refreshingly humble when you look at how beautiful the film looks.

He talked at a DOC NYC festival panel about the one scene he had to light, he lit with a flashlight as he doesn't shoot with lights. It is the very first scene of the film (and spoiler alert you might see it later). He dreamt about this scene and it took nine months to get the people involved, the Cartel, to give him the OK to film it. He met with masked men from the Cartel in a town square, allowed himself to be blindfolded and then driven into a remote forest. He did set up one ground rule with the Cartel that was important to him: that he not be thrown in the trunk of the car for the entire journey! This is an exceptionally brave filmmaker.

Matt Heineman surprisingly reveals this wasn't even necessarily the scariest scene to shoot; I'll let you know another when we get there. This film is full of incredible access and unbelievable scenes.

Now I'll break *Cartel Land* down the same way it is in my spreadsheet, only in text form. I have capitalized the tone of the scenes and plot points as we go through the detailed text.

OPEN OF *CARTEL LAND*—A character, wearing a scarf to disguise his face while making the lethal drug methamphetamine, talks to the Director: "We're poor, and the US buy the drugs," and we would do "clean jobs ... if we could." This perfectly sets up the film. It gives us the film's promise: that we will have unbelievable access to a drug Cartel and to a powerful inherent conflict, that because the drug cartels are making the drugs for the USA, the USA is implicit in this crime. An American father and son even taught the Cartel how to produce it.

There are no easy protagonists or antagonists in this film, and that not only feels like a new angle on drug smuggling but a unique take on endless stories we hear or see on TV about Cartels. There is also something else that is unusual about this scene and the characters, which I will reveal later.

TITLE—A sequence of the delivery of drugs across the Mexican/US border.

SCENE 1– time code 04:10. I should really call this a sequence because it takes you into a number of locations. Opens on a border line; we hear audio from a man in voice over, "There's an imaginary line between good and evil, right and wrong." We see one shot of him, Nailer, not talking just driving, and then a newsfeed explains what is happening in the US and introduces us to the issue: Cartels have taken over. The border control agents are overwhelmed, so concerned citizens are arming themselves.

We then move into a night scene, where we expect (or want) to see what vigilantes do; the shots are of vigilantes in infrared walking the border. This is an ACTION scene of these American vigilantes searching for the "illegals." It ends with no one being captured but a lovely audio edit where you hear the sound of spitting to telegraph to us that the scene is over. It then dips to black.

In this scene, we are presented with the US side of the story, in English. I wonder if this is because the Director and Editor were thinking of their audience and consciously trying to make it more relatable to English-speaking countries. The fact that these scenes don't have to be subtitled makes the whole film that much more accessible to a wider audience. But this arc, of the US border vigilante, of Nailer, is what I consider the B-story of the film and works only in comparison to the A-story.

SCENE 2–TC 07:23. At nearly eight minutes in, the backstory of our US vigilante character is revealed through interview. He explains and reveals OBSTACLES, most notably that vigilantes aren't always seen as a good thing. They're considered possible racists. His line, "No Government here … " is poignant, it's like the "wild wild west … " the police are 90 minutes away. This is the story beat, or the purpose of the scene and the goal. Is he the antagonist or is he your protagonist of this story? The scene ends with a line about the Cartels not caring about anyone, and a lightning storm, which gives us not only a sense of foreboding but a strong end to the scene.

SCENE 3—Music changes. In the previous scene we just heard the vigilante's justification for his actions: he does what he does because the Cartels are evil. So, putting yourself in the mind of a member of the audience, what do you want to see next?

We are taken on a journey through Mexico and a list of names is read out by a woman in interview intercut with a very EMOTIONAL scene of a funeral. Now we're seeing just how bad the Cartels really are—which is exactly what we wanted to know—the perfect time to be given this scene.

A man reveals the Cartel killed every member of a large family, even innocent teenagers and babies. Innocent workers killed for revenge as their boss's actions went against the Cartel, and the government doesn't do anything about it. A short music sting ends the scene as the graves are covered.

How are you feeling right now? Were the US vigilantes right? What do you want these Mexican people to do? What would you do? Do we need someone to seek retribution?

SCENE 4–13:36. We are introduced to a new character in Mexico who loads up his gun and talks about defending his community. He shows us images of his neighbors' heads cut off by the Cartel, on his phone, which suggests this may have been something that happened very recently. It INTENSIFIES the HORROR of the Cartels. We hear again how the government doesn't do anything. He asks us "What would you do?" the only time in the film that anyone talks to camera. So, "We decided the best way was to die fighting." Now as an audience we can breath a sigh of relief: we want this man; the community needs this man to avenge these innocent deaths.

You can feel the comparison with the similar language used by the US vigilantes across the border, but this time we want these Mexicans to fight this injustice. We are almost shouting a cheer as we hear from this character, and start feeling a warmth towards him...what a hero ... someone who is so motivated to protect his community.

He introduces us to archive footage of a first meeting of the town elders, where they decide to form a rebellion. What will happen? We are motivated to want the next scene.

SCENE 5—Music changes, we see guns and hear about the first attack in one town led by these elders. We wanted this ACTION, we wanted to see them succeed to drive out the Cartel from this town and we are left feeling HOPEFUL as the town is cleared of the Cartel in just three weeks.

Ask yourself how you'd feel if they didn't succeed?

Dr. Mireles, our "hero" character, appears in this scene wearing a mask. He then tells us that he might as well reveal his face, as the town knows it was him. He becomes the leader of the newly formed group, "Autodefensa" (AD). Recruits are given t-shirts and join Mireles.

What are you feeling right now as an audience member? Are you joyful and happy that they succeeded?

SCENE 6–18:00. The music changes again, signifying a new scene, and the new group, bolder and more courageous, moves on to the next town. We hear in voice over how they have taken six towns for three days at a time.

Chronologically this scene may not have happened in this way. After the first attack, people probably went back to their regular lives for a while. Other filming may have taken place but the Editor gives us what we want, he senses how the audience is feeling. We now know who the hero is, he has had one big win, so let's see what he'll do next. I think if he went home, or simply had some kind of meeting, we would have felt let down. The Editor is deliberately building here...why? I'll reveal my thoughts after the next scene.

We're at 18 minutes in and in Scene 6 the action INTENSIFIES TENSION. We hear how the government is often working with the criminals. The townsmen and women are joining in; we see vérité shots of breaking into

116   Case Study: *Cartel Land* Edit

houses. They handcuff the Templar Cartel, and it is just regular townspeople doing this. It's a huge ACTION scene.

SCENE 6 cont'd.—We're still in a town, but on the streets in exterior shots, not in the houses. So we're led to believe these all happened in the same location. But maybe they have used archive footage from other attacks. It does look slightly different to the trained eye. But only the trained eye would question it I think. This doesn't take us out of the film, but works very well to help the rising feeling of building tension.

We hear helicopters, a man points (just two shots) and then we see a group of what looks like the army arriving. Someone in voice over tells us it is indeed the army.

The absence of police/army or government has already been introduced as a beat of the story, so this arrival feels like a big moment. The army (or government, however you want to look at it) arrives on the scene and they have a very heated exchange with a member of Autodefensa. At least we think it is AD because Dr. Mireles is standing nearby. A powerful music sting is heard, driving the intensity of the argument, as the army tells AD they must disarm.

We're now introduced, for the first time, to the clear antagonist on the Mexican side of the border. Even the music directs us to feel this way. The army wants to confiscate AD's weapons, and we feel the very real push back by the community. Townspeople are asked by Mireles on loudspeaker to come out of their homes to defend the group. Everything is tense. Crowds brandishing sticks push army vehicles, a woman with a baseball bat screeches at the army.

The army eventually leaves without taking the weapons and tells AD, "It's on your head," washing their hands of responsibility for deaths and warfare. And yet we feel HOPEFUL. Why?

The music softens, there is clapping and we hear Mireles give a victory speech. Did the Director really capture a victory speech at that time? Maybe, but you feel the point of view of the Director and Editor here, in the music choice, in the sound design and in the shot choices. You feel as Mireles does. You're happy that the government didn't disarm the militia, or vigilantes, or whatever you want to call them.

Case Study: *Cartel Land* Edit

The scene ends with Dr. Mireles victory speech, warning the recruits not to act like the Cartels. Why is this warning included here, do you think? Foreshadowing maybe? The scene ends on sound punctuation, we hear hand claps with the sunset on a silhouetted man holding a gun on a hillside.

This is a high point of our A-story, a real turning point. This is a huge sequence of events, we're left feeling hopeful, we want to see who wins, we've just watched great action scenes.

So the filmmakers can keep us dangling here, knowing they've left us in a place wanting more. An apex.

I feel pretty certain this is the end of Act 1. We know all the characters, what is at stake, the obstacles. The journey has well and truly began for our protagonist(s?) to reach their goals.

When the film is at a high point of the A-story, the audience wants very badly to get to the next scene. This is the perfect time to return to the B-story, as the audience will hold on to the tension that's left hanging in the A-story.

SCENE 7–24:00. With one shot over a town, and a traffic sign on the highway, we're back with the US vigilantes. The music drops out under traffic sound effects. The radio newsfeed tell us, "Vigilantes are at an all-time high." We see our vigilante driving, but hear his voice over telling us his backstory. It reveals very quickly that he was not just a drug addict but a meth addict, the very drug the Cartel were making in the first scene of the film.

This is a big REVEAL AND SURPRISE. A huge revelation has just been given to us at 24 minutes into the film. If this had been revealed earlier it wouldn't have the same impact. You're given this news just when you need it, for that "Aha!" moment. The US vigilante was a drug addict. It plays into all of our preconceived ideas as an audience member, that those who protest too much have something to hide. To show someone who is strongly and passionately attacking an issue—and is so vehemently black-and-white about this issue—suggests immediately that maybe there is something more to their story. And indeed there was.

We hear a short line about the mental abuse from his father as he talks about cleaning himself up and trying to get work. All the while, we see him gear up and walk his patrol of the border. He talks about losing his job. We hear that he feels jobs have been lost to "illegals," and he wanted to do something about this. He says he apprehended "illegals," and we see shots of illegal immigrants being put into vans. This footage may be archive footage from elsewhere, or footage filmed with the police, as we don't see him in these shots. But the Editor or crew got footage for this one way or another, and it makes the scene work. We hear an interview from one illegal immigrant, just a few lines about how they are used by human traffickers. Then our vigilante almost responds to that comment by saying he has shifted his goal, now he only cares about drug traffickers not about losing jobs to illegals. As a character he has shifted his goal.

This has been told to us in a montage scene and it works thematically. We also are experiencing some EMPATHY, emotion that could also be compassion for a complicated character. The US vigilante is becoming a more complex character as we learn his backstory, and has a moment of transformation by the end of this scene.

Depending on which culture we're from or where we live, or our fundamental moral beliefs, we may be conflicted about this character. It starts with the surprise revelation about his drug addiction, how our vigilante used to capture illegal immigrants because he lost his job and then how he pivoted in his goal to just capture drug traffickers. Do we now have a better understanding of his cause? Could he be a protagonist after all?

Whatever we may be feeling the scene ends with a gunshot into the air, an act of threatening war or power, to remind us of the goal of the protagonists, and motivate us into the next scene. After all, that's what this whole film is about, a war on drugs.

SCENE 8—US VIGILANTE GROUP GROWS. A short scene, only about 90 seconds. More recruits have joined and are watching the news, and our vigilante talks about the US government being in bed with the cartels. We've heard the same argument from the Mexicans. We hear from the other recruits, about border walls, tall fences making better neighbors, the oath in the army that enemies are foreign and we are being invaded by cartels, the villains.

You could argue that this scene isn't necessary. But our main character has said he doesn't always agree with the other recruits. So do we remain sympathetic to his plight or are we further conflicted? Is he our antagonist after all? Maybe that is the only reason for this scene, the CONFLICTED emotions we have about this group as it begins to grow.

SCENE 9—MEXICO, NEW INFO, OUR PROTAGONIST IS A DOCTOR. Another "Aha!" reveal moment for the audience: our hero is a doctor. This has been slowly revealed to us, we didn't need to know this about our main character before, it was better to hold off on this great reveal as now we like our hero even more, who doesn't slightly hero worship doctors?

This is a lovely scene of Dr. Mireles with a little child. Why do politicians kiss children? To make them look great. This is a well-developed protagonist, we believe in Dr. Mireles's fight, his goal, we are now even more sympathetic to his cause and we want him to win. The scene ends as he watches a sad scene in his office where the Cartel have caught two young men, it gives us more context explaining who the Templars are as he comments on the clip. It moves the story on and this transitions us into the next scene...

SCENE 10–32:00. A night drive. Under moonlight, we hear an interview of a woman being kidnapped. It is SHOCKING. We're reminded of the terror of the Cartel. A female character tells a terrible story, that is hugely emotional, about how her family are killed in front of her and she is raped. It has been some time since we've heard the extent of the Cartel's evil. This is a devastating reminder of the terrible and heinous crimes that they commit.

The coverage of this scene, to cover the edits, are flames of fire. Our interviewee mentions a fire at the beginning of her interview, but other than that the coverage is symbolic. Fire represents destruction, hot, fear, "fired-up" emotions. It was a stylistic decision by the Editor. When I ask students if there is anything about this scene that they remember, they never say, oh that fire cutaway that didn't make sense.

So stop the film. What do you want to see next? How are you feeling? Fired up? Do you want revenge, justice for that woman? You want to see that next, and Matt Hamachek is going to give it to you.

SCENE 11—You are now totally motivated to want this next scene, I know I am. A scene of ACTION, the Director/Cinematographer shoots a real gun fight, an Autodefensa (AD) ATTACK, it is an action scene. They capture "Chaneque and Caballo."

SCENE 12—Music changes, and we see a newsfeed telling us that 28 towns have been taken.

120   Case Study: *Cartel Land* Edit

Mireles talks to the town. We feel HOPEFUL. Is it possible that they could take the whole state? There is a montage of attacks, seizing the drugs, more towns, people wearing AD t-shirts, photo shoots and magazines covers featuring Dr. Mireles, he really has been made a hero by the nation. The press celebrate his victory and Mireles makes a joke to a young reporter about not giving out his phone number because his wife would be jealous. This may not have seemed particularly important to you, but remember this later, as it's a hint, a subtle foreshadowing.

Remember how we talked earlier about spreading these throughout the film?

SCENE 13–41:00. SHOCK. A night scene, the AD crew watch the MEXICAN PRESIDENT on television. AD are on night patrol and capture a member of the Templar Cartel. We hear Mireles speak, "They can't hand this person over to the government as they don't do anything, they're just set free." CONFLICT. Dr. Mireles in darkness, whispering instructions, "to put them in the ground" after they have gotten information. The screen goes to darkness.

Have we as the audience been naive? This is war, but to hear our hero say those words is intense. Essentially, it sounds like he is ordering someone's death. What an incredibly strong turning point. Wow, our hero is flawed. We are conflicted. This is just the folly of war, but it is such rare access to actually hear a person giving the order to kill someone. It feels like a scene out of the Sopranos. But this is real life.

Maybe now is a good time to look at that spreadsheet in its entirety. Look at my example at the beginning of the chapter which is how I would usually construct all of this information. Look at what the story beats do for the flow of the story arc, the rising tension, the conflict, the emotion we're made to feel. Never too front-loaded with scene after scene of information or action, this film is giving us time for contemplation and reflection.

Most scenes have been motivated; there are obstacles and turning points, similar to the Aristotelian form of fictional storytelling. You can see this as a pattern when you break down and analyze the film in this way. We haven't been overwhelmed with information, just given enough to not be confused. Then, the relevant information is peppered in, right when we need it.

SCENE 14–42:10. STRUGGLE OF FAMILY MAN. We hear the bells of town to signify a new scene. Mireles enters a swimming pool and we see him with his family. We hear an interview with Mireles's wife. We're nearly 45 minutes into the film and it's the first time we have heard her voice.

She tells us this is the first time the family has been together for six months. We hear her own struggle and what she had to give up to be married to this fearless leader. The CONTRAST with the scene before of a bright family setting. We hear her obstacles—and therefore Mireles's obstacles—are the story beats of this scene. You hear from his wife just when you need it, we didn't need to see her before or know that he had a family.

This may be symbolically hinting at a dual personality, a leader of fighters and a father. We need this scene to be placed here because the last scene expressed the hero's flaw and we need to care about him again to feel sympathy and for the next scene to hit that much harder, and make more of an impression on us emotionally.

SCENE 15—SHOCK. Not even 2 minutes later, we see shots from over head of a field and hear a plane sound effect. Newsfeed states that Mireles has been in a plane crash. The question is raised as to whether it was an accident or sabotage; that is a question that doesn't need to be answered. You don't have to resolve everything, keep the film as tight as possible and if you can keep the audience guessing that can be thrilling for the viewer too. In the previous scene, you have just been told he has a family. Because of that, you're made to care about his family, even more about the accident, and the shock reverberates more intensely. You hear one sound bite from "Papa Smurf," one of the AD members, and then a great sound edit moves us from hospital monitor beeps which turn into gunshots and we see…

SCENE 16—Story beat of ACTION AND CHAOS of AD. This is completely motivated, as the audience has to know what happens in response to Mireles's accident. What sounds like news audio tells of chaos in the group AD without Mireles, we see a scene of action, of fighting, news reports tell us that the Mexican president wants to stop them. This is the first time the government talks about Autodefensa (AD).

Rising tension has been crafted so deftly in this scene spend some time watching it. The punctuation to end the scene is a member of AD crying. We are led to believe it's over a dead member of the group as they're wearing the white t-shirt.

SCENE 17—Mexico City in sunset, news audio talks about Mireles's accident and explains that he is currently in recovery. We hear his voice under images of the moon, what he remembers, his recovery with a walking stick. He tells us of spinal cord injuries and his face is paralyzed, again all in voice over (VO). Finally, he is worried for his family's safety, but he is worried more for his home region of Michoacán. We are given this information for a reason, make note of it.

Mireles now has serious OBSTACLES to his goal. The turning point in this scene is that he has passed his responsibilities to Papa Smurf, who we have seen earlier.

SCENE 18—We see Papa Smurf in ACTION. This scene shows AD raiding houses and looting. We hear VO from a member of AD saying that they're just taking back from these houses what the Cartels took from them. Huge CONFLICT, are we seeing AD resorting to the same tactics as the Cartel?

SCENE 19—TURNING POINT and building tension. A town meeting with Papa Smurf. People don't want AD in town, people are saying that Autodefensa are raiding houses (which we have just seen), flirting with women, the town wants peace, wants AD to be gone, there is shouting from the townsfolk and AD are thrown out. Music comes in and then…

Remember we are in Act 2 of the film and the tension should be rising as we're in the middle of the act. Eventually at the end of Act 2 we'll hit the climax of the whole film. Right now you're so involved in the film, asking yourself, "What could possibly happen next?" You have to find out, you have to keep watching. So much action. So, if we're wanting more of the A-story, the Editor can make us wait, keep us in this holding pattern of tension, and take us to the B-story. This gives us breathing room, we can't have relentless action, we need to absorb and reflect. Matt Hamachek knows us better than we know ourselves. Don't give it to us too easily; make us wait.

SCENE 19—Time code at 52:00 minutes, a 60 second, short scene. Our characters in the B-story are actually reflecting and considering the work of AD. We're back in Arizona, the US vigilante is with his wife, they're watching clips on their computer of the AD raids. REFLECTION. They're analyzing what is happening in the same way we are, but they show sympathy for Autodefensa, "They're taking back against the Cartel, it's the way it should be done up here."

I'm not sure that we, as the audience, are feeling the same way. It is an interesting joining of the A & B storylines that merge here. Is this scene something that the Director created, showing the vigilantes the clips, making this scene happen? Giving us a pacing moment that we definitely needed. Interesting ... I wonder.

SCENE 20–53:00. ACTION. Hearing the Mexican voices of drug traffickers (possibly) through a new digital scanner, the US vigilantes go on patrol. This is the most tension we get from our B-story, as they do find people crossing the border.

A similar commentary is made by Nailer, almost the same words that we heard from Mireles, "If anyone touches me we drop 'em." Is he maybe suggesting they should be killed if they try to escape? As they're led down the mountainside, music comes in, and we go to night shots where the police collect the immigrants. Nailer doesn't actually say to kill them however and that is a big difference. Notice the leader of the captor and how he responds to Nailer's question "Yo sabe?"

For me this feels like a high point in the B-story so we can then return once again to our A-story.

An interesting transition happens between scenes here. We hear the US Vigilante say, "Innocent people are being caught up in a war." We then cut from his headshot to Mireles's head shot in the next scene. Is the Editor saying are they similar people after all? The film is visually showing an almost literal morphing between characters.

SCENE 21–58:00. THE HERO RETURNS, very EMOTIONAL. Mireles gets recognized in the airport, we hear that his children are still scared and we see Mireles's father upset. We can see half of his face is paralyzed.

SCENE 22—HERO RETURNS TO THE COMMUNITY Mireles walks into a town celebration, he is struggling to walk with the help of his children. The music is beautiful, emotional and foreboding. Still wearing his AD white shirt he fires up the town folk with his speech. It ends on people dancing and dips to black. Are we feeling HOPEFUL again?

SCENE 23—Group meeting having dinner, all the heads of Autodefensa are present. CONFLICT is revealed as we hear that some AD members feel others are breaking into houses. Dr. Mireles tells Papa Smurf "We have to be careful not to become criminals."

SCENE 24–01:05:00. Music changes and we see a member of the AD with his weapons. This is a huge ACTION scene of AD capturing people, are they acting as criminals here? We see a man explaining how to use a Taser: "You take them and if they don't want to go you do this." There are gun shots, the cameraman is shot at as he jumps out of car, incredible filmmaking. Pure action flick, all the more amazing as it's non-fiction. After a car chase, they capture a guy when he has pulled over at his home.

At 01:08:00 a child is desperately crying about her father being taken. This is incredibly emotional.

The tension continues to build as they jump back in the car with the captured man in an unbelievable scene. The AD member looks like he's on drugs, is menacing, and enjoying teasing and poking a gun at the man's head as he questions him. There is no doubt in my mind that the AD here is acting like a torturer, a bully, and a criminal and possibly has used drugs.

Imagine filming that scene as the car is being driven, you're facing backwards, a (probably/possibly) loaded gun is in the hands of someone that looks half crazed. The scene ends arriving at a compound and we're left hearing cries of torture. We see men waiting handcuffed, and dark foreboding music comes in.

Take a breath, you need it don't you. This feels like the climax of the film for me. We had heard that criminals may have infiltrated the AD but now we're feeling that the Autodefensa are actually becoming the Cartel, or are at least as bad. But perhaps this is really what war is—there is no "good" side. But let's see, is this the climax? We still have 30 minutes of the film to go.

SCENE 25–01:13:00. Newsfeed about the Mexican President wanting AD to disarm. Mireles meets with Papa Smurf and other AD members, and they go to a larger meeting. The camera films the ground, subtitles are mid screen, and they reveal that the government hasn't agreed to any of their terms. TURNING POINT. In an AD meeting they discuss becoming legal by joining the government. They admit to robbing, kidnapping, etc., and the president says he will forgive them. Mireles does not trust the government.

It works perfectly for the film that there are no shots of people talking in this scene. Surprising, right? It serves to make the meeting more mysterious, you have this secret access, and if you read any good screenwriting book they will always advise that the hero should be somewhat mysterious. It gives the meeting more weight and importance. Just listen to what is being said, no need to see anything! Audio is so important, if you can only get audio from a scene you might be ok. Better to have good audio and no image, than no audio and a good image.

SCENE 26–01:18:00. CONFLICT AND OUR HERO HAS FLAWS. Dr. Mireles is in a public town square meeting, drumming up support for his group, as he doesn't want to capitulate to the government. The scene ends revealing he's an adulterer, and a possible manipulator, as he professes his love and affection for a young woman from the crowd. He also can't keep his hands off her. However, his last line in the scene is, "This is the fight of our lives, we'll fight to the death," and we get a real shift in tone. This also reminds us, just in time, that he is a fighter (as well as a lover).

You have entered the scene hopeful that Mireles will still stand up to the government, the middle of the scene we wonder maybe if he is an adulterer and not trust him, and by the end we're conflicted because he is still fighting and the only hope against the Cartel. How are we supposed to feel about Mireles now? We're conflicted. Surely our hero doesn't so easily show his affections for young girls, in broad daylight, on camera? Have we lost faith in our hero?

SCENE 27—Music changes, the US vigilante's news footage reveals violence has increased across the border and border controllers have been killed. This motivates more US recruits joining. RISING TENSION. Our main character also says he won't back down, mirroring Mireles's line in the previous scene. The scene ends with an infrared lightning storm.

For me this scene is also placed here because we haven't seen the B-story for 20–25 minutes. Yes, border controllers have been killed, which is new information, but this scene doesn't feel as strong as the rest of the film. Another comparison of stories is happening here, both are prepared to fight to the death. It is a small hike in tension and gives us a break in the A-story which allows the next scene to pay off more strongly.

SCENE 28—Back with Mireles, he is recording a farewell video on his phone in case he gets killed. Some of the AD have joined the government and are called The Forgiven Ones. Are they essentially a new Cartel supported by the government? More TENSION as Autodefensa split and symbolically kick Mireles out of the group. SHOCK as Cartels have infiltrated AD, we are given this information from an interview with the member "El Gordo." "I'm with the government and Viagras Cartel." Papa Smurf agrees the Cartels are involved but nonetheless happily puts on a police shirt and wields the government-supplied gun.

This could be the second climax of the film, ending Act 2, followed by 15 minutes of descending action in Act 3. Remember I mentioned I thought the climax came earlier? Well hey why can't a film have two climax points. Maybe this is a four-act film. Tarantino breaks filmmaking rules all the time. They are only rules (dating back to Aristotle) to help the novice filmmakers construct a story in a satisfactory way. If you're good enough, break them; make your own rules. Hamacheck/Heineman's structure works brilliantly well.

SCENE 29–01:28:00. Reveals FEAR. Mireles is going to leave. He goes to see his girlfriend; we hear the audio only of Mireles saying to his girlfriend that they're all out to get him. He talks about meeting her in the US, and that he has to leave. The audio confirms that he is indeed an adulterer. Depending on whether you think adultery is categorically right or wrong will influence your feelings about him, possibly making you mistrust him. Has our hero fallen?

SCENE 30—Music transitions into Mireles's wife driving, you are completely MOTIVATED now to want to hear from his wife. She says, "He isn't who you think he is, he has the power to convince like a movie star, he's always had women." From the shots you feel that the family are leaving too, Mireles has let them down, they're not driving together. The hero has fallen in this scene, his downfall OBSTACLE was his adultery. Was it also because he was like a movie star, too good to be true? We're left to make our own decisions.

SCENE 31—A rooster sound covers a music edit. Mireles is on a ranch and he speaks in English for the first time. Why speak in English? Did he make it over the border to the US?

I have asked many people about this scene. Rarely do any of my students notice the change in language, but it's a wonderful subtle shift, again a merging of possible stories. Did Mireles escape to America from the violence as he said he would? Maybe.

He is not with his family on this ranch, he has lost everything, he says his family was his motive to fight, but was it? This is what he is saying now, and it contradicts what he said earlier. Do you remember back in Scene 24 he said that whatever it takes, he would fight to the death? Did he put his family first? He does admit that it is all his fault that he is now alone.

SCENE 32—When everything else feels like it has gone wrong, who can provide hope? It's not our original protagonist, who has lost everything. But our B-story (possible) protagonist, the US vigilante, now takes center stage. We've never been sure how we feel about him throughout the film. And this is powerful, that through the editing we've been made to keep guessing, letting us make up our own minds. Whoever we are will decide if we liked him or not. I know how I feel about putting up borders, but was there a little sympathy for him, at all?

He now speaks philosophically and HOPEFULLY. He talks about people around the world taking the law into their own hands. He tells us, "Cycles do stop if you want to change them." He won't repeat his father's mistakes, he thanks his father for being a sort of opposite role model—someone he never wanted to emulate, which caused him to behave in the exact opposite manner. "People have to want to change." Nailer is the morally sound person by the end. What a surprising twist.

SCENE 33—The same scene as the opening, the only time we think we see the real Cartel after the opening shots. Cartel members are speaking in English too, saying that everyone has been corrupted. A scene that features an amazing directorial choice.

Cartel members say that AD and Cartels are the same, both funded by Cartels. "We are them." A huge reveal that the very first character we saw on screen is wearing a POLICE SHIRT. He must have been wearing that shirt in the very first scene, but of course we aren't given that reveal until now for the most fantastic pay off. "Now we are part of them. It's never going to stop." Hard words, impossibly sad.

This is how the film ends, ambiguously, with good and evil mixed up and part of the same whole. There are no easy answers here, just people mixed up in human suffering, and others trying to make a difference. Part of the reality that the film has shown us is that it's often hard to tell who is who.

SCENE 34—A FINAL SHORT SCENE (BUTTON) ON THE FILM. An update shot of Mireles in maximum security prison.

And we have a new update: in April 2017 Jose Mireles was released from jail.

Oh and did you guess which scene was the most harrowing for Director Matt Heineman to shoot? Not the Cartel making meth, or in the car with the crazy Autodefensa as he is driving haphazardly through the streets of Mexico with a loaded gun pointed at a man's head? Heineman had many but one of the most disturbing was the woman who talks about her husband who was chopped up in front of her while she was raped. Heineman talks about the effect on him and her, that she was left with a hollow stare, a look of trauma, that went right through him.

After the film was made, Heineman was sent a photo showing one of the meth cookers killed. That meth cooker had said in the film that being in a Cartel meant he needed to live like a king because he would be dead by 30. Was he right? What an immensely brave director to make this film.

11

Copyright Law, Third-party and Archive Material

So let's consider your research for your film. Perhaps you need footage to illustrate a point and you don't have anything relevant in your own footage or what is commonly referred to as rushes. Archive footage might work, or a news article, or maybe it's a police surveillance camera. These are all called third-party materials, and there are many categories. It's called third-party because you literally don't own the material. You can't just take anyone's artwork whether writing, photographs or clips from a TV show to illustrate your point, without first considering the ownership of that work.

Whenever you produce any work, as soon as it is made or created, it is copyrighted. This wasn't always the case. So why is copyright a good thing? You don't want anyone taking your film and word-for-word recreating it. You want to try to make some money from your hard work, so that you use those funds to make another film or even just make a living. Copyright not only protects you from people reproducing your work but from piracy as well.

You can buy clips, license the rights to use them for a fee from many stock library footage banks or TV networks etc. Dependent on what you're wanting to buy, licensing costs will range in cost from US$60 per second to US$1K per second at the most expensive libraries.

There are many ways you can find footage. There are the expensive stock footage libraries like Footage Farm, Getty's or the BBC Motion Gallery. There are museums, private libraries or going directly to television networks. Or what about YouTube? And what if you haven't got a big budget?

Also consider how long you want to license the footage, artwork or piece of music. Think about what uses you need. Where will your film play? In theatres, online, etc.? And what territories (US, Europe, Asia, etc.)? Maybe you think it'll only play in America, because it's a story about the American education system. Prices vary by outlet and time and region.

Some people say it's not until you want to sell your film that you need to acquire all the rights for footage, so you could potentially screen at some festivals without them. But what if you fall in love with an image and what if the distributor wants your film right away? What if they approach you after the screening and you don't want to delay the negotiation or contract?

One thing to note is to try to negotiate the same rights for every clip you use: territory, length of deal, and commercial uses. So that you don't have to be aware of every clip coming up for renewal at different times over the lifespan of your film's distribution.

Back to researching footage.

The owner of a copyright has six exclusive rights, according to Perdue University. Under copyright, no one can do these things:

1. Reproduce the work. No one can reproduce an artwork without the creator's permission.

2. Create a derivative work (i.e., a video mash-up or re-contextualization).

3. Distribute (i.e., the person who owns the work has the right to decide where it is first shown publicly).

4. Display the work publicly—remember today we have pop-up advertising, banner ads, etc.

5. Perform the work—this one is easy to understand for any dance, music, play, etc.

6. Violate the "moral rights"—meaning the protection of the artist's vision, for site-specific work, etc.

So what happens if you violate these copyright laws? Penalties can include injunctions, your work can be impounded and destroyed, damages could consist of the profits you have made on your work and more. You can also be fined for every item that is in violation of copyright. So each DVD or book, for example, could incur a fine: 1,000 books sold, 1,000 times your fine.

MUSIC

There can be ways we can use original video or film, or photography or any image under a different class of copyright law that may make it free for us (see Fair Use). Music however often presents different issues due to ownership and the way it is used.

Often we are using music as a score and not as material to be discussed as an object of critique or to illustrate an argument. So music deserves a special mention in regards to copyright. There is a complicated licensing process for musical works as they have two forms of copyright. *Sync rights* for the words and music composition, and *master recording* rights for the actual recording of the piece.

So if, like me, you filmed a musician singing a song they had written, in a studio or performance space that you booked, and you booked their time specifically for this recording, then you only have to pay or secure the sync rights for the song/music. But who owns those rights can take some research. Sometimes labels can own the sync rights and publishers own the master recording rights. Especially if the band is well known. You can hire Music Supervisors to help you research and negotiate with these companies, or they may have knowledge to suggest a band that may offer a similar track that could be used or discuss with you composer fees.

Or let's take another example. One of our characters in *Musicwood* played some music, noodling around on his guitar. To use this in the film, we had to try to find out if this was his own music. He told us that it wasn't, so we then had to track down whose music it was and get a materials release and make sure the musician owned the sync license.

When you finish a film, the distributor will often expect a script to be delivered alongside a clearance sheet for footage and a music cue sheet with

132 Copyright Law, Third-party and Archive Material

Cue #	Scene Description	start TC	end TC	Comments	STATUS
01	Intro	1:00:00:00	1:01:18:14	Clean Cuts original composition	
02	Main Title Theme	1:01:18:14	1:01:47:01	Clean Cuts original composition	
03	Onscreen performance: Kaki King	1:02:06:16	1:03:37:12	"Bone Chaos in the Castle" Master / Publishing credits: TBD	NEED TO CLEAR
04	Chris Martin at Gruhn's Guitars	1:03:37:12	1:04:28:15	Clean Cuts original composition	
05	Composition of Guitar GRAPHICS	1:04:40:06	1:04:56:05	Clean Cuts original composition	
06	Bob Taylor at The Factory	1:05:17:19	1:06:16:03	Clean Cuts original composition	
07	Onscreen performance by Bob Taylor	1:05:57:17	1:06:16:22	Title: TBD	
08	Introduction To Tongass / Greenpeace	1:06:26:04	1:11:01:14	JuxMusic: "Anything You Can Synthesize" by The American Dollar	
09	Introduction of Sealaska	1:11:09:14	1:12:03:12	Original Native folk music from KTOO Celebration footage.	
10	Dave Berryman Gibson Intro	1:13:25:10	1:14:36:05	Clean Cuts original composition	
11	Onscreen performance: Yo La Tango	1:16:41:15	1:18:26:20	"The Ballad of Yo La Tango" Master / Publishing credits: TBD	NEED TO CLEAR
12	The Whales / Going Into the Forest	1:19:30:21	1:22:50:11	Clean Cuts original composition	
13	The Ecology of the Tongass	1:23:06:09	1:25:13:14	APM Track "Incognito" Underscore_RNM_0025_00601	NEED TO LICENSE
14	Clear Cut Forest	1:25:34:20	1:27:20:23	Clean Cuts original composition	
15	Celebration Event	1:27:21:22	1:28:38:07	Original music from the live performance at the event onscreen.	
16	Seeing Sealaska Forestry Ops	1:29:17:05	1:30:34:12	Clean Cuts original composition	
17	Marching into Celebration	1:32:32:04	1:32:50:15	Original music from the marching performance onscreen.	
18	History of Sealaska	1:33:58:18	1:35:33:05	Original Haida folk music from early 90's documentary. Not cleared, not fair use.	NEED TO CHANGE?
19	Change needed on Sealaska board	1:35:44:05	1:36:14:03	Clean Cuts original composition	
20	Tom and Vicky Sidebar	1:36:14:04	1:38:51:23	Clean Cuts original composition	
21	Sealaska Visit Gibson	1:39:41:05	1:41:06:03	Clean Cuts original composition	
22	Intro to FSC; Bob talks to SA	1:43:16:03	1:44:31:02	Clean Cuts original composition	
23	Building a Guitar	1:46:23:21	1:47:51:15	Clean Cuts original composition	
24	Onscreen Performance: Sergius Gregory	1:48:09:09	1:49:40:08	"Push Me Down" Master / Publishing credits: TBD	
25	Madagascar Trip	1:49:51:09	1:51:30:13	Clean Cuts original composition	
26	Land Deal	1:51:34:16	1:53:38:08	JuxMusic: The American Dollar "Ether Channels"	
27	Flight in before Tree Ceremony	1:57:11:05	1:57:55:04	Clean Cuts original composition	
28	Drive TO Tree Ceremony	1:58:12:15	1:58:46:14	Pre Existing Royalty-Free Loop	

FIGURE 11.1 *Musicwood* clearance log for footage

time codes for the amount of time all material is used (see Figure 11.1). The music cue sheet will look similar to the clearance log, except music tracks will replace footage description. This is also prepared for the lawyer when seeking Errors and Omissions insurance which we explain further in this chapter.

THIRD-PARTY MATERIALS

There is good news for us documentarians and a little understanding of copyright law can go a long way. We are often working with low budgets, and making critiques or cultural commentary with our work; often we can't do that without depicting the art, news or video footage that was produced at the time.

One of the best guides to understand the parameters in using third-party material has been produced by The Center for Media & Social Impact, based at American University's School of Communication in Washington, DC. It is an innovation lab and research center that creates, studies and showcases media for social impact and has supported filmmakers in its reporting on Fair Use, Free Speech and Intellectual Property Rights. Read it because you breathe a heavy sigh of relief realizing if you can make a good case, or rather a good argument maybe that expensive clip can be used for free. This will be covered in more detail later in the chapter (refer to the appendix for their website).

But let's remember copyright laws and be mindful of them because before certain laws were passed anyone could have taken your private journal if they found it and published it. Food for thought.

If you are still concerned about what might constitute a copyrighted work, take a look at this handy table produced by Cornell University—a copyright chart on http://copyright.cornell.edu.

PUBLIC DOMAIN

Alongside Fair Use some footage, at least older footage, may not be covered by copyright at all. Some creative works might in the public domain—i.e., the public can use them for free, with no copyright issues.

> The public domain consists of all works that never had copyright protection and works that no longer have copyright protection. The public domain also includes most works created by the United States government. All works in the public domain are free for the public to use. Works published in the United States prior to 1923 are in the public domain.
>
> (Perdue University)

So we have unrestricted access to almost all of the films and media from government departments: from National Oceanic Atmospheric Administration underwater submersible films (which I've used), to maps by the Forest Service (which I've also used), to love letters from Theodore Roosevelt (which I haven't used). I'm not sure he would ever have written love letters, but you get my drift. Anything pre-1923 and anything made by the government are all available to use for free.

FAIR USE

More good news! Citing the US Copyright Office:

> The fair use of a copyrighted work, including such use by reproduction in copies or phone records or by any other means specified by that

section, for purposes such as criticism, comment, news reporting, teaching (including multiple copies for classroom use), scholarship, or research, is not an infringement of copyright.

In other words, if you are making a point, cultural commentary or argument you may be able to qualify the use of that clip as Fair Use, and thus the clip is free!

To determine whether the use of a work is a fair use, the US copyright office asks you to consider four factors: purpose and character of the use; nature of the copyrighted work; the amount and substantiality of the portion used in relation to the whole; and the effect of the use on the potential market.

Here's Title 17 of the US Code cited from the US Copyright Office:

> Section 107 of the Copyright Act provides the statutory framework for determining whether something is a fair use and identifies certain types of uses—such as criticism, comment, news reporting, teaching, scholarship, and research—as examples of activities that may qualify as Fair Use.
> Section 107 calls for consideration of the following four factors in evaluating a question of fair use:
>
> ▶ *Purpose and character of the use, including whether the use is of a commercial nature or is for nonprofit educational purposes*: Courts look at how the party claiming fair use is using the copyrighted work, and are more likely to find that nonprofit educational and noncommercial uses are fair. This does not mean, however, that all nonprofit education and noncommercial uses are fair and all commercial uses are not fair; instead, courts will balance the purpose and character of the use against the other factors below. Additionally, "transformative" uses are more likely to be considered fair. Transformative uses are those that add something new, with a further purpose or different character, and do not substitute for the original use of the work.
>
> ▶ *Nature of the copyrighted work*: This factor analyzes the degree to which the work that was used relates to copyright's purpose of encouraging creative expression. Thus, using a more creative or imaginative work (such as a novel, movie, or song) is less likely to support a claim of a fair use than using a factual work (such as a technical article or news item). In addition, use of an unpublished work is less likely to be considered fair.

▶ *Amount and substantiality of the portion used in relation to the copyrighted work as a whole*: Under this factor, courts look at both the quantity and quality of the copyrighted material that was used. If the use includes a large portion of the copyrighted work, fair use is less likely to be found; if the use employs only a small amount of copyrighted material, fair use is more likely. That said, some courts have found use of an entire work to be fair under certain circumstances. And in other contexts, using even a small amount of a copyrighted work was determined not to be fair because the selection was an important part—or the "heart"—of the work.

▶ *Effect of the use upon the potential market for or value of the copyrighted work*: Here, courts review whether, and to what extent, the unlicensed use harms the existing or future market for the copyright owner's original work. In assessing this factor, courts consider whether the use is hurting the current market for the original work (for example, by displacing sales of the original) and/or whether the use could cause substantial harm if it were to become widespread.

The Center for Media & Social Impact, based at American University, has created a statement of Best Practices in Fair use available online. They worked with Documentary organizations and filmmakers to produce four classes of situations, with their informing principles and limitations that filmmakers can apply to their footage to consider whether it can be deemed Fair Use.

One thing that is extremely important to note is that Fair Use is not a defense to claims of violation of privacy or publicity rights. And while copyright is protected under Federal Law, privacy changes from state to state. So be very clear you know what these are when it comes to casting, locations, research and third-party materials, etc. So let's look at the difference between them.

PRIVACY

What is the difference between privacy and copyright, and why do I care as a filmmaker? The Library of Congress provides a great explanation to the difference between privacy and copyright:

> Privacy and publicity rights reflect separate and distinct interests from copyright interests. While copyright protects the copyright holder's

property rights in the work or intellectual creation, privacy and publicity rights protect the interests of the person(s) who may be the subject(s) of the work or intellectual creation. Issues pertaining to privacy and publicity may arise when a researcher contemplates the use of letters, diary entries, photographs or reportage in visual, audio, and print formats found in library collections. Because two or more people are often involved in the work (e.g., photographer and subject, interviewer and interviewee) and because of the ease with which various media in digital format can be reused, photographs, audio files, and motion pictures represent materials in which issues of privacy and publicity emerge with some frequency.

Let's consider four kinds of privacy:

1. **APPROPRIATION OF LIKENESS**—using an unauthorized commercial use of a person's name or image without their consent. This usually refers to a celebrity and a filmmaker is benefitting from their likeness. Comedy (parody) and news have different rules.

2. **INTRUSION ON RIGHT TO SECLUSION**—This does not include public spaces, but does include hidden cameras and long lenses shooting through windows, for example. This is violating a person's right to solitude. Again, if doing a highly investigative journalistic piece then there are different rules. In 2017, some states have changed their rules for journalists as well, especially regarding agricultural companies in the Midwest. These corporations and factories are arguing that they have the right to privacy, and that journalists will also be trespassing.

3. **PUBLIC DISCLOSURE OF PRIVATE FACTS**—Publishing images or text concerning information about a person's health, financial, sexual, license plate, underage, address. Again, if deemed "news" you may be able to avoid this.

4. **FALSE**—False light publicity. You can be exposing someone to ridicule or incompetence or mental health issues. Must have substantive evidence. If true, you must be able to cite sources.

When I was trained at the BBC any factual information I was presenting had to have two credible sources—credible sources being newspapers or books, etc. Wikipedia is not deemed "credible."

Lauren Greenfield, director of the documentary *The Queen of Versailles*, was sued by one of the major characters in the context of false light publicity. The case was eventually dropped because it was proved that the director never said that the character was a bad business-person.

Presenting anyone in a false light, even if true, has the potential to be highly offensive. You have to be especially careful of any editing that could be seen as potentially misleading or damaging. In *Queen Of Versailles* Greenfield let the character speak for himself. If you do this in an interview, in vérité or a court case, then their own words will offer a POV, especially if it is obvious you haven't cut into the sound bites on-camera. Be careful of that. If you want to read further, there is a very well-known case against the filmmaker Joe Berlinger by Chevron Oil which is especially interesting. This is also discussed later in the chapter in conversation with my own lawyer.

RELEASES

Having participants sign a personal release form allows you to legally use that person's interview, likeness, etc. If you can't get a paper copy be sure to get them to at least release themselves on-camera, saying their name and that they are happy to be filmed for your project.

Personal releases, location releases, third-party materials releases—we have included examples in the Appendix (at the end of the book). There are also useful film community websites that allow you to print blank releases that you can adapt for your own production.

WHEN A RELEASE ISN'T POSSIBLE

So let's say you have done a good amount of research on finding all the rights holders for footage you have found online (a term called "due diligence"). This done, you now think because of the argument or commentary you are making in your film that this third-party material can be used without consent.

You've also received photos and have a release from the photographer, as well as some of the people that appear in the photos. But one person wasn't contactable, you just can't track that person down. So you have some risk.

Also you have used some music in the film you haven't paid for or enquired about licensing because you're making an argument about how society is reflected in the music, maybe about how punk music is an example of how young people viewed the government in Washington DC at the time.

All possible scenarios that pose some risk. You think you're probably ok, but that piece of music might be recognized even though you can't find out who owns it, so what can you do to protect yourself? First you should try and consult with a music clearance company, there are experts in the field. And if it isn't music you consult an entertainment lawyer, but you can actually do even more than that by buying a type of insurance known as Errors and Omissions (E&O) insurance.

E&O insurance is an insurance plan—in case anyone tries to sue you and your film. You will have to do your due diligence in researching the origin of all footage and music. This means that as you gather all of your releases, music licenses and archive rights you will have done your best at attaining releases and discovering owners, ideally with paper trails. Before airing your film, most TV networks expect to see all your releases and legal documents, many of them require E&O, and you'll have more peace of mind about that footage you "acquired." E&O will cover the lawyer costs if someone tries to sue you. It can ensure you don't lose all your life savings, your home or make you bankrupt.

For *Musicwood*, we worked with the incredible lawyers at Donaldson + Callif in California. They've represented huge documentaries such as the aforementioned *Queen of Versailles, Inside Job, Weiner, Jane* and many, many more. They helped us make sure everything in *Musicwood* was cleared, and helped us enormously with Fair Use on our third-party material.

We were honestly very surprised at how much footage we could use that was deemed Fair Use. Michael C. Donaldson gives great advice on Fair Use for filmmakers:

> You never have to pay a penny if you understand Fair Use. *Room 237*—a third was clips from *The Shining*. Yes, we got a call from Warner Bros. and we talked to them, but not a penny was paid. In the film *Los Angeles Plays Itself*, there are no other materials in the film besides clips. Every clip was Fair Use. You can't be afraid of this.

Encouraging words, so essentially if you abide by Fair Use laws you may be OK.

So as a reminder here is a quick basic three-question checklist regarding Fair Use rules:

1. Does this item illustrate your point?

2. Do you only use as much as you need?

3. Is it a clear connection between the item you're using and the point you're making?

Our lawyers also helped out with other complications. With *Musicwood*, we had agreed to show the final cut to all the major parties involved in the film before we screened publicly. Our film highlights some tricky situations about procuring "legal" wood, and after screening the film, one company—not happy with how they were being portrayed—sent us a cease-and-desist letter.

This came as a surprise to us, but at the time we were extremely worried. This was all happening right when we were about to have our festival premiere. When you're going up against huge corporations and you're a small production company it can be scary, so have wonderful lawyers. We did! This was all happening right when we were about to have our festival premiere. When you're going up against huge corporations and you're a small production company it can be scary, so have wonderful lawyers. We did!

After much legal wrangling, we altered some of our text cards at the end of the film. The important thing is that I didn't walk away feeling I had succumbed to the pressure from Gibson, just that we had reached a compromise. What a relief.

ERRORS AND OMISSIONS INSURANCE

To secure E&O insurance, insurance companies will only accept and consider "Fair Use Opinion" letters from specific lawyers. Make sure the lawyer you are using has represented a number of films, get a referral, look them up. I love that our lawyer's mantra is to not be afraid of Fair Use.

So once you've found the right lawyer, how do you go about getting E&O insurance?

The first step is to create a "clearance log" of all of your material by time code. Essentially the clearance log is a list of every single clip in your film, how long it lasts and the name of owner or source. Your lawyer will use this log to easily see footage duration and ownership. You will also need to provide this for all the music in your film. This is called a "music cue sheet" as mentioned earlier.

As a reminder the checklist found at cmsimpact.org, provided by American University, is a great tool to use at this time. The university department has done a tremendous job with aiding and supporting filmmakers, and I can't talk highly enough of their extremely helpful document. The University, working with others, have worked hard to make sure there are some strong protections for documentary makers. But we are working under a new government every eight years and laws change frequently. The checklist will give you some definitions as to what you need to do in the process of filmmaking but your lawyer will be your safety net.

Donaldson + Callif are specialists in their field. They represent documentaries day in and day out. I don't know what I would do as a filmmaker without the D+C partner Chris Perez. Remember what I said earlier about your support system as a filmmaker. I consider them to be part of that team.

Please note this is a helpful starting point *only* and you can not use this chapter in any way to support your argument for using third-party material or for privacy cases when discussing your own work. It is useful in as much as having some understanding of the broad parameters which govern laws in regards to documentary making. I'm hoping Chris will be writing his own book soon. Chris Perez provided the exceptionally useful information below about areas of concern for documentary filmmakers. When these notes appear written as first person these are helpful notes from Chris himself.

JOURNALISM

A documentary may be considered a work of "journalism," and this can have consequences in a number of different areas.

First, for purposes of ethics, journalists are held to a certain standard of newsgathering and reporting. This is less about the law (although ethics are sometimes reflected in the law), and more about standards and practices for first-rate practitioners of journalism. For example, when you hear the classic debate over whether someone is to "reveal their sources," this is as much about journalistic ethics as it is about laws related to journalism.

Second, regardless of whether you consider a documentary a work of journalism, it's still going to be subject to the same legal standards as any news journalist would be subject to. For example, when it comes to telling a story about a real-life individual, you have to consider their personal rights; namely, whether you violate their right of privacy, libel, etc.

The main difference that I see between most print journalism and documentary films is that documentary films are more inclined to allow their interview subjects to make statements of fact. This isn't always the case, as many documentaries often use a narrator's voiceover to make statements of fact in the same way that a newspaper journalist would. However, where that narration isn't present, the documentary filmmaker still has to be concerned about statements of fact made by their interview subjects. The documentary filmmaker, like the print journalist, must engage in "neutral reportage," which is a defense to defamation if the publisher of the information (in this case, the filmmaker) cannot verify the statement entirely. If the documentary filmmaker presents the statement made by the individual as unverified, and the average viewer understands that they have to take this statement with a grain of salt, then generally speaking the filmmaker has done the job of aiding the viewer in understanding the context of the statement.

HIDDEN CAMERAS, PHONE CALLS AND DOOR STEPPING

Hidden cameras, recorded phone calls and door stepping all implicate privacy issues but have different factors at play.

With all of these issues, while the right of privacy varies from state to state, the basic question being asked is whether the person has a "reasonable expectation of privacy," which itself is based on a number of considerations. You have to consider, among other things: (1) where the action is taking place; (2) the manner in which the action is recorded; (3) if a conversation, the relationship between the individuals being recorded (e.g. the conversation may be considered confidential if between a doctor and patient or lawyer and client); and (4) if a conversation, the manner in which the statement was made.

With a hidden camera, the intent is to go into a traditionally "private" context and record something that you wouldn't normally be able to record.

However, if you were to bring a hidden camera out onto Times Square and record the crowd there, no one would have a right of privacy, because that it is a very public place.

With recorded phone calls, you have to consider not only the privacy rights of individuals but also whether the states in which the conversation is being recorded are "one-party" or "two-party" consent states. In a one-party consent state, only one party (i.e., the caller) needs to know that the call is being recorded. In a two-party consent state, unless you have the consent of both parties, by virtue of recording the call, you will have violated the wiretapping statute in that state. The act of recording the call is the violation—not the publication of that call in a documentary.

Door stepping is a gray area. Often it involves going onto someone's privacy and capturing someone in the privacy of their home. You have to consider that the individual's home is one of the most private places they can be. However, you can imagine someone walking from the doorstep out onto the public street and being questioned. In that case, they have quickly transitioned to a public area where anyone can put a camera in their face.

SATIRICAL WORKS

The first thing is to ask is whether the material is a parody, satire or a joke. People often confuse these concepts. A parody is an imitation of a work that comments directly on the work and therefore is allowed to take quite a bit from the work that is the subject of the comment. A satire comments on some broad aspect of society. Often, it is evaluated liberally under the Fair Use doctrine. Neither one has to do with humor. A joke is all about getting a laugh and gets no special break under copyright law.

Let's start with the jokes because most people aren't too sure what a joke is, and I haven't been able to find a case which defines it. But dictionaries will help us here. A joke is something that is said or done to evoke laughter or amusement. It can be a one-liner or an amusing story with a long-awaited punch line. A parody or satire does not have to be funny. The difference between a parody or satire on the one hand and jokes on the other is crucial, since jokes are not generally copyrightable whereas parodies and satires are.

Most people don't want to be laughed at. But they can't do much about it. The question one should ask is this: Was this an invasion of one of the personal rights of privacy, slander or false light? The reason that none of these rights are invaded is because no one is misled into thinking that the comic is making a statement of fact. The comic doesn't slander someone or put them in a false light if everyone who hears the joke understands that it is a joke rather than a statement of fact.

Satire is often thought of as a sub-sect of humor, but actually does not necessarily have anything to do with humor. A satire mocks social conventions. When courts are presented with a satire case, they don't say: "This is a satire, so we will give it extra latitude." Rather, they painstakingly set out the manner in which the new work comments on some social condition and use that as a significant factor in their analysis. It is almost as though satires are a favored subset of Fair Use.

A parody has general latitude under copyright law to take from another work because a parody must comment on the work that is being parodied, so people must recognize the underlying work in order to recognize what the parody is commenting on.

The clearest definition of a parody is the following:

1. A new, copyrightable work,

2. based on a previously copyrighted work,

3. to such an extent that the previous work is clearly recognizable,

4. but not taking more from the copyrighted work than is necessary,

5. that criticizes or comments on, at least in part, the subject matter or style of the previous work, and

6. is not likely to hurt the value of the previous work.

Humor is absolutely not a requirement. A true parody does not have to be cleared. The courts are clear on that.

TRESPASSING

It's important to make the distinction between two acts here: (1) the act of trespassing, which occurs by going onto someone's property without permission; and (2) the publication of audiovisual material captured in the course of a trespass.

In the first act, you have trespassed once you enter the property without permission. However, from a practical perspective, it may not be worth anyone suing you for trespass unless any actual damage has flowed from the trespass or a related claim. Did the trespasser break anything? Did the trespasser cause any emotional distress? Did the trespasser cause other trespassers to follow?

With the second act, let's say you made a documentary film that includes footage captured while trespassing. The owner of the property may sue, but it's important to note that a court will not assess damages that flowed from the trespass (e.g., damage to property) to the publication of footage captured during the trespass. HOWEVER, you still need to run your use of the footage through the same personal rights analysis—namely, privacy analysis—that any other footage would be run through. For example, did your footage capture anyone in a private situation where that person would normally have a reasonable expectation of privacy? This is a somewhat separate question from the concept of trespass. It really is about what we see on screen.

RECREATIONS

There are plenty of "pitfalls" and, more generally, things to be aware of.

Recreations of real-life events should be placed in the same category as films based on a true story. If the average viewer is to construe a recreation or a film based on a true story as having actually occurred, then you need to make sure that you are not violating anyone's personal rights.

In terms of personal rights, when I'm reviewing a film based on a true story, I'm mostly looking at: (1) the right of privacy; (2) the right of publicity; and (3) defamation and libel. And when you are doing these analyses, the first question is always going to be whether the character in the recreation or film is recognizable as a real life individual. If they are recognizable, then you go into the analyses. If they aren't, then you have a much wider latitude to make up events because, clearly, this character isn't anyone in particular.

Whether a person is recognizable in a character is based on a multitude of factors, but it's important to note that changing someone's name is often not enough. There are considerations to take into account, including one's profession, their physical appearance, their position in society and the people portrayed around them. If I make a film about Hillary Clinton in which I name her husband Dan Johnson, but Dan is an ex-President from Arkansas who has been married to Hillary Clinton for many years, everyone is going to know that it's Bill Clinton.

We've already discussed privacy rights above. But generally speaking, if the average viewer sees the recreation or film as true, then you have to consider the privacy rights of the real life person on whom the character is based.

The right of publicity (often called personality rights) is the unauthorized commercial exploitation of someone's identity. The right of publicity is curbed by the First Amendment, which allows filmmakers to tell their stories. So if you are making a film that portrays readily accessible facts and events, then you have a great deal of leeway in not violating someone's right of publicity, which is more about the commercial value of someone's identity. It's mostly applied by celebrities, but everyone has a right of publicity.

Defamation is (A) a statement of fact (B) made about an individual that is (C) false or misleading and (D) damaging to an individual's character or reputation. All of these "elements" must be satisfied for there to be a viable defamation claim. You can make statements of fact about somebody that are negative but true—that's not defamation. You can have a negative opinion about somebody—that's not defamation. You can have a negative, misleading statement about someone, but if isn't damaging to their character or reputation, then it's not defamation.

The law also permits for a certain amount of "fictional embroidering" when portraying real individuals. Courts know that not every event in a film based on a true story is true. Most of the dialogue is going to be made up. Whole events will be added to make the story more compelling. The bottom line is that you have to actually meet the elements of one of those personal rights claims to be in trouble with regard to the use of real individuals in a film.

12

Brain Trusts, Test Screenings and Outreach

It is a good idea, a very good idea, to hold test screenings before you complete your film to make sure the film works on a number of structural levels for your audience. These screenings can serve two purposes and we took advantage of that.

First, it is a way to help refine the film, to react to how the audience feels about how the film is working. Second, screening the film to an interested audience who will then feel invested in its success; to use each screening to build up an active and engaged community around the film, ready for the final release.

Instead of referring to these screenings as just test screenings, we called them "Brain Trusts." We like this phrase; it feels more inclusive and it really is using the collective minds of this small group of people. This is a way to get critical feedback on your film in an intimate environment, often involving people who are passionate about the issues that your film covers.

Marc Schillers, founder of distribution and consultant company BOND/*360*, says:

> When people ask me what the "call-to-action" should be for their film, I always have the same answer—"Get your core fans to tell ten others

Brain Trusts, Test Screenings and Outreach 147

to go and see it." And because of this, when I'm asked what the most powerful community building platform is for independent filmmakers, my answer is never Facebook or Twitter or Tumblr. It's the personal email lists of the filmmaking team. Nothing is more powerful when it comes to getting people to see a movie.

Yes, you can ask for email sign-ups on your website, but there's nothing better than a direct face-to-face request to ask for email addresses. We were able to do this while still in production, by using our Brain Trust survey forms and asking for email addresses. (more on these later). In this way, as soon as the film came out we already had a team behind us that could spread the word about the film. They'd seen it evolve, been actively involved in shaping it, and were really invested in it—there's no better marketing than that.

If you find organizations that can use your film to help address their goal, then there are a lot of possibilities. They'll *want* to stay connected and may send out news about the film to their contacts, as they'll want to support your work (which in turn supports their work). It's a great way to build a symbiotic relationships with an interested, engaged core audience.

These win-win relationships can play a key component in your distribution. Your film supports their work, and hopefully they will then share information about your film—release dates, screenings, etc.—to their very active, passionate and involved member base. Beyond word-of-mouth to their supporters, they could hold screening parties, show the film at their conventions, etc.

For social issue documentary makers, there's a great resource called the Encyclopedia of Associations, which lists every non-profit in the US by keyword and subject area. Most libraries keep it in their reference section.

As mentioned in Chapter 8, our Kickstarter research on organizations was also very detailed. We already had 22 groups actively sharing information about the film. We also reached out to authors who had written about the area and we isolated the core audiences for our film:

- Music schools

- Luthiers and Guitar groups

- Native American groups

- Outdoor groups, fishing, camping and hiking

- Local and National Environmental organizations

- Forestry groups

- FSC (Forest Stewardship Council) certified, forested landowners.

Look at our audience map in the crowdfunding section and have fun creating this. It really is a positive exercise and you'll surprise yourself with the groups of people who will be interested in your film. It isn't always the people that come obviously to you.

There are other organizations that can also help with outreach for a fee, and work as social impact producers. Here are just some of them. You can refer to the TV network PBS POV blog where they list engagement strategists for more:

Caitlin Boyle at Filmsprout—www.filmsprout.org

Sara Kiener at Film Presence—www.filmpresence.com

Angela Alston at MocaMedia—www.mocamedia.tv

Working Films—www.workingfilms.org

Picture Motion—www.picturemotion.com

How did our Brain Trust screenings go? *Musicwood* is a thriller, but it's also a social issue documentary, so outreach was very important to us. We wanted to reach not just advocates but activists, people that would take the film to places we couldn't reach without their help. If you have a call to action for your film, these people can use your film to build momentum and can even get laws changed. We've seen this done.

Our very first Brain Trust screening was of a 30-minute cut of the film to what we now consider as partners in Washington DC. We wanted to involve significant NGOs who were working on the relevant issues, so we invited representatives from the Environmental Investigation Agency (EIA) and Greenpeace, possible investors, people who might donate services and even friends who just loved documentaries. Everyone who attended seemed genuinely happy to be there and grateful for the invite. It was a small intimate group for this first screening, and this led to many productive, long and supportive relationships for the film.

We made a list of talking points and asked everyone to complete a survey, which asked questions about structure as well as the impact of the film. It also collected their email addresses and we then added them to our Member Database.

Some of the survey questions went along these lines:

- Did you get a sense of the beautiful area from the footage in the film?
- Did the film make you want to do something and get involved?
- Did anything drag, was confusing or unclear?
- Would you recommend the film to others?
- Does the open work for you and make you want to continue watching?

Once we had a 90-minute rough cut of *Musicwood*, we held another Brain Trust screening in Portland, OR. This was an expense to us, but we felt it was incredibly important to get feedback from people in the heart of logging country. It was also an opportunity to hear from Native American tribes who lived close by.

Wend Magazine (who wrote about our Kickstarter fundraiser) allowed us to use their offices and members of the Portland Numa tribe attended, as well as 25 other active community members. We agonized about whether we should spend this money, but screening the film to Native American tribal members was important to us, and this screening gave us some critical feedback: among other things, that our open of the film wasn't working at all.

Be sure to evaluate the feedback you are getting. Thom Powers (of Toronto Film Festival, DOC NYC, *Stranger Than Fiction* podcast fame) offered some great advice about test screenings: listen to the problems they have and not always the solutions. There's a big difference between a note that you get from one person and feedback that you keep hearing over and over again. We continued to hold Brain Trust screenings with every new cut of the film. *Musicwood* wouldn't be the film it is without them.

13

In Conversation With

Fork Films Funder, Women Make Movies Distributor, DOC NYC Film Festival, PBS POV Television Strand Exhibitor

In this chapter we will hear from four major members of the documentary filmmaking community: a funder, distributor, film festival and television network. Kat Vecchio of Fork Films, Debra Zimmerman of Women Make Movies, Raphaela Neihausen of DOC NYC and Justine Nagan of POV all answered questions that I hope represent many of the questions you would have liked to ask.

FUNDER: FORK FILMS

So let's start with what I know. I have applied for multiple grants, many times got to the final rounds, and have also been awarded generous funding. With every grant, festival or funding application you will be required to start with a written summary, or synopsis, of your film. So let's start there, and use applying for Fork Films as our case study.

Fork Films is a production company and film funder; they funded 16 films in 2017 with generous awards in the range of US$10K to US$50K. All great news for us filmmakers. We chat here with Kat Vecchio of Fork Films, Director of Grantmaking, but first I'm going to quote their mission statement, as I'm sure it will incentivize you as a filmmaker.

151

> In the belief that film has a unique capacity to shed light, evoke compassion and stir action, Fork Films invests in and creates media that make an important social contribution, with a particular emphasis on material that has been overlooked, people who tend to be underestimated, and stories that have been left out of the mainstream historical record. Fork Films awards grants to full-length non-fiction films that foster a culture of understanding and work towards a more peaceful and just society, while utilizing powerful and artistic storytelling methods. Specifically, we seek films that promote peace building, human rights, and social justice, with a particular emphasis on projects that bring women's voices to the forefront.

Abigail E. Disney, CEO and President of Fork Films, believes art matters more than ever in this polarizing time: "Art builds empathy and coalesces. The films we select exemplify Fork Films' commitment to fostering a culture of understanding."

First, be mindful of who you are applying to. Fork Films is a film grant. Although your film may fit perfectly with their mission—to foster a culture of understanding—your synopsis should be cinematic and entertaining (refer back to the Research chapter—Chapter 1). Your proposal shouldn't just be a description of how your film relates to human rights issues, but should describe a film that an audience will find engaging, moving and will drive them to action.

Read film synopses on websites such as HBO, POV, ITVS and Showtime. Get familiar with how to market your film. Can your non-filmmaker friends and family understand your proposal? They are your audience too.

As with most grants, when applying to Fork Films they also need to see a work sample and a detailed budget. Make a 10–15-minute work sample that is as polished as possible; this can make or break your application. You will be describing in your application your next steps in production and how you will use the grant funding, so be specific. Think of this as a relationship with a funder that you hope to build for the future. How can you make them share your enthusiasm for the project? And remember, they know how to make films, so be authentic, knowledgeable and creative.

I was once told by a funder that they pull out the budget and lay it alongside the proposal and examine both at the same time. So having a strong budget is incredibly important. I have been told anything below US$250K can make funders concerned; the average for a documentary feature generally varies between US$350K and US$800K, and the higher-end budgets can make them equally concerned. I was also once turned down because my budget was too low. Seriously, learn from my mistakes.

So be realistic, but not overly ambitious. After all, you will have to raise the funding for this budget. If you have a reduced rate for any crew member, explain why. Is it a deferred cost, or "in-kind" exchange of services? This may also cause concern for funders if you haven't been clear as to how you are saving money (refer to the Budget chapter—Chapter 4).

Another very common request from funders awarding filmmaking grants is the need to have a clear idea of the audience for the film and how to reach them. We made an impact report for *Musicwood* (an analysis of impact on the audience), which was immensely useful to send out to funders when the film was complete. This is a great way to stay in touch and show how their support was so important. Also refer to the audience map from the Crowdfunding chapter (Chapter 8). Remember, the work that you put in for your crowdfunding campaign will prove useful in many different areas. So don't just say that you want the film to reach everyone. Do your research.

There are several pertinent elements of Fork Fund's criteria that may distinguish them from other grants. They look for strong characters and relevance of the story, why the story needs to be told *now*. They need to feel confident that the filmmaker and team are capable of completing the film. They will fund projects in development, production, and post-production, but generally only award two development grants per round. You can go to their website for more detailed information: www.forkfilms.net

I've enjoyed specifically writing this chapter as it's meant I've caught up and chatted with many members of the New York filmmaking community, so you are hearing directly from them and not just me or my anecdotes. Here Kat Vecchio, Director of Grantmaking for the fund, met with me to answer questions.

> **Kat:** We've been offering funding to independent filmmakers since 2010, but only created the open call process we use now in 2014. So

in a way we are still a pretty new funder. First off, the filmmakers need to fill in a short application which is reviewed by at least two people. If you can't explain your story in only a few words then it might mean you don't quite know what your story is about yet. A filmmaker with a strong film and story line will be able to write it and condense it.

Usually a third/quarter of all applicants make it to the next round. Good news, and then even more good news. We use the Core application process, which is a new application process that formalizes applications across a number of grants. So if you apply for one grant you may be able to use most of that body of work for another grant. Check out the Documentary Core Application project through IDA. Another documentary organization that supports filmmakers.

Of the 300 applicants on average, roughly 100 filmmakers are invited to the second round, where we gather more information from the filmmaker. Then about a third of those make it to the final round. This year it was 32 applications, reviewed by a seven-member board to grant 16 awards.

Our application numbers doubled that of two years ago. And the quality was incredible. I think that's why we funded more than we ever have with 16 films. On average we fund 10 to 11 films.

The mistake filmmakers often make while writing a proposal is that they have an issue in mind they want to make a movie about. They stick with that issue, explain the problem but don't come up with a strong story and characters. Filmmakers need to be able to see a story, to construct a story with the characters they have found, to know their characters well before writing a grant application. When a filmmaker applies for a grant, they need to explain and expose the narrative arc, each character's story and what's beyond the issue/idea of the documentary.

The filmmaker also needs to be honest about the difficulties they might encounter during the creation of their project and be able to come up with reasonable solutions for them. We often see potential problems in an application, and if the filmmaker addresses these head-on, it gives us more confidence in the project.

Grant applications have specific rules you have to follow, and each grant is slightly different. Surprisingly, a lot of people don't read the rules carefully and apply without following them.

Often junior filmmakers—who may only be junior in experience in the filmmaking world as they may be reporters or authors, for example—might have a great application, but may not know how to make budgets. They may leave out incredibly important costs in post-production, for example. So Fork Films prefers to see a team working along side the junior filmmaker. It's hard for filmmakers to wear two hats: the creator and the producer/accountant hat.

It is useful to list all the other ways they're thinking of raising money. All the grants they're going to apply to must fit their project mission. Don't forget, we at Fork know a lot of the other funders. As a note, grants that are focused on "emerging filmmakers" are not often talking about first-time filmmakers. So the filmmaker's goal of raising money needs to be somewhat realistic. Have a real funding plan. Maybe it includes private investors. Bring in someone that can review and help prepare the budget.

If a proposal comes with a very low budget, the filmmaker needs to explain that. If the budget doesn't include the editing fee, the filmmaker needs to explain that the service is offered in-kind, or donated, or whatever the reason is that it can be offered at no cost. So remember the budget and the proposal need to walk through the whole project for the funder to understand their approach, and to trust that the film can be made.

Also, please stop changing your [film] title. Even if there isn't a good one right away, keep with one working title until you have the final title. In the industry, it makes it very difficult to remember all projects if their titles change every day. Remember that while working on your film, you are creating a network around you of supporters and they need to be able to remember you.

It always surprises me that people think we don't fund films made by men. Women are 50% of the population so all it really means in our guidelines is that they have to be represented. It's probably unlikely that we fund a film made all by men, featuring no women characters or women in the crew.

Let's talk about films that did well for us. *Babushkas* [full title: *The Babushkas of Chernobyl*] was a really good example of how the filmmakers brought an issue to us in a new unique and surprising way. We don't often fund environmental films, but look at how those old women survive living in Chernobyl. And they just didn't want to leave. It was about homeland, and not underestimating people, so many layers. It was about characters more than the issue.

Topics like health-care, incarceration, drug abuse and women's reproductive rights are all huge and important issues in the US today and there have been amazing films about those issues. So if you have a film that revolves around those issues make sure you've seen those films before you apply. Tell us about your approach and why we haven't seen it before. How can your film move the conversation forward? How can you engage the niche audience?

Also we love films that are layered. They might do a few things simultaneously. It might not be the person you expect who is fighting for an issue, or it might reach across the divide and develop a culture of understanding.

Not many filmmakers are like your production company, Maxine. Helpman Productions is a non-profit, so maybe only one or two grantees are in that situation. So I want to explain that there are many benefits of having your grant paid through a Fiscal Sponsor. Think about the auditing trust that has to take place if a funder is writing a check for a large amount of money to a new filmmaker. That filmmaker is essentially an unknown property. And there are many benefits in regard to accounting if you use a Fiscal Sponsor. You only pay tax on the money you spend, because the Fiscal Sponsor will hold the funding until you need it in whatever year you need to pay it.

Also it gives you some gravitas if your funding comes through a Fiscal Sponsor—that is, many Fiscal Sponsors have been in the business a long time and have a good track record. You may be new to filmmaking and new to us. Also some of them offer other benefits, like promoting your finished film on their social media or in their newsletters. So there are a lot of benefits.

The old adage is true that with one funder comes more funding, it's a vote of confidence. And with more funding you get to the next step with your film, and a better proposal.

DOC NYC FESTIVAL

We are very lucky here in NYC to be surrounded by wonderful documentary communities. The two I'm going to concentrate on here are the ones curated by Thom Powers and Raphaela Neihausen. The *Stranger Than Fiction* screening series is a wonderful weekly event that runs every season and introduces you to newly released or festival films from around the country and around the world. It's a great way to meet the directors and hang out afterwards chatting to other filmmakers and Thom and Raphaela. It's such an intimate event and you really do feel like your part of a community.

Then DOC NYC festival, which not only premieres amazing films but programs unique and informative documentary panels. Speaking from experience I'm always learning something new from these industry panels. With 250+ films and events, presented by 200+ filmmakers and special guests it's the biggest documentary festival in the country. It is held every November, and full disclosure I have often worked as a screener or led the filmmaker Q&As post screenings.

Many of you will know Thom's name from the Toronto International Film Festival where he programs the documentary films and his Pure NonFiction podcast. Raphaela, who also highlights a documentary of the week on WNYC Radio, is the co-founder of both DOC NYC and the *Stranger Than Fiction* series and has very kindly answered questions about the festival below.

> **Raphaela:** DOC NYC regularly receives almost 2,000 submissions. We are witnessing an ever-rising trend in the sophistication of storytelling, cinematography and craft. Partly because there are increasing resources being put into documentaries as philanthropists and investors see the form as a powerful way to convey a message.

Basil Tsiokos and his team do a tremendous job reviewing all submissions and making sure each one gets a fair shot. At DOC NYC we show over 100 feature documentaries, so we're programming with lots of different motives. New York arguably has more documentary filmmakers than any other city in the world. That's an important factor for us to serve that community and their output. But we're also trying to showcase films from around the world that we think will connect with local audiences.

We have two formal competition sections called Metropolis (NY stories) and Viewfinders (distinct directorial visions). We also have an evolving list of categories that in the past have included Sonic Cinema, American Perspectives, International Perspectives, True Crime, Fight the Power, among others. You can always visit the archive page of the website and see the categories for each year.

For any festival, it's important to pay attention to the kinds of films they've played in the past to have a sense of whether yours might be a good fit.

DOC NYC is more than just a showcase of films. It's a gathering place for filmmakers from all over. We have a concurrent 8-day industry conference called DOC NYC Pro where filmmakers—both established and emerging—come to learn the latest creative and business trends in documentary.

Documentaries have always inspired passionate conversations and debates. Increasingly we see those conversations ripple out more widely into the media and propel change in large and small ways. It's exciting to see the formats multiply for documentary. We see a flourishing of short form work as well as an expansion of ambitious episodic series.

We receive many more submissions than we can fit into our program and that inevitably means leaving behind many worthy films. That's obviously a painful part of the process. Fortunately, there are many other documentary and specialty festivals to give films another chance.

We try to stay in contact with colleagues around the world, scouting for recommendations. We try to visit at least one country where we've never been each year to grow that network.

We've had filmmakers find distribution, get their first press quotes, and galvanize social media awareness (from being in the festival). But sometimes the best thing that can happen is just letting the subjects of the film experience it with an audience. It's often very emotional and cathartic for a film subject to hear an audience respond with empathy, recognition and love. What's exciting about the festival is that you can witness those emotional high points over and over again.

WOMEN MAKE MOVIES DISTRIBUTOR

It's not always easy as a first-time filmmaker to get a meeting with distributors (although we did after our premiere and had conversations beforehand, so bear that in mind). Now that we can that we can consider all types of models of distribution within this digital landscape it can be difficult to work out your distribution strategy. It's great to have the opportunity to hear first hand from a distributor about the business.

As filmmakers we can start building a groundswell of attention around our films to find our own audience through social media and going out and finding them ourselves. So let's not think of the old paradigm of you "must" get a theatrical distributor, making a handsome one-deal sale, they handle everything for you and you can walk away. Long gone are those days. You will see our case study for *Musicwood* in the Distribution chapter (Chapter 15). We didn't get a theatrical deal but we did have a limited release in theaters, we still managed to get amazing reviews and *Musicwood* did get a North American and International distributor.

So don't think of distribution when the film is finished or just when you're in your festival run, think of the distribution at your pitching stage, when you have enough principal photography shot to make a trailer and your 10–15 sample scenes.

We had the pleasure of chatting with Debra Zimmerman, Executive Director of Women Make Movies, on exactly what to pitch, when and so much more.

Women Make Movies is a fantastic non-profit organization that supports filmmakers not only as a distributor but a fiscal sponsor (see funding chapter). They offer a Production Assistance program and host some of the most informative filmmaking webinars that I've heard. They were founded in

1972 and they have been working primarily in documentary distribution for the last 15–20 years.

Zimmerman contends (and I've heard this mentioned in many conversations) that fewer than 10% of documentaries will hit those theatrical, big consumer markets; ones that do are most often the US$1 million-budgeted documentaries. But there is a big world out there and many opportunities for the other 90%. Women Make Movies was one of the pioneers in the non-theatrical market and as emerging filmmakers this may not be a market you have considered.

At its core, Women Make Movies is an educational and semi-theatrical distributor. Zimmerman wants to be clear about the difference between these markets. In semi-theatrical, the general public can access the film, i.e. screenings at media arts centers, museums, galleries, festivals but unlike the typical theatrical release, it is not for an open-ended run; rather it is for a set number of screenings, usually one or two days or nights or a set number of screenings at a festival.

The educational distribution model often comes after semi-theatrical. This method can offer a longer lifespan for the film and opportunities for long-term distribution. This is exciting for distributors like WMM and filmmakers alike.

Colleges and universities are obvious educational markets, but so are other non-profit organizations and agencies, hospitals, prisons, labor unions, the US Army, women's organizations, conferences and libraries. Think of any organization that might be able to use your film to educate their members, clients, patients etc. This can result in a more long-term strategy for your film; they may be in a curriculum for a very long time.

As an emerging filmmaker you may never heard of these markets. So Debra Zimmerman often explains the context and scope of these markets and talks to filmmakers about three distribution goals: fame, fortune and good conscience. Fame, obviously is the road you may be taking in building your career as a filmmaker, getting top influencers to recommend your films and introductions to top tier festivals, which all help you achieve funding for your next film. Fortune speaks for itself: yes you want to make money, you want to be able to live and make a living. And finally, good conscience. You may want to make your film for a particular audience (we have talked about why being specific about your audience is important in previous chapters). You may be passionate about this audience; you may want to change policy and make a concrete impact, which is your film's legacy.

Sometimes filmmakers may need to choose between a festival that gives a film more exposure to the industry as opposed to those who will help the film's impact on policy. Quite a few years ago, the Danish documentary *Enemies of Happiness* won the Best Film at IDFA and then the Sundance World cinema prize, and WMM chose to play it at Silverdocs (now AFI Docs) and the Human Rights Watch Film Festival because these festivals have strong connections to Washington, DC. Capitalizing on those connections offered access to outlets such as *The Wall Street Journal*, and members of Congress to try to influence US policy towards Afghanistan.

WMM works on unique and individual distribution strategies for each film. They concentrate and have years of expertise in the semi-theatrical and educational market but have worked on limited theatrical releases and can work in tandem with theatrical distributors or broadcasters.

Zimmerman also gave us a couple of pointers about what to look out for when working with the large aggregators in today's market. Netflix and iTunes may not be able to offer marketing opportunities for your film unless it's successfully become one of those top 10% of documentary films, those million-dollar budgeted films. Yes, pre-sales with Netflix can happen and they can offer upfront money deals for their "originals" but they will want worldwide rights. Debra Zimmerman stressed that filmmakers should be aware that that is one pot of money for everything—that is, the life of the film will stay with Netflix because the rights they take preclude sales to others for a good number of years.

But let's keep looking at the other 90%—the films that may not be one of the 16 playing at Sundance, but have the potential to succeed elsewhere. WMM values these voices and Zimmerman is worried with the current political climate and the attacks on women and diverse voices that these films are needed more than ever. With the big four tech and big three digital companies, how can your film succeed and be seen outside of the properties that threaten to monopolize the marketplace?

Independent films are tough to market. If the films' subject is tough to market then you need to make a really really great film. And sometimes filmmakers find it very hard to market their films themselves. WMM understands this and knows how to help.

There are very real advantages to working with distributors. It can be hard to break through the noise and reach an audience, so strategy is important. Some filmmakers are fantastic at outreach and marketing their films and have large social media followings. But others may be fearful of speaking engagements and Zimmerman understands that "salesmanship isn't always easy for artists." It can be helpful for filmmakers to work alongside a distributor for this reason, and she talks about a multiplication effect on audiences when it's done properly: if filmmakers have that skillset, it does help the success of the film but distributors can also help immeasurably in this area. For instance, WMM has worked on two new films on domestic violence—*Private Violence* and, more recently, *A Better Man* (which recently premiered at DOC NYC). "Since WMM worked with *Private Violence* a couple of years ago, when we acquired *A Better Man*, we already had an amazing database of contacts and therefore its much easier for a film to reach the organizations and influencers in this area."

So if you are considering approaching Women Make Movies what do they look for? For distribution, they seek out films with a feminist perspective; films that reflect women's interests. For their Production Assistance program, the subject can be anything. But for both programs the films needs to have a woman director. There can be a male co-director or male producers. The key is that the artistic vision is usually from the director and they are looking to expand opportunities for women directors.

While in production and raising grant funding working with WMM as your Fiscal Sponsor/Production Assistance program is a great way to be introduced to WMM. But even if you're not part of that program, WMM are happy to view a very serious rough cut, before it's locked, before it's submitted to festivals. This essentially means an almost fine cut, an *almost* locked cut. Within the Production Assistance Program, WMM can also advise on the editorial content of the film, and that can be a huge asset.

Zimmerman receives look books, trailers and treatments. But—bearing in mind she gets sent requests all the time—she says she'd initially prefer a short description of the film and the film's trailer.

Before any of this though, remember to do your homework. Is WMM the best place for your film? Do they represent films like your film? One of the biggest potential downfalls of a filmmaker is not doing their research into distributors. Is this distributor right for your film?

In conclusion, with a lot of distributors out there—both well-known and lesser-known—WMM have a long legacy of distributing extraordinary, women-centered films. When you receive distribution offers for your film, Zimmerman suggests taking a look at the company's catalogue. Are there films similar to your own? Are there too many films similar to yours? "The distributor may not be the largest company, but if someone is really passionate about your film they may spend more time working on it," she says. To contrast this idea, she even told me about a conversation she had with a well-known sales agent who was going after a film that they hadn't even seen yet. So sometimes the smaller company can really be passionate about your film and work hard representing it.

Talk to other filmmakers about their distributor experiences and get recommendations. Zimmerman told me: "There has to be trust both ways." She says that when a festival programmer chooses a film it's like "going on a date." But the relationship between a distributor and a filmmakers is more like getting married. At the end of the day, a filmmaker and their distributor have a real relationship, and it's a relationship that might continue for your entire filmmaking career.

TV NETWORK—PBS AND POV

How do you want to get your film out publicly to a wide audience (not the more limited audiences of film festivals)? Where should it screen first? Have you already harnessed a great audience on social media? Are you considering going straight to a digital streaming platform such as Vimeo On Demand. Or are you aiming for a TV broadcast, on a strand that has access to millions of viewers? POV on PBS has access to 97% of the country, with an average of 2 million people per broadcast. TV still currently pays the most upfront for the rights to transmit your film (unless as we've mentioned you get the million dollar Netflix deal), and often will buy digital rights for an amount of time—generally three years. Refer to the chapter on Distribution (Chapter 15) and the Broadcast TV section in Chapter 18 for a list of networks.

There isn't just a single way to exhibit your film these days. I had the pleasure of meeting with Justine Nagan after a Women Make Movies panel. Women Make Movies has offices in NYC. We chatted earlier to Debra Zimmerman about distribution, but WMM also act as an arts organization that supports filmmakers. Their panels are often available as webinars to screen online, making them a great resource no matter where you're located.

American Documentary is the non-profit media art organization that programs POV. POV is television's longest-running showcase for independent nonfiction films, premiering 14–16 programs every year on PBS. Since 1988 POV has presented over 400 films to public television audiences across the country.

To quote their website they are known for "their intimacy, their unforgettable storytelling, and their timeliness, putting a human face on contemporary social issues." The strand airs on Monday nights at 10pm on local PBS stations. Many films that POV have screened appear on my top films list at the back of the book (see the selected Filmography in the Appendix). Some examples include *Big Men*, *If a Tree Falls*, *The Overnighters* and the fantastic shorts *Hotel 22* and the Oscar-nominated *4.1 Miles*. So if you're based in the US watch the strand; if you don't know what they transmit how will you know if your film would be a relevant fit for POV?

The POV website splits their films into the following genres: Adoption, Arts and Culture, Class and Society, Criminal Justice, Environment, Family and Society, Gender, Health and Aging, International LGBTQ, Music, Politics and Government, Race and Ethnicity, Religion and Spirituality, War and Peace, and Youth. I have left the History genre out of the list because generally that subject tends to play on their sister strand, Independent Lens, funded by ITVS.

Not only does POV transmit documentaries, they have funding rounds, very akin to grant cycles. But don't confuse them with grants as they are buying the rights to your film. Often (and I know this from working in development for the BBC), it's hard to get a meeting or audience with the TV networks. So this open submission is a wonderful way to ensure that a TV network really does consider the project you may have spent five years making. They are an incredibly important part of the American documentary eco-system. Think of your submission as a pitch packet, we have already talked about writing TV treatments and how important realistic budgets are to the commissioners.

But POV are not just a TV strand; they really are an arts organization that supports documentary filmmakers. They screen short films, maintain a comprehensive website of resources and have a very active blog. Up until a few years ago, they produced a yearly list of the top 100 documentary films that I made a point, annually, to refer to.

Justine Nagan is the Executive Director of AmDoc, and works alongside Chris White who is the Executive Producer. I was able to chat with Justine recently. At the time of writing, Justine is the Executive Producer for the series POV on PBS, and America Reframed on the World Channel. Justine is passionate about diversity, using documentary as a tool for civic dialogue and social change. She worked for many years as the Executive Director of Chicago's Kartemquin films (known for the famed director Steve James's films).

The PBS strand POV looks for films that challenge assumptions, surprise audiences and have strong points of view. They focus on films that have real opportunities for outreach and engagement, and diversity of style. They co-produce as well as acquire and, at the time of writing, they pay approximately US$170K for production and US$40K–90K for acquisitions. With average funding being between US$50K and US$120K.

POV gets 12,000 projects in open call. They choose the top 40 for 16–17 slots a year. They do not expect all rights, just US broadcast and limited streaming rights for four years. Of the 15 films chosen two-thirds are acquisitions. Of these films they don't get involved early in the production but would want to see a fine cut. They only want to see completed films—so no rough assemblies when applying. Half are foreign films with strong points of view from the filmmaker so they are open to co productions.

The staff make themselves available via email to answer specific questions before the open call (in spring or early summer) every year. But do remember they receive 12,000 submissions, so familiarize yourself with the films they program and read the submission guidelines thoroughly. Don't waste that important email asking an obvious question—they are busy with a small team. Always include the title of your film and logline when asking relevant questions by email. If the POV staff are interested in the film it's a great way to begin that dialogue.

POV screen high-crafted films and not all are focused on social justice. POV tend not to commission survey/essay or talking-head films, preferring instead personal films (no celebrities), or characters with a strong point of view—i.e. meaning less narration and more vérité filmmaking. They will consider applications from domestic and international filmmakers "that," as Justine says, "reflect the range and diversity of American voices."

So what has Justine Nagan seen a lot of lately? We asked her directly.

> **Justine:** The beauty of the call for entries is that we receive a truly eclectic [or "diverse," "varied"] mix of documentaries. Submissions come from all corners of the globe—from the Democratic Republic of the Congo to Denmark to rural America—covering all facets and walks of life. There are, however, times when we see more of one subject than another. This season's special series on the Syrian war and global refugee crisis, for example, highlights how world events activate filmmakers. Seeing a surge in docs on these concurrent crises, we thought it necessary to program a series highlighting the topic.

Areas that haven't been covered or seem to be off the radar…?

> **Justine:** Of course, our filmmakers' backgrounds vary, and we see more of some than others. With their strong public funding infrastructures, Scandinavian filmmakers are probably overrepresented (but all love to them) while filmmakers from developing countries might make up a smaller portion of the submissions. That sometimes means we see fewer stories from these areas, whether in Central America or Central Africa.

Would a film on Brexit be commissioned?

> **Justine:** While we cater to an American audience, we believe our mission of presenting bold storytelling isn't limited to a strictly "American" story. That means a film on Brexit is on the table, so long as it has a strong point of view that puts a human face on a contemporary issue.

America Reframed on the World Channel

Justine Nagan also programs for America Reframed. These are all American stories but the season runs to 26 episodes so there are more opportunities to broadcast here. At the moment, licensing figures are in the mid-4s, but Justine is hoping to improve the licensing budgets. "The social-issue documentary series presents an array of personal voices and experiences through which we learn from our past, understand our present and are challenged to seek new frameworks for America's future" (PBS website).

Independent Lens, or POV or BOTH?

The other documentary strand, well-known on PBS, is Independent Lens, funded by ITVS's Open Call. You can apply for both POV and ITVS, and most money will be obtained through their Open Call process. Independent Lens will often schedule films in the Winter every year as opposed to the Spring/Fall for POV.

Somewhere between 1% and 3% of Open Call applicants receive funding. Amounts average between US$150,000 and US$350,000. Open Call is not a grant. ITVS provides a co-production investment in your project. Since 1991, they have funded 533 Open Call programs, including the recent films *I Am Not Your Negro*, *Newtown* and *National Bird*.

ITVS, and therefore the Independent Lens strand, support projects at various lengths 30 and 60 minutes etc. POV will schedule 60-minute and theatrical-length documentaries. Both strands work with filmmakers on community screenings. "ITVS filmmakers don't just want lots of eyeballs on their films; they want to make a positive difference in the world...Since 2005, this national screening series has reached 350,000 new viewers for Independent Lens, while generating awareness and action on a range of topics."

So does your film fit the ITVS mission of stories that take risks and tackle important issues? They will fund works-in-progress, which differs from POV but your crew will need to have a person with experience in a principal role: Director, Co-Director, Producer or Co-Producer.

It is open to US residents or citizens only and they will fund historical, essay, narrated survey films, etc. They have quite different parameters to POV when it comes to commissioning guidelines so make sure you familiarize yourself with these.

Funders/Sponsorship/Advocacy, etc

Sponsors cannot fund your PBS film, similarly to the BBC, as this may bring into question the integrity of the work. If you have a funder with no editorial input on the film then that may be fine, but they will be vetted by POV's legal team. This also goes for anyone in the Special Thanks section of the credits—What did they do for the film? Do they have journalistic integrity? Have all your funding roles been clearly laid out in writing (as they will not accept any advocacy films)?

Shorts Digital Platform—POV Digital

POV Digital are open to shorts. They are also pushing the form forwards with a number of interesting projects

Working with the *New York Times* they produced *Hyphen-Nation*, an interactive project featuring a diverse range of American citizens who describe their struggle to belong in a nation that both embraces and rejects them.

Since 2010, POV Digital have partnered with StoryCorps, who record and preserve the voices of everyday people, one conversation at a time. Together they have produced over 30 animated shorts based on StoryCorps audio recordings.

The Whiteness Project is an interactive investigation into how Americans—specifically those who identify as white, or partially white—understand and experience their race. Each video interview is paired with a statistic that provides a greater societal context and offers an opportunity for self-reflection by the audience on their own thoughts about race.

POV Digital also partnered with the short-form digital content creator NowThis to launch Snapchat-native documentaries, and the numbers were great.

If you are looking to make shorts for POV think about how the platform for the film could be expanded outwards. Is there series potential? Are there possibilities for community interactivity? See also ITVS digital in the digital streaming section of the book (Chapter 18), where we interview Pam Torno, the series producer of Digital Initiatives at ITVS.

14
Festivals

Festivals are competitive. The top tier festivals are extremely hard to get into, there is a saying that it's harder to get into Sundance than it is Harvard. I don't know whether that is true but it feels like it.

Know this, be aware of this because it can be an expensive process and a little disheartening, especially after all the hard work of making the film. The good news is that there are so many more documentaries that are being made well, which means there's more of an appetite for documentaries being recognized as being "films" and that audiences care about them.

These are some interesting figures recently published for Sundance 2018 on the website Documentary Business: 1,635 documentary features were submitted to Sundance with an almost split 50/50 between international and US. Some 47 films were selected for screening, which is a 2.9% success rate. These odds are slightly higher for fiction films, as a higher % are programmed. The success was higher for US films, with 37 selections and 4.9% acceptance rate. Of the 47 selections 28% had had prior funding from Sundance Institute Documentary Program.

Where and when you choose to premiere your film is very important. It's the first step in the life of your film and can influence what other screenings you might have at other festivals etc., and what sort of distributors will be interested and so much more.

So try to plan ahead and have a strategy of film festivals you want to enter. This will save you a lot of time, money and effort. This may seem daunting, but you can certainly have a strategy that lists your top picks, and by application date, location etc. and then can adjust your strategy as you move through your application process, when you're either accepted or rejected.

Film festivals are often recognized by how impactful the film can be on your career. Will industry be there? Press distributors? Sales agents? Networks? For every festival the cache is to have a world premiere of your film, to have the first public screening of your film.

As an unknown filmmaker, most of the top tier festivals (Sundance, SXSW, Tribeca, Toronto) will only consider your film if it will be a worldwide premiere. For the next tier (LA, Hot Docs, True/False, DOC NYC, etc.), at the time of writing and from research of their catalogues, they will be fine if your premiere were a top festival, but if you haven't screened in a top festival, being able to offer your world premiere will make your film more attractive to them.

APPLYING/PREMIERING

We made our own specific list of festivals from word of mouth, the POV blog (mentioned in the previous chapter), online articles, attending festivals and talking to other filmmakers. Also distributors gave us their own list of recommended festivals, which was a huge help.

We started with a list of twenty festivals, which continued to grow. We made a spreadsheet with the submission deadline, cost to submit, the dates each festival ran and the location of the festival. We didn't apply to everything on our list, just the ones that seemed most relevant, and the ones we might be able to attend (see our festival list in the Appendix).

Here I would note it can be very helpful to look at the websites of films that mirror your own. Where were they successful? Where did they win awards? Odds are that your film will be successful there as well. Do you know any filmmakers who had already screened films at these. We managed to do this and it was a great idea to help us keep the festivals at a manageable level because entrance fees can become unwieldy.

Remember you've been building your Members' Database, with the emails and addresses of all those great crowdfunder supporters and brain trust participants. List them by location, and if you have a significant number from one area, highlight that festival.

Using the great application platform Withoutabox will allow you to complete one application that can be used to apply to many festivals. Give yourself enough time to fill out the extensive application (use all that PR language you've been developing), to upload pictures and encode the HD file of your film to a size that can easily upload (thankfully now most festivals accept Vimeo).

When applying to the medium or smaller sized festivals, email them and ask if they'll give you a waiver code for the submission fee. This may only work once you've played at the larger festivals and they see how successful your film has become, but you'll be surprised how many will reply with Withoutabox waiver codes.

One of the more complex aspects of applying to film festivals is trying to make the deadlines. We were advised that as an unknown filmmaker you should never submit a rough cut, because you are competing with finished films, and the top tier festivals won't allow you to resubmit with your finished film.

We submitted a rough cut of *Musicwood* to Sundance—we were convinced that this rough cut was so nearly finished that it would be worth it—and needless to say, we were not accepted. We then went to work for another year on the film, and the finished film was drastically different from what we submitted. Again learn from us: never submit a rough cut to the most important film festival in the world, never never never. You are competing with the best filmmakers in the world, and they are overwhelmed with submissions. What a waste of an expensive submission fee.

Also most festivals list an early deadline, a regular deadline and a late deadline—your odds of acceptance go down quite severely with each deadline. Don't wait until the end; try to get your submission in early! Remember you are competing with well-known filmmakers.

If you know or can make a connection with a festival programmer, by all means reach out to that person and see if they will give your film special attention. But remember there are a lot of filmmakers doing the same thing. If you're not sure, err on the side of caution. At the end of the day your film's merits need to stand on their own, so only ask a question that doesn't waste their time and is necessary.

With *Musicwood*, we finished a "festival cut" (just needing final graphics and sound mix) of the film in May. We had only just made the Toronto late deadline and weren't able to re-submit to Sundance, which, although months away, was the next big festival. One of our advisors suggested we apply to DOC NYC, which had Toronto programmer Thom Powers as its founder. Thom had seen *Musicwood* in our Toronto application, and was able to give us a very quick acceptance. This was an amazing feeling! We had been accepted to a major doc festival very quickly!

We finally decided to premiere at DOC NYC for a number of reasons: as NYC filmmakers we would be on our home turf, and we knew the major doc distributors are based here (see Distribution section). As it turned out, this was the perfect decision. Since it was in NYC we could pack the theater with friends and supporters, our Q&A was incendiary—we had representatives from all the groups in our film—and Thom gave *Musicwood* special mention in the press.

So what would we change next time? We would keep a closer eye on festival deadlines, make sure we apply for the early deadline and never apply with a rough cut.

PREMIERE NIGHT

You did it! Remember to celebrate your first festival premiere, you got this far and you got in, well done. We had a cocktail reception beforehand with a musician playing for the audience. This makes the night stand out and an event for all of your supporters. We also made sure we'd be remembered by giving out a gift to the audience—an eco-friendly guitar pick with our details on it (see Figure 14.1). I still think the guitar pick is cute and am still handing them out.

You want to save nationwide press for your "big" rollout, your premiere in cinemas, on TV, Netflix—wherever it may be. So do *some* press at your festivals to start building the buzz, but save some energy and $$ for the big push later (be sure to also refer to our Press and Marketing, and Distribution and Selling sections in Chapters 17 and 15 respectively). We were told that hiring a publicist for festivals other than Sundance, Toronto and maybe SXSW is a waste of money. But remember some sales agents will want some press to notice you at film festivals to get your film sold. It's a delicate balance: enough to get noticed to sell your film to a distributor or studio like Netflix but not to use all the big international outlets—save that for your release whether on air or online or both. Some sales agents believe you have to have a festival premiere to sell your film, so remember to practice how you talk about your film—and find some fun asides to mention as well. What is the story about your story? Your Q&A is pretty important.

Make sure to check in with the theatre where your film is premiering. How many seats does it have? Is the poster displayed properly? Are there postcards in the lobby? Are there postcards at the festival info booths or HQ? Reach out to your festival contact if things aren't set up properly. When you arrive, make sure the festival publicist knows that you're attending the festival and are available for interviews, go and visit the press office, say hello.

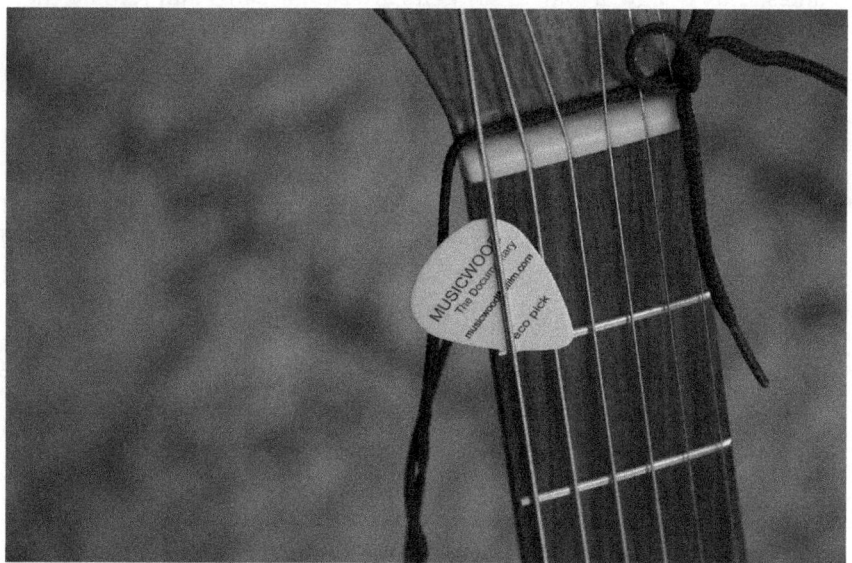

FIGURE 14.1 Our a gift to our Premiere Night audience members— an eco-friendly guitar pick with our details on it

That will remind them that you're there and put a name to a face; there's nothing like meeting someone in person.

If you're attending the festival and of course you will be on your world premiere night, make sure the programmers know you are doing a Q&A. We saw a filmmaker get forgotten at one festival when she showed up for her Q&A and so it didn't happen. And her film was fantastic, it was a real shame. Q&As can be very engaging and make for a special night for the audience. One of our Q&As was filmed and had more views on YouTube than the film festival's own promotional trailer.

When you can, and just as your Q&A starts, hand around a clipboard (with a pen attached!) to gather emails from everyone, let them know that this way they can keep up to date with any new developments in your doc, and stay informed of what's going on with the film. This is a great way to build up your mailing list with more patrons or an engaged audience.

DISTRIBUTORS AT FILM FESTIVALS

Some festivals have major doc distributors attending, often speaking on panels. This is a great way to say hello after their panel and remind them that your film is playing. There is more information on distribution in Chapter 15.

Research to find out if distributors will be at your festival. It's guaranteed at the top tier—Sundance, Toronto, SXSW, etc.—but they will also send representatives to festivals like DOC NYC, Hot Docs, True/False or Big Sky. If they are going to be at your festival, call individual distributors and invite them to your screening. Bearing in mind that emails are easy to ignore, mail them invites and then follow up with a phone call.

We were also given some tips for international festivals:

- ▶ IDFA's the world's most important doc festival in terms of international sales, so that's a great place to begin. They do look for theatrical films but it's not the starting point for them. They don't go for celebrity names or really huge political issues like other festivals.

- ▶ Internationally after IDFA look into CPH:Dox and Berlin

- Berlin, which screens approximately 400 films, is known for it's political engagement, often showcasing work that focuses on political hotspots or social exclusion.

- Nearer to home, Hot Docs (Toronto) has some great industry attendance.

- Toronto Film Festival is for films that are generally thought to get theatrical distribution.

If you're lucky enough to screen at Sundance, Toronto, Cannes or SXSW, maybe IDFA and Berlin too, get a sales agent as the major distributors, TV networks and streaming platforms will all be there. We were told this may not be necessary at other festivals, and the sales agent may not attend either.

THE FESTIVAL CIRCUIT

You've premiered your film, people are starting to buzz about it, and now you're getting accepted into other festivals. This is a great feeling, all your hard work is starting to pay off. You want to go to as many festivals as possible, but be careful, this is *expensive*.

Some will offer a screening fee, some will offer to fly you in and pay for expenses. Screening fees could be US$250, US$300, US$500, and the smaller festivals are more likely to pay you a fee than the big ones. The top tier festivals don't pay, but once you move to less well known festivals, you should definitely ask for a screening fee; it's kind of a well-kept secret. Once you play a few festivals and show up in their programs, you'll start to receive invites from other festivals and when invited you won't have to pay entrance fees.

Also keep in mind that every festival is going to want materials from you: your film screener (whether DCP, Blu-ray, HD QuickTime file on a drive), poster, postcards. Ask the festival coordinator for their FedEx or UPS shipping account numbers. And plan your festival schedule carefully, sometimes there might be overlap so make sure you have enough copies of the film and you can ask the festival to ship your materials straight to the next festival.

Start to think of your international markets too. Approach international distributors now that you have your premiere date (more in Distribution section—Chapter 15). You should have already begun to approach your national distributors before you have your premiere festival set as they may want to advise you on festivals and be very much part of the strategy.

Make a timetable of your festival run—we did this for the first 6 months initially—and carefully evaluate which festivals you will attend. Will they pay anything towards your costs? And then you can start planning what you're going to do once the festival period has ended. This gives you a lead time of 4 or 5 months to set up the next phase.

As with most of the sections of this book, you need to be constantly thinking ahead. Is your next phase theatrical (screening in cinemas), semi-theatrical (community, or other specialized screenings) or educational, or will you be going straight to TV and digital? If you're doing community screenings, consider trying to schedule them around your festival run (if they're in the same place) so that you're not paying twice for travel.

PRESS AT FESTIVALS

Publicity at festivals can make a difference with building your screening audience, but potential distributors only go to certain festivals, so, as said before, save your press budget for your theatrical tour or TV premiere, or day and date release on digital platforms.

That said, certainly try to get local press if you're attending a festival and want a full screening. For the most part, you don't want to rely on just the festival to get you the press and audience attendance (except Cleveland Film Festival, which got us great press and a packed audience every night and a great Rotten Tomatoes Review!).

Try to get press contacts from the press person representing the festival. We were lucky enough to do that a few times; it was a great help. Sometimes you can offer to work in tandem with the publicist of the festival. Definitely contact them if you're attending the festival, let them know you're available for interviews, etc. Festivals might get you mini-reviews (those are capsules, not full reviews), like a paragraph in a paper on the fest's top 7 films, top 10 films, etc. We often got these and they were great to share.

For each town we attended, we wanted to have a large local audience (otherwise why go?), so we piggy-backed on the festival press, made our own individual press releases and reached out to press ourselves. For some festivals it worked, at others it was a struggle. I was more successful with press in the UK about this story; possibly because Europe is more open to stories about saving forests and writing about environmental issues? Who knows.

What would we do differently with the festival circuit? We spent a lot of money on festival submission costs, travel, meals, lodging, etc. We learned so much through this experience that I wrote an article for *IndieWire* called "Lessons Learned As a First-Time Feature Director on the Festival Circuit" (included here later). I still use this as my guide for festival strategizing. I would love to get into Berlin film festival in the future. They televise the opening night on National TV. Previously the countries cultural minister and the mayor of Berlin spoke on the importance of culture as an assertion of free expression in the face of repression, which sounds pretty amazing as a festival mission statement.

We ended up attending some festivals that we didn't need to, and sometimes going to the wrong festival in regards to who attended, when they overlapped. Perhaps we would spend less time and energy on PR at certain festivals and concentrate on enjoying just attending. Next time we'll plan our schedule on an even more of a micro scale, piggybacking festivals with our semi-theatrical screenings, and attend fewer festivals overall, there's definitely a few we wouldn't go back to.

25 TIPS FOR THE FIRST-TIME FEATURE DIRECTOR ON THE FESTIVAL CIRCUIT

You might be wondering why this tips list is included. It was an article I wrote that contained so much of what I had learned from the festival circuit with my first feature, that it now acts like a great cheat sheet. A refresher that I find incredibly useful before entering festivals.

I had only been on the festival circuit once before, with a short film, and even then I only applied to five festivals. So this time it really felt like the beginning of a steep learning curve. And when you're in the thick of it, it's all happening so quickly and there are constant choices and decision making experiences. There were so many times I thought, "If only someone had mentioned THAT to me!" Hopefully you will find it helpful and encouraging, almost like having a mentor in your pocket or as your cheer leader as you show up at your first festival. There was a lot to learn, so what did I learn about festivals?

This one I have mentioned already but I can't underline the important of it enough.

1. ONLY enter festivals when your film is finished. Yes, we all hear about rough cuts getting into festivals, but don't, seriously, submit that rough cut. Remember, you're going up against finished, polished films. When you've shown at least 10 people and they've all said it's done, go for it. No rough scratch tracks, no GFX still to be commissioned. Done done done. We learned this the hard way, we really wanted to get into Berlin, and you only get ONE chance to enter. We submitted a cut we thought was pretty close to done, only to work for another year on the edit.

2. Make PR materials BEFORE your festival run. Look, we know how it is, you've been scrambling and taking up absolutely every minute of every day until your premiere getting the film to be the best it can. You're madly outputting days before the screening and hoping against hope that everything looks and sounds ok. But in all of that you NEED to get a designer (or yourself) to make imagery for your film. Make a postcard, make a movie poster, make a flyer. You're going to need this stuff. And have your tag line, and short synopsis, and long synopsis, all this will save you time in the future.

3. Think hard about where you're having your world premiere. Premiere status is your currency as you do festivals, and it can be hard to figure out how to make it work. We had the lovely Thom Powers wanting to screen *Musicwood* at DOC NYC, but since we are somewhat a music film, we also loved the idea of SXSW. Ultimately, because we knew our premiere was going to be intense and controversial (see our YouTube Q&A for more), and DOC NYC was so supportive, we decided to premiere in New York, our home town. We were able to fill the theater and it was an amazing experience. Following that, SXSW were absolutely lovely to us and considered our film. But remember: once you hold your world premiere elsewhere your following screenings won't hold as much gravitas to the big festivals.

4. And while we're talking about it, check out DOC NYC. People may not have cottoned on to the fact that you can get great access here that you

might not get at a huge, long-running festival. We made lots of connections: Cinema Guild, First Run, IFC Films, Gary Hustwit, etc. We had distribution offers for digital, VOD and educational straight after our premiere at DOC NYC, so not bad, not bad at all.

5. Know what each festival is known for. It's hard to work out a festival strategy as it's not always easy reading about which festivals have particular genre favorites. But look into it, check the line up of films from previous years. Entering festivals is expensive, so if you have the time, do this. Big Sky has a large Native American population. Cleveland has a very strong European presence. Santa Barbara has a fantastic Social Justice Award for documentaries. These are just a few tips we picked up.

6. Start looking into international distribution BEFORE your festival run. Distributors want to be involved in your festival strategy if possible, include a note about where you are considering premiering. One of the international guys said we should have brought them in *before* our festival run—who knew? So don't just think of US distributors, think globally too.

7. So what happens when you do get into festivals? Remember to celebrate. You have made a feature film! This is a major accomplishment! And you're in festivals! Don't lose sight of that. Many festivals have submission numbers of over 5,000 and upwards, so you've got to celebrate. There's so much always to be done on the film that we would lose sight of that quite often. We would post mantras around the office, to remind us about the great journey we were on. We especially liked this Sean Penn quote about the process of filmmaking, "Even if it doesn't end up 'in' the film it definitely ends up 'in' you." We have gained such a rich story on this journey, and we're eternally grateful for that.

8. Figure out your festival goals. What are you really looking for from festivals? People to see the film? Press? Distribution? All of the above? The big fests do get distributors to take notice, but others might be tougher. Reviews from press rarely happen, but some festivals were actually fantastic at that. Cleveland were incredible, and Santa Barbara got us great press, helped by the fact that we were nominated for an award. Go into the festival knowing what you want to get out of it.

9. Get people to your screenings. Somehow, in the rush to get our film finished in time for our premiere, we never stopped to consider the fact

that we were expected to help get people to our screenings at certain festivals! We had never done this before, and just sort of thought that once our film was in a festival, the work was over. This is NOT the case. You'll be reaching out to press, social media, people on the street—anyone you can think of to get to your screenings or write about it.

10. Know the distributors. We had some great responses from distributors but there are so many of them out there. There are a number of places to search for a list of distributors; the chapter of this book, and Film Forum has a detailed list of feature film companies as does the Toronto Film festival.

11. Build your audience. People are seeing your film! At every screening we attended, we would pass around a clipboard for every audience member to sign. Now we've built up a great email list for those towns to get the word out about the next phase of *Musicwood*, from events, to theatrical releases and iTunes. Also, you might meet some great advocates for your film who will want to help promote it—put a star by those names.

12. Get noticed. Think about how to go the extra mile for your festival screenings to get noticed. And maybe don't spread yourself too thin. Decide which festival you MUST go to. We were scheduled at three festivals at one time and we missed out on going to Sarasota. We wished we could have been there.

13. Connect with some outreach partners. Find some groups that have the same goals as your film and connect with them to get the word out. It's a win-win!

14. Keep the crowd-funding love going. We ran our Kickstarter campaign in the early days, mid-2011, and it was an instant community builder. We felt supported and found the people that would encourage us all the way through our festival run. It was wonderful meeting some of those early supporters at festivals along the way; some might even want to be ambassadors for your film—tap into that if you can.

15. Very young festivals will invite you, and they will have teething troubles. We love the DIY nature of young festivals but maybe say "Yes" only if it's part of your strategy, because every fest takes energy. For example, maybe it's your hometown and there's a real reason you want to attend.

You do really want to "attend" as many of your screenings as possible as that causes buzz around the film, but only if it's part of your strategy.

16. Think BIG. Our film was a feature film. It may be a documentary but it was made to be cinematic, with pacing and visuals designed for the big screen. Try to think big in your press releases and blog pieces. We wrote a press release for every town we visited. We had mixed success, sure, but it did get us in some big papers like the *Chicago Sun-Times*.

17. Do Q&As after the screenings. This seems like a no-brainer, but make sure the fests and theaters know that you will be there and doing Q&A's. We saw a few tough spots (thankfully never with *Musicwood*) when the film ended and the audience left because no one had mentioned there was a Q&A. Then when you're doing that Q&A, tell stories about your film because people really engage with stories. They love those behind-the-scenes tales that offer funny or thrilling stories about making the film.

18. If you're gonna tour with the film, put the tour together EARLY. We self-distributed our theatrical screenings and we had three separate big tours with the film. First with film festivals, then music festivals (awesome!) then a theatrical screening tour in the Pacific Northwest then the Northeast. Because we couldn't arrange all of our theatrical screenings together in one month we had to do ad-hoc flights to cities, and this got very expensive. If you have the time and know that you will be doing a theatrical tour I would say start planning this straight after your premiere. Some filmmaker friends hired a van and took off around the country with their film—not a bad thought.

19. Do full-week theatrical screenings when possible. Two of our theatrical screenings weren't full weeks and that makes it hard to get press. Think of all the competition you're up against for events in New York, so you need press. In that case, it's even more important to make a special event of it and attend, so think how you can do this in a way to make an impact. We had major bands play before a screening—we did a Q&A with invited members to join a panel, with someone from our outreach partners. This helps with PR as well, because the other people involved will help promote the event.

20. The very big feature distributors know that documentaries often have a lukewarm reception at the box office so think of unique ways of

distributing and how to raise income. We were lucky in being able to sign with Cinema Guild for our digital and educational distribution. With them handling those paths, we could focus on a limited theatrical release to generate the reviews; we had our theatrical release tie-in day and date with our digital distribution.

21. Have a team! It's the only way you can keep up with festival requests, press and outreach. Interns are wonderful things: talk to local schools or advertise on craigslist and get some help, even if it's part-time. You are going to need it, because there are forms to be filled and materials to be created for every single screening, every single press request. We heard from a filmmaker friend who got an intern who proved her mettle and quickly became the film's AP. Check in periodically to make sure your interns are getting what they want from the internship too, maybe build in some training days.

22. Before you arrive at any screening check the cinema size and tickets sales. We did a ton of outreach and PR for a screening at a festival without checking this and arrived to find out the screening theater was pretty small. Subsequently, we packed the room. If we'd thought to check ahead, we could have adjusted our efforts accordingly, or asked the festival to give us a larger room. Conversely, if you know you'll be screening in a huge room, you can step up the press push. If things aren't looking good, start offering free tickets to press folks. You might have to cover ticket costs but it'll be worth it for PR.

23. Consider a sales agent. This is a tricky one, because we heard advice from both sides. Some folks said they wouldn't have had any success without a sales agent. A significant filmmaker said they didn't want to give up a cut of any income for something they were essentially doing themselves anyway (DIY!) but he had a huge reach as a filmmaker already. We didn't work with a sales agent because we had some pretty good contacts with the TV world. But a few doors didn't open for us and in hindsight a sales agent would have been great; bring them on EARLY! We were told a sales agent would be more useful than PR at festivals. Save the PR for when the public can access the film.

24. Recognize you're not alone. Just when you feel worn out, read this line from Joe Berlinger at Sundance: "The best decision I made in preparing for Sundance occurred with my most recent experience with *Under*

African Skies when I decided that you can't control the fate of your film, so I decided to actually enjoy the festival experience and to experience the work of my colleagues." Talk to other filmmakers, embrace the sense of community, enjoy it, make those friends for life. Get advice from those filmmakers about other film festivals, find out which ones will treat you well and make you feel it's all been worth it.

25. During the early days of our festival run, we attended a Q&A with actor and filmmaker John Lurie. We managed to have a quick chat with him in a bar afterwards. As novice filmmakers, we asked him for one piece of advice as we began to get our film out into the world, and without missing a beat he said, "Just don't deal with any assholes." Life is too short.

15

Distribution (or Selling and Income)

When you think of distribution for your film, there are a number of markets to consider—for example:

- ▶ TVOD including iTunes, Amazon, Google Play, Vimeo On Demand known as Transactional Video on Demand because people pay per view.

- ▶ Subscription VOD digital streaming, Netflix, etc.

- ▶ AVOD or advertising-based VOD is still a new market. It has the goal of having a consistent stream of people watching your videos (and thereby seeing the advertisements).

- ▶ Short documentary digital platforms that work like TV networks in as much as they pay a small acquisition fee (Vox, Slate, NYT Op-Docs, ITVS digital)

- ▶ cable video on demand (VOD)

- ▶ educational

- theatrical screening ticket sales

- semi-theatrical screening fees

- broadcast TV rights

- and, believe it or not, profit from DVD sales (not much, but yes we did make profit on DVD sales).

We go into more detail on each of the distribution platforms above in other chapters. See "In Conversation" with Debra Zimmerman and Women Make Movies for semi-theatrical and education (Chapter 13). Theatrical plus TV and streaming have their own chapters later in the book (Chapters 16 and 18). The other markets will be expanded on in this chapter and we include a list of distributors.

One of our consultants asked us a great question that really helped us focus our distribution plan: What did we want from our film? Money, critical acclaim or to make sure the film is seen?

Unbelievably, we didn't care that much about money. We kind of still don't, except we like to eat, and we should at least be filmmakers that can eat! We wanted critical acclaim, so we would have an easier time getting funding for the next doc. And as *Musicwood* was a social issue film, we wanted the film to be seen (I mean who doesn't) and for the film to support a campaign to conserve the old-growth trees of the Alaskan rain forest.

We premiered at the DOC NYC film festival (as detailed in Festivals, Chapter 13) and among the distributors that attended were some big hitters: IFC, Kino Lorber, Zeitgeist, Cinema Guild, First Run, HBO and CNN. We had some great success. Oscilloscope came to our screening. HBO asked to screen our film. We chatted with IFC and Zeitgeist, had interest from Cinema Guild, and First Run asked for a meeting. Later we had conversations with Autlook and Filmstransit too.

So you've finished the film, opened in festivals, made sure distributors have seen your film, and now you're having meetings with distributors. This is incredibly exciting! These meetings are kind of like a job interview, with both parties evaluating the other and seeing if it will be a good fit. As such, make sure you prep adequately before going in to any meeting. Look into

186 Distribution (or Selling and Income)

the distributor, research what films they have acquired—do you know anyone that has worked with them?

Refer back to the finishing of your film section in Fair Use (Chapter 11). Have you got your paperwork intact? All clearances checked with your lawyer? Your music cue sheet and releases? Hopefully any outstanding issues have been cleared up so that you are free to deliver your film in its current form to your distributor so that they can begin to sell it for you, and you can begin covering and recouping your costs.

We were advised that these are good questions to ask in a distribution meeting:

- ▶ How much will be spent on promotion and advertising?
- ▶ Are they are offering theatrical distribution?
- ▶ If there is theatrical, what is the minimum number of cities that you will open in?

Keep in mind all of the potential screening platforms and markets (listed at the top of this section) when you're thinking of distribution. Try and hold onto your semi-theatrical rights, rights to sell your own DVDs (less important now) and even possibly to sell downloads for community screenings from your website. These are all places where you can make a good return. We did a live stream on *Huffington Post* when we opened the Yale Film Festival and it didn't affect our distribution deals, which was awesome.

If you can retain the rights to sell downloads and streams from your website, Vimeo On Demand will let you sell your film directly to your audience (they absorbed VHX, which used to allow you to sell from your website for a 10–15% fee). If you think your audience is large enough and you have a good following on social media and have a huge email list (and so on), then you may want to just use this method.

Other films go a step further with merchandise and with consumer DVD, community screening kits, educational licenses and merchandise. The film *Age of Champions* set up a simple online store using Shopify. They sold more than US$300,000 in DVDs, kits and merchandise directly through their website. They eventually went onto raise a significant income through website traffic. So think about what you might want to do with your website and if you want to retain rights to do this.

Unless you have a huge social media presence, you generally will have to go through a distributor to get on digital platforms such as iTunes, Netflix, Amazon Instant and Google Play. Some distributors have direct deals with digital platforms, while others have to go through aggregators that represent a package of films to sell to the digital platforms. For example, Cinema Guild has a direct deal, while Filmbuff is an aggregator that other distributors will use. As an individual film you can also be offered deals from aggregators. We were offered a deal from Filmbuff, and we might consider working with them in the future. Distribber is another VOD aggregator that you pay to get onto these platforms.

With *Musicwood*, we had a pretty clear idea of what we wanted to do:

- ▶ We wanted a limited theatrical release to ensure we got critical acclaim.

- ▶ We wanted a large semi-theatrical run to make sure we could get out to a non-traditional documentary/film watching audience. We knew who our core audience was—Native Americans, music lovers, guitar makers, tree lovers, outdoorsy types. I wanted the film to tour in music festivals, which meant holding back some distribution control.

- ▶ We wanted to sell our own DVDs through our website.

Because our film had such a huge music aspect to it, we thought that music festivals might be a good way to reach a large section of our core audience. These days, a lot of music festivals have a film element to them, so we worked hard to build screening opportunities at Bonnaroo, Newport Folk Festival, Wilco's Solid Sound Festival and we opened in Portland theaters the week after their Pickathon Festival. We also screened at NAMM in LA, a massive music manufacturers conference which has an attendance upwards of 100,000 people.

We have made a fairly comprehensive lists of documentary distributors in this chapter; rights issues will vary and some distributors will allow you to create a hybrid distribution plan which affords you more control. I would say try to have the deal made as soon as possible **before** your festival premier, as your distributors have a better chance of collecting your semi-theatrical screening fees from all the film festivals. We took our time as we were so new to this, which meant we lost out on some fees (the festivals are more likely to pay when you have a distributor).

I've split the next section into **National** and **International Distributors**, as it was quite a different exercise negotiating for the rights for various territories.

NATIONAL

All Rights Distributers

Here are some of the largest distributors that offer comprehensive packages, including theatrical:

- Magnolia
- Sony Picture Classics
- Oscilloscope
- Participant
- Strand Releasing
- Music Box Films
- IFC
- The Orchard
- Janus
- Abramorama
- Grasshopper
- Cinedym
- **Zeitgeist**—they smartly let the festivals do the curating for them. They only take five films a year theatrically.
- **First Run**—lots of releases a year, generally an all-rights deal, but will sometimes negotiate.
- **Cinema Guild**—they do theatrical but educational rights are a major part of their business.

Hybrid Distributers—Cable, VOD or Semi-theatrical, Educational and Digital Only (Not Theatrical)

- **Women Make Moves**—semi-theatrical and educational, etc.
- **Gravitas**—digital and educational deal.
- **Film Buff**—digital distribution aggregator (iTunes +).
- **Distribber**—another aggregator.

All distributors will generally charge US$2,500 for digital set-up costs.

There are three digital release windows that you will generally follow if you want to make income from iTunes and Amazon before you move onto the subscription services, otherwise known as SVOD like Netflix (see below). Also, be careful about TV deals: if you're still waiting for a response from TV then hold back on these digital deals if you can as so many networks have their own digital platforms now. So you might want to negotiate for a clause in your digital deal to protect you from losing the TV deal later on (i.e. for a period of time the film can be taken down from the digital platforms).

Digital Release Windows

1. iTunes and Amazon

2. on-demand cable VOD

3. 3–5 months later, subscription SVOD: Netflix, Vudu, Hulu.
   Netflix generally offer in the region of US$10–40K for acquisitions (they pay a lot more for originals).

iTunes, Amazon, Google Play, Xbox, etc. are transactional VOD (TVOD) as mentioned earlier—i.e. you press a button and pay to play. The aggregator will often charge a one-time fee for digital set up and they will take in the region of 30% fee for royalties. Depending on your distributer and if they are not aggregators they go to iTunes with one or two titles a month direct (some distributors cannot approach these platforms direct but use aggregators).

For the SVOD services like Netflix and so on, at the time of writing you still need an agent or distributer to approach those services.

Educational Distributers

Not all University departments buy screening rights—for example, Music and Science buy very few films for their departments. See earlier, as some distributers offer hybrid rights deals.

- **Bullfrog Films**—educational only.
- **Passion River**—VOD, educational, home video, DVD, not all exclusive

DVDs

Yes, still possible and selling through your website. Remember some of the stores for e.g. Best Buy have replacement fees and return fees; Walmart will only take films that have made US$1 million at the box office or are Sundance winners.

INTERNATIONAL

In Europe there are approximately 15 theatrical releases a week.

Roco Films International

www.rocofilms.com

Annie Roney (Managing Director and Founder)

They also do educational.

Autlook

www.autlookfilms.com

Peter Jager

Dogwoof

www.dogwoof.com

Oli Harbottle

UK, but have expanded into US.

They try to tie in UK and US releases with a short window.

All rights, DVD, broadcast.

10 to 20 films a year, one a month.

They want universal subjects, the Sarah Palin doc (*The Undefeated*) and *After Tiller* were deemed too American.

Queen of Versailles did well for them because of the characters and portraits.

Cats and Docs

www.catndocs.com

Catherine Le Clef

Represented *The Woodmans* and *The Staircase, 5 Broken Cameras*.

Not theatrical, TV mainly, and suggest Dogwoof for theatrical.

They won't take on environmental films or music docs as they're hard to sell.

First Hand Films

Esther Van Messel

acquisition@firsthandfilms.com

Wide Management

Anais Clanet

infos@widemanagement.com

Films Transit International

www.filmstransit.com

Jan Rofekamp

Scorpion TV

www.scorpiontv.com

David Cornwall

...and a few other international distributors: **Rise and Shine**, **Java**, **Visit Films**, **Variance**, **Altitude (UK)** and **Madman (Australia)**; **Wild Bunch** is a French sales, finance and distribution company.

OUR DEAL

With *Musicwood*, we used a consultant to help advise us on the kind of rights we could hope to keep control of (selling DVDs through our website, keeping semi-theatrical rights etc.).

We had meetings and calls with First Run and Oscilloscope and got offers from The Orchard, Cinema Guild, Passion River, Gravitas and Filmbuff. We were thrilled. We made another shareable spreadsheet on Google Drive with all of the offers we received for *Musicwood*. This way we could contrast the deal memos, and now we have a great information archive for our next film.

Many more distributors approached us that we hadn't heard of or we had been advised against, so be careful: definitely do the research.

We signed a deal for educational and digital distribution to be handled by Cinema Guild, and we desperately wanted international distribution. We had conversations with Films Transit and Autlook, and eventually signed a deal memo with Scorpion TV.

Be careful when you think of your release strategy. We didn't schedule our theatrical release for months after our festival run. This enabled us to chase all the TV deals before we did a day and date release digitally with

Distribution (or Selling and Income) 193

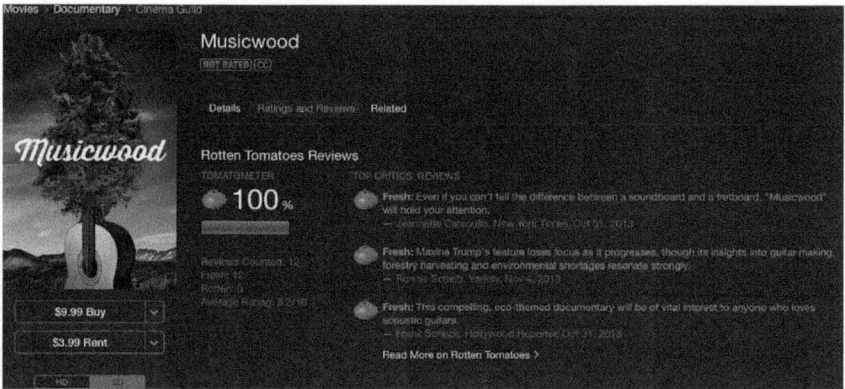

FIGURE 15.1 *Musicwood* **on iTunes**

our theatrical run. It was a way we could smartly use a big PR push for all platforms together (except TV of course) and allow us time to strike a deal with TV.

We kept hold of our DVD rights and would sell DVDs at festivals, right after the Q&A. Our DVDs are now carried in a select number of guitar stores around the country and on Taylor Guitars' website. We made our DVDs with Acutrack, at a cost of US$3.50 each, which included recycled plastic cases. We currently sell the DVDs for US$19.95.

We've now held over 100 screenings and counting for *Musicwood* around the country, whether festival, theatrical or to Native American audiences in Clan Houses. We had an additional sales of screening fees to Universities that came through Cinema Guild.

Through our distribution deals, sales of screening fees through our website and DVD profit, we actually managed to recover most of our production costs and pay back our US$35K investment to our production company Hitman Productions. This felt good!

We should have secured our distribution deal earlier, we held out trying to get theatrical deals because we wanted reviews. The distributors are more likely to get you screening fees at festivals. So maybe I would pay to rent some theaters (known as "four-walling") as soon as possible, rather than waiting on distributors if I decide to have a theatrical run in the future. That's up for debate.

SEMI-THEATRICAL/NON-THEATRICAL DISTRIBUTION

We chatted with the distributor Women Make Movies in Chapter 13, so do read our detailed interview with the Executive Director Debra Zimmerman. Woman Make Movies are very well known for working in semi-theatrical and educational distribution.

We didn't use a semi-theatrical advisor or booker. But some films do very well using semi-theatrical distribution instead of looking for a theatrical release. Alongside festivals, using libraries, community screenings, museums, one-night special event cinema screenings and so on are all deemed semi-theatrical—any other way the public accesses your film in a theatrical environment. We successfully added music festivals to our semi-theatrical list as mentioned earlier, and see my *IndieWire* article online about tips for film screenings at music festivals.

In the future we might consider using online web-based platforms like Tugg or Gathr that allow you to set up screenings in theaters. If you have contacts who are keen for the film to play in their town, they can request the film to play at a theater for one night using these platforms.

The documentary *Girl Rising* used Gathr and was incredibly successful. They had 1,300 requested screenings, selling 66,000 tickets in 169 cinemas, all without advertising.

Our distribution consultant told us that one documentary didn't make any money on their theatrical run for a week, but made US$1.3 million after 100 theaters booked them through Gathr and Tugg. They marketed their film as an action film and not a documentary. They charged US$20 a ticket for a special event Q&A and reached out to their 50K person mailing list. They made at least US$500 each screening. Sign up for Peter Broderick's informative newsletters for more.

EDUCATIONAL

Luckily for us we used Cinema Guild as our educational distributor. There are thousands of colleges and universities in America. Using a distributor means inclusion in their printed catalogue sent out in time for every academic semester, they can harness reviews from video librarian, and they attend academic conferences representing your film alongside their current slate. The fee from the distributor is higher for this market than the digital distribution to iTunes for example, and can be as high as 75%.

Kanopy and Hoopla is an educational digital platform otherwise known as patron driven acquisition (PDA) where students and academics use their library cards to access your film. There is a payment method and analytics that the platform itself provides, but this allows you to bring your film directly to this market although at a lower dollar amount. Hoopla is for the public library system where anyone with a library card can access your film.

16
Theatrical

Why bother with theatrical releases when documentaries notoriously don't get great tickets sales? After speaking on a panel at Sheffield Doc Festival the distributor Dogwoof's Oli Harbottle pointed out that, as an indie distributor, the term "theatrical doc" is something of a misnomer. "That's not where money is made. It's completely an awareness platform," he said, later adding that, for Dogwoof, theatrical success often means wide editorial coverage and social media impressions. "When a film is released in the cinemas, we're looking at how many pre-orders we had on iTunes, and on Amazon for DVD, because that's the purpose of us doing theatrical. I would say 1 in 10 films makes money at the box office theatrically. It's a very expensive exercise to get films out there."

Manori Ravindran, reporting for *Real Screen*, wrote more about the successful distribution strategy of Dogwoof (*Blackfish* and *Weiner* distributor), which releases about 18 films a year in the UK. They consider the whole lifespan of a film from the outset and work out windows to broadcast on TV, digital platforms and DVDs. In order to monetize films, the indie looks increasingly at collapsed windows, day-and-date releases, short windows to DVD, and also working with broadcasters and SVOD platforms on short windows.

"There are very few docs that warrant traditional theatrical release. The [*Houston* doc] is being treated as a tentpole doc that will be treated in much the same way as a proper movie," say Simon Chinn from Lightbox Entertainment and Red Box Films talking about their Whitney Houston documentary.

Shame Simon had to say "proper" movie. I think we should be thinking about all of our documentaries as movies. Don't let other filmmakers down by making just the traditional talking head formulaic documentary; let's push the definition of non-fiction filmmaking.

But Chinn did go on to say that as the producer they did raise the entire budget for their Whitney Houston documentary through theatrical pre-sales at the Cannes Film Festival. "That's a new thing for docs, to be able to pre-sell in that way," he said. "And it does show you how the market and theatrical audience has changed for docs, because that never used to be possible 10, 15 years ago."

So, as one distributor put it, they see it as a loss leader to help the film gain attention. And that's exactly how we felt. We wouldn't have gotten the critical acclaim we did without a theatrical run and that was important to us. We also used our theatrical release as a PR vehicle for our digital release because we were releasing on iTunes and Amazon on the same day. Filmmakers can debate endlessly on whether this is important or not, so work out what you want and your best strategy for getting it.

As mentioned in the last chapter, we decided to go with a hybrid model of distribution, which is more work for the filmmakers, but allows you more control of your film. We were lucky enough to have some theaters approach us directly to do theatrical engagements. If you don't get this opportunity then you could use a theatrical booker, but they are expensive, and you will need to have significantly budgeted for that.

We planned our theatrical tour (see Figure 16.1) and managed to plan community screenings around the same time and within the same tour. Some of these communities had invited us to screen in their area so they paid for our travel and expenses. In the future I would like to tie in our film festival tour too, as it worked really well.

Remember the outreach groups and communities from our very first Brain Trust: EIA, Greenpeace, etc.? Well, because we had bought them in early, they actually sponsored some of our theatrical screenings in DC, and through their contacts, got us a great audience of interested NGOs.

We weren't always booked for a full week run in theaters. Sometimes it was just three days. But whatever the run, expect your income to be about a third of all ticket sales, the theater then takes the rest.

When you have your theatrical run booked check the time slot for the screenings (you don't want to be screening only at 2pm on weekdays). Make sure the theater is displaying your poster properly, we also created a poster with all of the reviews that we stood on an easel for the opening night premiere at the theater in NYC (after all we were a *New York Times* Critics Pick!).

It's extremely important to test your screening Blu-ray or DCP too at the theater as every theater is different, and the sound quality and image can vary. Even Christopher Nolan still does this.

In every town where we screened the film, we would research local environmental groups and try and work with them, give them an opportunity to attend the screening and be involved in the Q&A. This gives the audience an opportunity to get directly involved in the issues while they're motivated to take action, or join a local group, etc. This built a great symbiotic relationship with these organizations.

We also flyered as many guitar stores as we could. Use any resource you can to get "relevant" email addresses (no one wants to be bothered with email junk that they're not interested in). This might sound like a lot of work, but it was enjoyable reaching an interested and involved audience.

What would I do differently in a theatrical release? Not much. I would possibly four-wall in LA to get the press and reviews. Four-wall means paying a theater to take a run of your film. I would then hold one-night ticketed events in as many theaters as possible (refer to the "Semi-Theatrical" section in Chapter 15) and plan that tour straight after our festival tour ended. I would have a PR and marketing machine working with me throughout the whole run.

As I've said before, consider your goal for the film. There is an excellent case study on self-distribution in *IndieWire*: "How We Made $1.5 Million Self-Distributing Our Doc: The Six-Step Playbook." I refer to it in the marketing section (see Chapter 17); they have no critical reviews on Rotten Tomatoes but they sure made a ton of money.

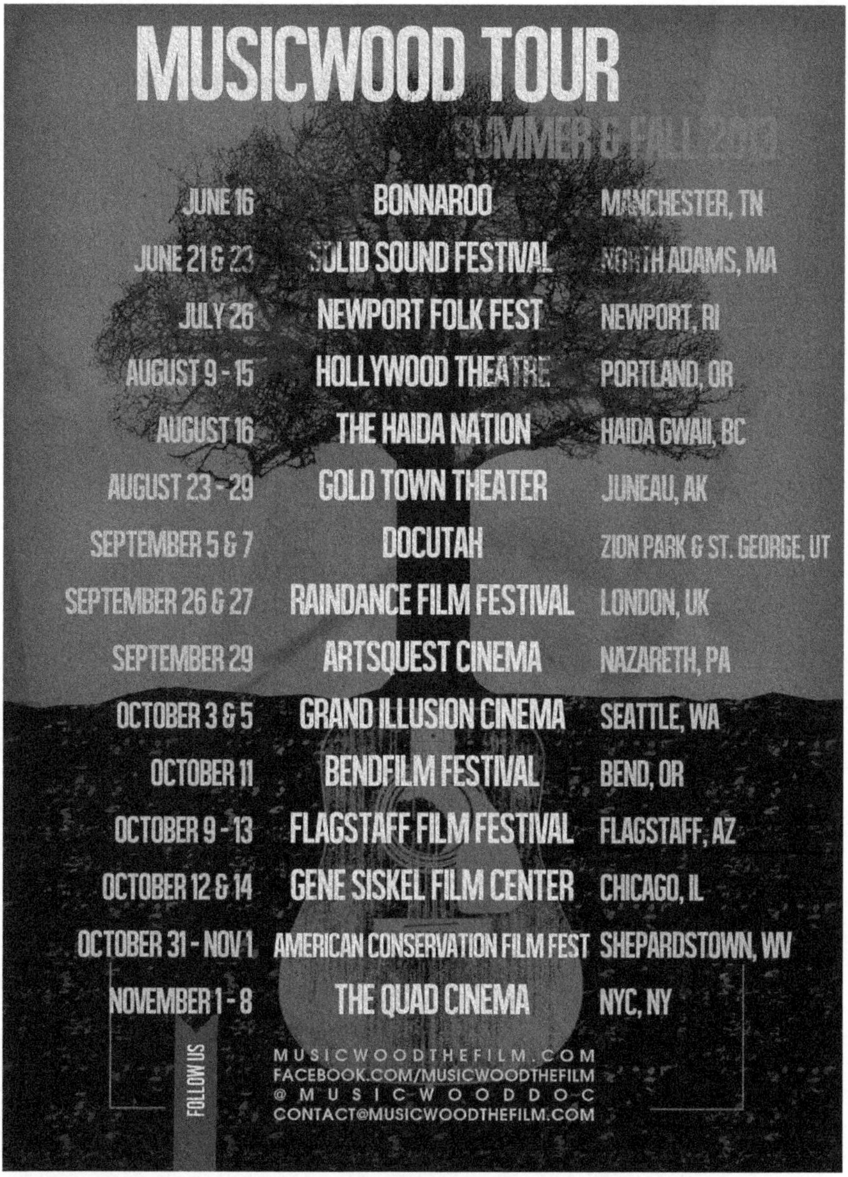

FIGURE 16.1 *Musicwood* tour poster, fall 2013

THEATERS IN OUR THEATRICAL RUN

Below are the theaters in our theatrical run. You could also refer to our full screenings list at www.musicwoodthefilm.com.

Chicago

Gene Siskel Center www.siskelfilmcenter.org

New York

The newly renovated Quad Cinema www.quadcinema.com

I would also suggest the Film Forum or Lincoln Center before you four-wall elsewhere.

Film Forum takes a DVD screener to consider but is very competitive www.filmforum.org

Seattle

The Grand Illusion. You might have luck at SIFF or North West Film Forum too; we got responses from all three theaters.

info@grandillusioncinema.org

www.siff.net

www.nwfilmforum.org

Washington DC

www.landmarktheatres.com/washington-d-c/e-street-cinema

The E Street Landmark Theater is a great theater and they're opening new theaters all across the city.

Portland OR

Hollywood Theater (beautiful theater) www.hollywoodtheatre.org

Juneau, Alaska

Gold Town Theater www.goldtownnick.com

Nashville (who kindly got back to us but didn't take the film because the film was in the Nashville Film Festival; next time I would go with the theater)

Belcourt Theater www.belcourt.org

Los Angeles

We didn't take the film to LA as you have to four-wall there.

This is the theater that is most supportive of four walling:

La Laemmle Theaters www.laemmle.com

17

Press and Marketing

At a film panel I recently attended the discussion was centered on how singularly important marketing is for your film and what we should be concentrating on most. At a second panel we were asked to consider the best spokesperson for our film and the stories that can be told to build an aura around it and help with publicity. I have heard that Marshall Curry thinks of his marketing as soon as he begins filmmaking—and look how successful his films have been. Refer back to the introduction to this book and the research chapter (Chapter 1) on the question of who needs your film.

We heard Tom Quinn (previously a founder of the distribution company RADiUS-TWC and Head of Acquisitions at Magnolia Pictures) talk about how the filmmaker themselves can sell their own film by the way they get up on stage and talk about it. This can help a distribution company believe that the film will be successful. So when you come out on stage at a festival for a Q&A remember this could be your chance. "You" are often the best person that can sell your film.

And then what about your press materials? The first line of your press kit is the most important: it will probably be your tag line and the description will be used over and over again as your elevator pitch. It's called an elevator pitch for exactly that reason: a situation might occur where you find yourself travelling a few floors in an elevator with a producer, and that's all the time you have to pitch your film. This is important stuff. Your press and marketing will be the first thing the public will see or read about your film. Here's ours:

> *Musicwood* is an adventure-filled journey, a political thriller with music at its heart.

From very early on in the pre-production of our film we were thinking about our audience. How the heck were we going to get guitar players and Native Americans to watch our film? Neither audience is especially known for going to the theater in large numbers.

Musicwood relates to conflict resolution on some larger level; it gets into politics, it gets into our future sustainability and looks at ownership of resources. In this world where people want easy entertainment and escape, it was a hard film to market to a mass audience. So to reach a wider audience, we tried to promote the drama of the film rather than the documentary aspects.

Think, as well, about your Vimeo/YouTube description for your trailer. This can begin the process of marketing the film. Who are you making the film for? What's the audience? Are there a number of different types of groups that will be interested? All food for thought and preparation for the next steps.

Ideally, we would have liked to include another line about the conflict in the film: "An age-old battle between the white man and Native Americans." But since one of our primary goals was to make a difference with our film, we took it out. To really make a difference, we needed to keep everyone in the film involved in the issue, talking and negotiating. The CEOs from the competing guitar companies, the Native American Corporation and Greenpeace, are not natural bedfellows and that's what makes the film so interesting.

We used a PR company, who pretty much used the press release we had written. (After all, we're the most passionate people to write about our film, and they didn't see much to improve on.) They got us trade press, etc., but we had a very small PR budget and we did a lot of the work alongside them.

THEATRICAL MARKETING AND PRESS

In general, you want the most publicity when the most people can go and see your film, whether it's theatrical distribution, or television or whatever platform you're streaming on. We had done a lot of self-motivated press for festivals (as detailed in Festivals section—see Chapter 14), but we really saved up our big national and trade press campaign for our theatrical run. As mentioned previously, we were simultaneously releasing digitally (a process known as "day and date") on iTunes and Amazon, so we saw it as our big release into the world.

There is a difficult balance here because distributors have said that press at a festival helps films get a deal; those big laurels help think of the lifespan of your film: festivals, theatrical possibly, then TV or streaming.

"The mainstream press…will only talk about a film once, so you release it theatrically—six months or three months before broadcast—that's the hit. Some of the most important outlets that will write about film, the timing is off, and if you're in TV and you want to get that television audience, that press attention goes for theatrical," John Hoffman at Discovery, explained. "It's nice to see a film you love getting good press attention, but you are possibly compromising audience for the television [broadcast] because you're not syncing that unpaid promotion." Remember, TV networks buy most rights so think about what you want to do with your film and have a strategy.

This subject also appears in the Festivals chapter (Chapter 14); in regards to how much press you want to garner for your festival run, don't go for the big guns unless you have a deal and are releasing very soon after the film premieres, which is exactly what some films do, it's a good idea. Get advice. If you can, get good trade press (i.e. *Hollywood Reporter*) at festivals but leave the broadsheets like the *New York Times* until later. That's one plan.

We saved the biggest push for our New York theatrical release, treating it as a huge premiere special event, which came months after our festival world premiere.

We wanted to really make a splash, but had no budget for P&A (print and advertising), so we had to get creative. One of the things we came up with in a brainstorm session was an idea for guerrilla marketing that got everyone really excited. We made printed caution tape, with the film's release details on it, to wrap around trees in New York City. We put the tape around large trees in strategic places all over town. It stayed up for days and people sent us photos and shared on Instagram, etc.

Another idea that worked well from our festival screenings was giving out our customized guitar picks. They were a bigger expense than postcards, but hopefully not as easy to throw away, were eco-friendly, and would get people talking about the film.

We had all of our Kickstarter contacts, and now email lists from test screenings, Q&A sign-ups and more. We offered discounts for screening RSVPs from certain relevant communities (like the staff of the Guitar Center or hiking groups, for example), and we reached out to all of our core audience groups (as listed in earlier chapters).

We didn't only flyer around town; our great intern put up posters in music schools (Guitar School, New School, etc.), outdoor equipment stores, music venues—anywhere that made sense).

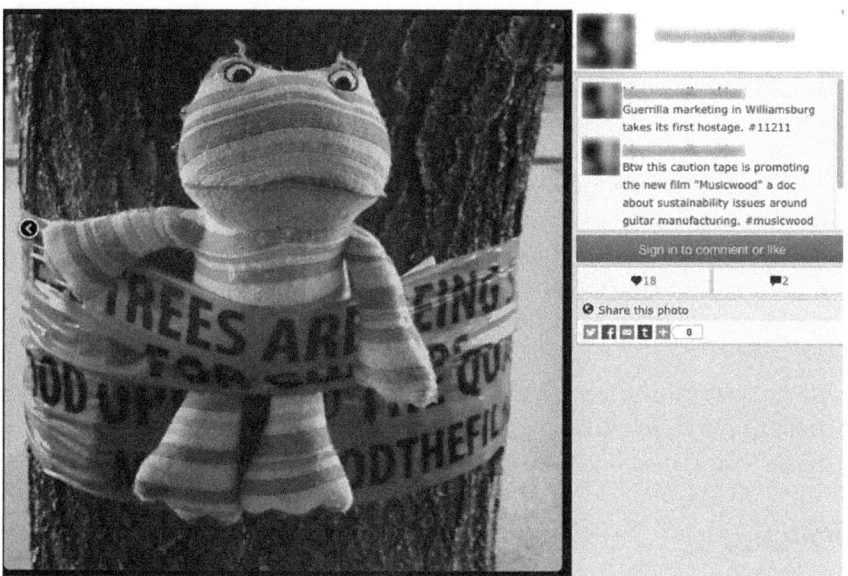

FIGURE 17.1 A stranger's photo on Instagram having fun with our guerrilla marketing

Another idea we tried, which admittedly didn't work as well for us, was booking panelists to join us on our Q&As after the NYC screenings. The idea was that the panelists would be a draw to interest more people to come to the film's screening. It had worked for a friend's film, so we mirrored his idea. We opened in theaters when it was bitterly cold in NYC, there was a New York election that night and, as we said, our money for P&A had run out. Even having one Q&A attended by a well-known band with a devoted fan following didn't really get results.

Some strategies for getting folks to the NYC screenings worked, some didn't, but in the end we had a successful two-week run at The Quad Cinema and received some amazing reviews. That was our goal.

REVIEWERS

If your PR team didn't do a great job in getting reviews, there are a certain number of Rottentomatoes.com reviewers (though not many) that you can email directly through the site. It takes time, but it's a little-known secret, so dig through the listed contacts there—it'll be worth the extra few reviews. I think we got four extra reviews by doing this.

BLOGS

We also made different press releases for different blogs: environmental blogs, guitar, music, outdoor enthusiasts, and so on. We had our contact list from our Kickstarter research and so were in a good place to use that information to reach out to people who had already spread the word and to others who hadn't, and now we had a better chance of coverage with a completed film.

We got less blog attention than we thought we would, again possibly as a result of our difficult subject, or people feeling tired of environmental stories, our lack of contacts, or our PR team not being able to reach them.

OVERALL

So how did we do for press? We were a *New York Times* Critics' Pick, which was thrilling. *Huffington Post* live streamed the film. I wrote two articles for

IndieWire and we wrote a third article for magazines. We got written about in national newspapers *The Independent* and *The Scotsman* and the magazine *Time Out* (plus others) in the UK.

With our PR company, we got great trade press from *Variety*, *Hollywood Reporter* and Thompson on Hollywood, for example. If you can get *Variety*, they do a full review, not a capsule, which is great. And we now have a 100% rating on Rotten Tomatoes!! Whoop whoop!

What would we do differently for press and PR? Well we're pretty stoked with the results; we really did reach our goal. Next time we would start with a bigger PR budget and hopefully a P&A budget too, so we could afford to pay two PR companies to reach local press and larger national outlets. Booking two companies is apparently quite common. You can also pay PR Newswire US$600 to carry the story of your release, which other news outlets can then pick up. We would also have enough lead time for printed magazines, as it can take 6 months to get the slot you would want to work in tandem for your release.

Maybe next time we'd also like to raise more money.

You can see all of our press on our website—www.musicwoodthefilm.com/press.

18
TV and Streaming

You may have been lucky enough that your distributor will be selling your film to TV networks or streaming sites. Your film can also be sold via sales agents working on your behalf—Submarine, Cinematic Media, and Film Sales Company are some companies. These agents will approach you or you can approach them before you have your festival premiere so that they can attend with you and represent your film. They do generally only attend the major festivals however.

DIGITAL STREAMING

You may have been fortunate enough to have found an agent to represent you that could sell your film to the streaming platforms. Please note that it is useful to be aware of the opportunities of releasing your films at different times on the digital platforms. See Chapter 15 under the header "Digital Release Windows." At the time of writing Netflix and Amazon "originals" do need these agents to open that door for you. Agents can get you that access and if those platforms are interested they will pay a lot of money for "originals". However, if these streaming platforms acquire films they pay a lot less. Hulu have also now started to release documentaries, they have just negotiated a deal with CNN Films to be their streaming partner and are doing some interesting work..

We have previously discussed the screening windows for iTunes, Amazon and Vimeo On Demand before the film goes to Netflix etc. This is a window to raise royalties from rentals that your distributor (or yourself with Vimeo On Demand) can raise. These dollar amounts will greatly reduce once your film is available on Netflix as fewer people will need to rent your film. This is important. If Netflix acquire your film then they will often pay one price for all rights and offer a lot less for acquisition deals.

You may have pitched your film at IDFA or Sheffield Film festivals at their pitching markets and received pre-sales funding from these platforms, but this is quite rare for unknown filmmakers. Not unheard of but, as we have mentioned, if you want this pre-sale funding then align yourself with an experienced producer. "Who is on your team?" is often a question you'll hear, as many funders are nervous if you have no film experience. Or make sure your scene selects that you screen are so fantastic people will *have* to have meetings with you.

Once you premiere at a top tier festival, if you have a great film you will receive distribution offers or sales agents will negotiate on your behalf with these platforms.

Do note that we are discussing theatrical length documentaries. There are many more opportunities for short documentaries to pitch direct to platforms such as Slate, Vox, NY Op Docs CNN and ITVS digital.

Slate and Vox have pitch sections on their websites, and note that Netflix are also acquiring mid-form documentaries—refer to the titles on the 2017 and 2018 Oscar short documentary nominations for examples.

We were fortunate enough to ask Pam Torno, the series producer of Digital Initiatives at ITVS, a few questions about their pitch process.

> *ITVS Digital Open Call programs such genres from Arts & Culture, Democracy & Rights, Diversity & Identity, Health & Environment and International stories. Are there any areas that you aren't seeing explored by filmmakers and would be interested to see proposals on these subjects?*

(Continued)

(Continued)

The Digital Open Call application process is open to short nonfiction stories on a wide range of subjects—as long as they're in the zeitgeist, reflect the world we live in, and have a unique point of view. Those are the attributes that we think will spark online conversations and help us build a dedicated audience for Indie Lens Storycast, the new YouTube channel we've launched in partnership with PBS Digital Studios. We're not looking for specific topics, but we do want to make sure that many perspectives are represented on Indie Lens Storycast. At ITVS, diversity in front of and behind the camera is core to our mission.

After the initial application round in Digital Open Call you state on the website that the top 10 to 15% of applicants will be asked to submit additional materials for further review. What percentage of proposals reach the funding stage?

Depending on the number of applications submitted anywhere from 2–5% end up receiving some level of development funding, so it is a highly competitive process.

It's exciting that ITVS digital awards development funding of up to $30,000 for digital series. Often this is a similar amount that feature documentaries receive from funders. Do you expect to see a production bible in the application, which includes detail such as what other episodes would include?

Once we select the digital story proposals we want to develop for potential exhibition on Storycast, we'll be sharing basic formatting conventions and guidelines with those filmmakers to help them optimize watchability and keep viewer retention high. We also plan to monitor our channel metrics to see what's keeping our audiences engaged. Our goal is to learn from the data we gather and share knowledge with the filmmakers we support so they have the skills to produce stories that can thrive in the YouTube ecosystem.

Apart from the fact Digital Open call would like series proposal submissions what would you say is the main difference between the ITVS "Digital" Open Call funding and ITVS Open call funding, apart from duration of projects?

The Digital Open Call funding initiative was designed to give filmmakers an opportunity to tell their stories in the public digital space, as opposed to public broadcasting. It's become our content pipeline for Indie Lens Storycast, so those who want to apply should have a strong sense of how their story will appeal to a younger, digital native audience and be willing to work with ITVS to craft a series or a short doc that's consumable to YouTube viewers.

(Continued)

> When did this fund begin and how many proposals have you funded so far?
>
> Open Call has funded eight projects since it began in 2015
>
> The website features short descriptions of each project you have funded so far. Do you ever accept submissions for one-off proposals rather than series?
>
> We do see the opportunity to present standalone shorts on our YouTube channel. We'll be working with filmmakers through the development process to help them shape their story direction and figure out its optimum length, whether it's a one-off or a series.
>
> When you talk about Digital Open Call being only open to pre-production projects, that lends heavily on a great application (as no film clips will be available). Any tips on how to write a great proposal? Do filmmakers submit look books?
>
> Some applicants make the mistake of applying with ideas that are underdeveloped. Even though this is development funding, we still expect filmmakers to do their research, demonstrate that they have credible access to a subject, and come to us with a well-conceived story and approach that has potential to draw a big online audience. It's equally important that they understand our mission: we're looking for urgent stories with social impact, and we want to hear from underrepresented voices.
>
> It's great in the submission information that you mention, on average, applicants spend 1–2 weeks completing their applications for Digital Open Call. I've only written for the ITVS Open Call and that is quite detailed. What are the differences between applications, and is there a lot of difference?
>
> Filmmakers selected through Digital Open Call receive support to develop a pre-production idea into a proof-of-concept pilot. It's not a production agreement, so the amount of materials we request from applicants and the internal review process is a little smaller in scope. However, our standards of quality for the proposed content remain very high for both open calls.

US TV NETWORKS

There is still often more money available from Broadcast TV than digital platforms except for the lucky few. Both myself and my Producer have a background of working in TV. We pitched to a number of the TV networks ourselves, although there were some that we didn't have contacts for, like Showtime or EPIX, but we knew our film probably wouldn't be a good fit for them (see later in this chapter for genres of documentaries they program).

Musicwood features a Native American corporation unsustainably logging vast areas of a unique US rain forest. It's a complex reading of a situation that upends your traditional expectations of Native Americans. Essentially, we're saying that Native Americans are just like the rest of us; they have corporations that use up and spit out the best natural resources just like many Western corporations. The hope of the film was that Native Americans who adhere rigorously to their cultural values would be able to pressurize their corporation (they are all shareholders) to act differently than the industrialized nations in the rest of the world. You'll have to watch the film to see what happened.

All this makes the film quite controversial and, unfortunately, controversy doesn't sell well to TV networks in the US. For example, most of the Washington, DC networks—Discovery, Nat Geo, Smithsonian TV, etc.—will avoid any controversy in their programming. So, very few networks in the US were interested in the film. HBO asked to see it. CNN watched it, as did Al-Jazeera, and all of the networks did get back to us, which was great.

Through our international distributors, Scorpion TV, the national Russian TV network bought *Musicwood* to show nationally in Russia and on their cable channel here in the US. AMC Asia also picked up the film, as did TV networks in Australia and New Zealand. We were also streamed on airline in-flight entertainment channels such as Quantas, Finnair and on Indonesian airlines.

US TV Network Opportunities

Here is a brief description of the Broadcast Networks in the US that buy feature or one-off hour-long documentaries. Generally, it is helpful if you are an emerging filmmaker to align yourself with an established Executive Producer, Producer, or Consultant Producer to introduce you to the executives at these networks. You will pay those producers but they will be able to get a response from John Hoffman at Discovery or Courtney Sexton at CNN. I've met many of these executives at film festivals so make sure to attend where you can do the same, and hear them speak on panels and so on; it's a great way to introduce your project. As mentioned earlier you may also be introduced to them at pitching sessions at festivals. Practice pitching, make a good sizzle video with examples scenes of your film and be ready with your synopsis if, after your elevator pitch, they seem interested.

Discovery networks (and their digital channels such as Science and TLC) all take feature documentaries.

National Geographic are now in the business of producing high-end cinematic one-off, event documentaries.

Showtime, **EPIX** and **ESPN** commission big name portrait docs; these will rarely appear on Netflix as they have their own streaming platforms.

HBO—25 to 40 films a year. If they acquire, they generally pay more than Netflix acquisitions (not to be confused with Netflix Originals). They have a hold back for digital distribution as they have HBO GO.

CNN commission or acquire 8 to 12 films a year. *Our Nixon* was a huge success for them. War, politics, the environment are interest areas for them. No music docs.

A&E only commission films—no acquisitions. Look for big, cinematic, character-driven pieces.

PBS's POV look for films that challenge assumptions, have surprising, strong points of view and no celebrities; 16–17 slots for films a year. See Chapter 13 for a much more detailed conversation with the Executive Director Justine Nagan. Justine has given us some great information about this important strand and PBS Documentary in general.

Independent Lens on PBS have a similar amount of slots as above. As stated in Chapter 13 they will fund historical, essay, narrated survey films and so on. They have quite different parameters to POV when it comes to commissioning guidelines, so make sure you familiarize yourself with these.

Other PBS opportunities include America Reframed, NETA, American Public Television and PBS American Masters (music and arts). Each local PBS station has their own rights too and there is an opportunity to underwrite your screening (raise your own funding to do this) to access these numerous local stations.

Other outlets for documentaries in the US include:

- Ovation
- Smithsonian
- MSNBC (politics)
- CNBC (business)
- ESPN (sports)
- OWN
- Fuse
- Russia Today

EUROPEAN TV NETWORKS

Sky Atlantic takes 12 films a year. All acquisitions. *The Crash Reel, Act of Killing, Manhunt* are examples. And the Sheffield film festival (Sheffield Doc | Fest) is very important to them.

UK networks *all* want big feature docs. Europe is a big market for documentaries, so how can US stories be broadened out to these markets? Denmark, Germany etc. all have TV broadcasters that commission or acquire documentaries. So remember to apply to those great European festivals (see the Festival list in the appendix).

The Canadian Hot Docs film festival would introduce you to the European markets (many TV networks and distributors attend), as would the myriad European film festivals and representation from an international distributor, so there are a number of avenues to explore.

BBC STORYVILLE

We've given some detail already in this book about US broadcasters, so this section will expand out from the US and provide more information on a well-known European broadcaster. Rarely will one broadcaster budget your whole film and often you will be looking for co-production funding from a number of places.

Storyville is a very well known documentary strand on the BBC in the UK. Mandy Chang is now at the helm of BBC Storyville. Chang originally hails from Australia and worked at the TV network ABC but created documentaries for the BBC TV strand Arena for a number of years in the UK. Jo Lapping works alongside Chang and has been with Storyville for a number of years working with Kate Thompson and Nick Fraser before that.

Although some of their best-rated films have been about Iran, Gadhafi and Mughabi, at the time of writing they currently have seen a lot of submissions about the war-torn countries of Iraq and Syria. Murder was also very in vogue at the time of *Making A Murderer* and the *O.J. Simpson* documentaries. So they may feel these genres have been quite well served for a while.

Preferring films with great characters that have stories unfolding, they would take historical documentaries in the context of a character's story, an example being *My Mother's Lost Children* about an eccentric Jewish family thrown into turmoil when two stolen children reappear after 40 years.

Essay films, biography or straight current affairs are unlikely to be commissioned by them as they look for character-led films. They specifically want more women filmmakers and diverse voices.

Generally, Storyville covers 15–20% of a film's budget and they do try to support you in finding further funding if they come in early and are making a co-production.

BBC Storyville programs approximately 24 films a year, both commissioning and as acquisitions. They attend IDFA, SXSW, Tribeca, Hot Docs, Berlin and festivals like the Human Rights Watch. They are becoming more open to new directors and first time filmmakers. With *Pussy Riot* they came on early because they knew of the director's previous work. They are happy that you approach them at any time with clips of the film and a two-page treatment at most which talks about the ambition and scale of the film.

Storyville is a strand like POV that is so well known it is competitive. Prepare a great trailer or sample of scenes, don't waste the initial email pitch, make it unturndownable and good luck.

19

In Conclusion

Throughout this book I've mentioned many things we would have done differently. Making *Musicwood* wasn't a simple swim in the pool; we were often barely keeping our heads above water—and that was even when we were supported by our awesome team.

We wore many hats, my producer and I. So many that often we had spread ourselves too thin and we made some expensive mistakes. But we threw ourselves into the deep end and have now learned how to swim and make sure we use the support of symbolical floats. Joining film groups and finding your people is essential. There are many in New York, from Film Fatales to Filmshop. And in other areas look on Meet Up; I'm sure there will be other film lovers that will share your passion in your town. Join the great doc online discussion forum, the D Word, tune in to Women Make Movies webinars and attend your local film festivals. Forge strong relationships, where you give back as much as you gain. The generosity we experienced from some filmmakers is unforgettable.

I have spent a significant section of the book on funding, crowdfunding especially. Learning to pitch and raise money for films isn't an easy skill set for anyone. We need to make a living and we want filmmakers to be able to give a voice to characters that only they may be able to find or have access to. We hope you are successful and remember to bring your patrons along with you.

And even if your film doesn't get the distribution you hoped for, you have made a feature film; what an accomplishment—you have learned so much, your next film will be the better for it.

In the same way equipment has become more consumer friendly and made it possible to make more films, we now have more access to our audiences through streaming platforms. So put your film on Vimeo On Demand or use Distribber and get it seen.

As a wise person once said, "Success is not final, failure is not fatal: it is the courage to continue that counts". The storyteller Ira Glass expands on this:

> Nobody tells this to people who are beginners, I wish someone told me. All of us who do creative work, we get into it because we have good taste. But there is this gap. For the first couple of years you make stuff, it's just not that good. It's trying to be good, it has potential, but it's not. But your taste, the thing that got you into the game, is still killer. And your taste is why your work disappoints you. A lot of people never get past this phase, they quit. Most people I know who do interesting, creative work went through years of this…And if you are just starting out or you are still in this phase, you gotta know its normal and the most important thing you can do is do a lot of work.

I do want to say features aren't everything. Yes this book is angled mainly at the feature documentary process, but series and the new medium form (as opposed to short or long form) is an exciting area and funders are wanting series so there are more opportunities in the marketplace. Features are hard, time-hogging, oftentimes none-money-making vehicles but I love them.

For my next documentary, *To Kid or Not To Kid*, I'll be doing a triple-somersault high dive from what I've learned, so make sure you check it out. I know these notes will be helpful to me as I move forwards, and I hope they'll be helpful to you too. Be creative, be lucky, work hard—and enjoy the process. Remember what Sean Penn said: all of your stories you gather along the way, whether they'll end up on screen, they end up in you.

Thanks for reading the book and I'll be looking out for your next film too. And if you want to work with me as a consultant, email: contact@helpman-productions.org

SPECIAL THANKS

To all the fantastic contributors to this book: our amazing lawyer at Donaldson + Calif, Chris Perez, Pamela Torno of ITVS Digital, Kat Vechio of Fork Films, Justine Nagan of POV, Debra Zimmerman of Women Make Movies and Raphaela Neihausen of DOC NYC Film Festival.

A big thank you to Marshall Curry and Matt Hamachek for their genorosity and immense encouragement. With every film they make I learn something new. Gary Hustwit who gave his time and knowledge for free. Our film consultants, Doug Block and the D-Word, and Peter Broderick. For bringing together the NYC doc making community and making it what it is: Thom Powers and Raphaela Neihausen. The brilliant Bruce Sheridan for believing that Focal Press would be interested in my book. The Cleveland Film Festival programmers who made us feel like royalty, and all the fantastic film festivals out there that have programmed great panels, where we learned so much and met so many great people.

The great organizations in NYC that make me feel like there is a whole documentary world out there when I'm editing alone in my basement: Filmshop is a special organization, Women Make Movies have amazing webinars, Film Fatales, NYWIFT, Stranger Than Fiction at IFC. And the online film resources: *No Film School*, *IndieWire*, IDA and many more. My students who produce incredible work and Chair of the Documentary Department at New York Film Academy, Andrea Swift.

My amazing film, book and life editor, Josh Granger; none of this would be possible without you. Our *Musicwood* friends Bob Taylor, Larry Edwards, Scott Paul. The Haida, Tlingit and Tsimshian tribal members in Alaska and Haida Nation on Haida Gwaii. Our amazing interns and PAs. And last, but by no means least, *all* of our amazing Kickstarter supporters; Alison and Jean Lavenant went above and beyond. And my new Fairy Godmother—you know who you are. And to all my family who were brave enough to take part in my new film, *To Kid or Not To Kid*.

Thank you, Simon Jacobs at Focal Press publishers for recognizing the need for this book and your patience waiting for my additions, with every new piece of advice that I gathered and deemed essential. To the authors who helped me make my first film: Sheila Curran Bernard and Michael Rabiger. And the editor Sandra Stafford (another documentary lover) and John Makowski at Taylor & Francis.

Appendix

USEFUL LINKS

American University Code for Fair Use Best practices:

http://cmsimpact.org/program/fair-u

Fair Use Check List produced by Cornell University:

http://copyright.cornell.edu/policies/docs/Fair_Use_Checklist.pdf

No Film School blank release forms:

http://nofilmschool.com/2016/08/grab-every-filmmaking-form-youll-ever-need-these-99-free-templates

This is a great article on self-distribution:

"Attention, Filmmakers: Here's How to Self-Distribute Your Film"

www.bit.ly/1C5v9qf

A case study on DIY digital distribution:

"Indie Game: The Movie: The Case Study"

www.bit.ly/ISaoFj

A full list of distributors:

"I Love Docs, Distributors & Sales Agents"

http://www.ilovedocs.com/resources/distributors-and-sales-agents/

MUSICWOOD FILM FESTIVAL SHORTLIST

We shortlisted these festivals and didn't apply to them all. If you are having conversations with a distributor, they will have a list of which ones they attend and will want you to apply to those too. You'll also see from our list below we geared our strategy to wildlife, music and environmental festivals, so you will want to gear your strategy to your film's core audience.

Berlin (Germany)

Big Sky Film Festival (MT)—known for its Native American audience

Cleveland International Film Festival (OH)

CPH DOX (Denmark)

DokuFest (Kosovo)

Edinburgh Film Festival (Scotland)

Environmental Film Festival (DC)

Environmental Film Festival at Yale (CT)

Full Frame (NC)

Hot Docs (Canada)

Jackson Hole Wildlife Film Festival (WY)

BFI London Film Festival

Los Angeles (CA)

Mexico International Film Festival And Awards (Online Only)

Mountain Film Festival, Telluride (CA)

Nashville Film Festival (TN)

Newport Beach Film Festival (CA)

Palm Springs International Film Festival (CA)

Raindance Film Festival (UK)

San Francisco International Film Festival (CA)

Seattle (WA) or any other big name West Coast fests

Santa Barbara International Film Festival (CA)

Sarasota Film Festival (FL)

Sebastopol Documentary Film Festival (CA)

Sheffield Doc/Fest (UK)

AFI Silverdocs (DC)

Sonoma (CA)

Sundance Film Festival (UT)

SunnySide La Rochelle (France)

SXSW (TX)

Telluride (CO)

Thessaloniki Film Festival (Greece)

Traverse City (MI)

Tribeca Film Festival (NY)

True/False Film Festival (MO)

Vail Film Festival (CO)

Visions du Reel (France)

New York Film Festival (NY)

Leipzig DOK (Germany)

Asheville Cinema Festival (NC)

Wild and Scenic Film Festival (CA)

SELECTED NON-FICTION FILMOGRAPHY

Fight the Power

Edward Snowden

Gasland

The Invisible War

The Thin Blue Line

Editorial

Enron

Inside Job

No End In Sight

Economic Injustice

Dark Days

Overnighters

Princess Shaw

The Corporation

War

The Kill Team

The Pat Tillman Story

The Road to Guantanamo Bay

Humorous

Anvil

King of Kong

Overnight

Vérité

City of Ghosts

Cutie and The Boxer

Sweetgrass

Crime Drama—series

Making a Murderer

The Jinx

The Staircase

Hero's Hubris

American Movie

Client 9

The Fog of War

Intimate Portraits

Brother's Keeper

Catfish

(duplicated as excellent vérité film) Cutie and The Boxer

Faces Places

Marwencol

The Queen of Versailles

The Way We Get By

Food/Cooking

Jiro Dreams of Sushi

King of Corn

Kings of Pastry

Activism

5 Broken Cameras

Food Inc

The Garden

Environmental

Circle of Poison

Crude

Musicwood

River Changes Course

The Babushkas of Chernobyl

The Eagle Huntress

Courtroom Drama

Paradise Lost Trilogy

The Staircase (series)

Women's Rights

After Tiller

To Kid or Not To Kid

Trapped

Vessel

Action

Big Men

Cartel Land

Sports

Crash Reel

Hoop Dreams

Murderball

Senna

Tickled (But Not Really)

Undefeated

Word Play

Touching The Void

Children and Teens

Born Into Brothels

Garbage Dreams

Horseboy

Only the Young

Paradise Lost Trilogy

Racing Dreams

Rich Hill

Spell Bound

To Be and To Have (foreign film)

Family Drama

Capturing the Friedmans

Stories We Tell

Tarnation

Toto and His Sisters (foreign film)

Hybrid Documentaries

Exit Through the Giftshop

Man on Wire

Project Nim

The Arbor

The Imposter

Music

Kurt Cobain: The Montage of Heck

Musicwood

Searching For Sugarman

Some Kind of Monster

The Defiant Ones (series, but what the heck)

LGBTQ

How to Survive a Plague

Memories of a Penitent Heart

Strong Island

The Times of Harvey Milk

Incarceration and Essay

13th

The House I Live In

Art House and/or Filmmaking Technique

Baraka

Koyaanisqats

Room 237

Sherman's March

The Salt of the Earth

Unrest

Waltz With Bashir

Biopic

Iris

Listen to Me Marlon

Weiner

Animal

Buck

Blackfish

Grizzly Man

March of the Penguins

Kedi

Religion

Going Clear

One of Us

Political

Bowling For Columbine

Fahrenheit 9/11

Street Fight

Travels With George

Box Office Smash/Oscar Winners

Citizen Four

Twenty Feet From Stardom

Undefeated

Wolfpack

Great Use of Archive

Our Nixon

The Donner Party

The Kid Stays in the Picture

The Weather Underground

Other Formats

DJ Khaled's Snapchat Story

Classic Documentaries

Grey Gardens

7 Up series

Harlan County USA

Don't Look Back

Gimme Shelter

RELEASE FORMS

Materials Release

LICENSE TO USE MATERIALS

PROGRAM (*TENTATIVE TITLE*): _____

1. For good and valuable consideration, the receipt and sufficiency of which are hereby acknowledged, I irrevocably grant Hitman Productions LLC and its parent, subsidiary, affiliated and related companies (the "Producer") the right, in perpetuity, throughout the universe, in any language, and in all media now known or hereafter devised, to use (in whole or in part) the:

_____

(collectively, the "Materials") in and in connection with the preparation, production and distribution of the Production, and any version thereof, as Producer may determine in its sole discretion. I authorize Producer to use the Materials as set dressing and/or on-screen props and to edit, crop or juxtapose the Materials and to incorporate and license others to incorporate any part or all of the Materials into the Production or any version thereof and/or any other production. I further grant Producer the right to use the Materials for the purpose of advertising and promoting Producer, the Production or any version thereof or any other production in which the Materials are incorporated and/or the exhibitors (including, but not limited to, institutional promotion) and sponsors of any of the foregoing in any manner whatsoever, including, but not limited to, product integration, commercial tie-ins, and implied endorsements. Without limiting the generality of the foregoing, I agree that the rights granted hereunder shall include the perpetual, worldwide right of Producer to edit, telecast,

cablecast, rerun, record, publish, reproduce, use, license, print, distribute or otherwise exploit, in any manner and in any medium or forum, whether now known or hereafter devised, the Production or any version thereof and/or any other production in which the Materials are incorporated, in whole or in part, without any monetary compensation to me.

2. I represent and warrant that I have the sole right and authority, as copyright owner in the Materials or authorized representative of the copyright owner, to grant the rights granted to Producer hereunder and that the consent of no other person, firm, corporation or entity is required to enable Producer to use the Materials as described herein, and that such use by Producer will not violate the rights of any third parties. I agree that I will not assert, maintain or assist other persons in asserting or maintaining against Producer, its successors, assigns and licensees any claim, action, suite or demand of any kind or nature whatsoever, including but not limited to, those grounded upon copyright or trademark infringement, invasion or privacy, rights or publicity, other civil rights, or for any other reason in connection with Producer's use of the Materials in the Production or other productions as herein provided.

3. I will indemnify and hold harmless Producer, its successors, assigns and licensees from and against any and all claims liabilities, demands, actions, causes of action, costs and expenses (including attorneys' fees and court costs) whatsoever, at law or in equity, known or unknown, anticipated or unanticipated, arising out of Producer's use of the Materials as provided herein, and for breach of any representation or warranty made by me herein. To the fullest extent allowable under any applicable law, I also hereby expressly waive any and all so-called "moral rights" in the Materials as used in connection with the Production that may now be or may hereafter come into existence.

4. I understand that Producer will be relying on this License and expending money in connection with the Production and that I shall not be entitled to terminate, rescind or cancel this License for any reason. I acknowledge that no payments resulting from the Production shall become due and owing to me for any present or future uses or exploitations, and I hereby release Producer from any claims, obligations or liability relating thereto.

5. Producer shall be under no obligation to actually use the Materials in any manner.

6. In the event that Producer is in breach of any provision of this Agreement and/or any other agreement entered into by Producer and Licensor, Licensor specifically acknowledges and agrees that the damage, if any, caused thereby will not be irreparable or otherwise sufficient to entitle Licensor to injunctive or any other form of equitable relief. Licensor's rights and remedies in any such event shall be strictly limited to the right to recover monetary damages, if any, in an action at law. Without limiting the foregoing, Licensor shall not be entitled by reason of any such breach to terminate or rescind this Agreement nor to enjoin, restrain or otherwise impair Producer's exercise of any of the rights and privileges granted or to be granted to Producer hereunder, nor to restrain, enjoin or otherwise impair Producer's property or assets or the development, production, exhibition and/or exploitation of the Production or any advertising, publicity or promotion in connection therewith.

7. I will not at any time issue, authorize or participate in any news story, magazine article or other publicity or information of any kind relating to the Production or Producer or disclose any confidential information, including without limitation the terms of this License, without Producer's written consent in each case. Additionally, I have no right to use the names, trademark, logos, or trade names of Producer or the names or logos related to the Production for any purpose whatsoever, including but not limited to, publicity, public relations, merchandising or self promotion purposes without the prior written consent of Producer.

8. The rights granted herein shall inure to the benefit of Producer, its licensees, successors, and assigns.

9. This License constitutes the entire agreement and understanding between the parties regarding this subject matter hereof, and cancels and supersedes all prior or contemporaneous agreements, communications and understandings (whether written or oral) between the parties relating to the subject matter hereof. Licensor confirms that Licensor has read and fully understands this document, and has not signed it in reliance on any statement, opinion or representation by Producer or anyone acting

on Producer's behalf or otherwise. This License can only be amended by a written document signed by all parties hereto.

AGREED AND ACCEPTED:

_____ Print name

_____ PRODUCTION COMPANY

Date: _____

By: _____ Name/Title

_____ Signature

Adult Release Forms

ADULT RELEASE—DO NOT FORGET A MINOR RELEASE FORM which will be worded differently

APPEARANCE RELEASE ***PROGRAM (TENTATIVE TITLE)***:

_____

1. *I irrevocably grant to ………………………. ("Producer"), its licensees, successors, agents, sponsors and assigns all right of every kind, nature and description including, but not limited to the following unrestricted rights, throughout the universe and in perpetuity to copyright, publish and utilize my name, likeness, image, voice, biographical material and contents of any interview I provide, both on and off-camera ("Materials"); to use everything within the grant of rights, including any property, real or personal, in whole or in part, in book(s), article(s) and other print and literary use(s), television, radio, film, theatrical, videocassettes, sound recording, new media, whether on the World Wide Web, internet, CD-ROM or otherwise, educational use and any so-called subsidiary and ancillary rights and uses, as well as any sequel(s), remake(s), additional or repeated use(s) of the Materials, including the right to publish, produce, distribute, exhibit, broadcast, cablecast, webcast, transmit, edit, dub, exploit and otherwise sell, lease, license or dispose of the Materials in any manner and by any means, method, process or technology now known or hereafter developed and to utilize any of the above for the purpose of advertising, trade and publicity of the Program.*

2. *I agree that Producer may use, incorporate and/or record on film, tape or in any other media any material(s) and performance provided by me and/or the company or organization I represent. All of the grant of rights herein is for good and valuable consideration, receipt of which is hereby acknowledged. I warrant and represent that nothing that I do or provide shall violate or infringe on the rights of anyone else.*

3. *I acknowledge that the results and proceeds of my services shall be deemed a work made for hire.*

4. *I hereby waive any right that I may have to inspect or approve the finished product or products or the advertising copy, marketing material or printed matter that may be used in connection therewith or the use to which it may be applied.*

5. *I hereby release, discharge and agree to hold harmless Producer, its legal representatives and assigns, and all persons acting under its permission or authority or those for whom Producer is acting, from any liability from any and all claims, demands, costs, legal fees or causes of action that I may now have or may hereafter have for libel, defamation, invasion of privacy or right of publicity, infringement of copyright, whether intentional or otherwise, that may occur in connection with any of the rights granted hereunder.*

6. *I acknowledge that Producer is under no obligation to utilize my services, property or material herein provided.*

7. *I hereby warrant and represent that I am of full age and have every right to contract in my own name and to grant the above.*

AGREED AND ACCEPTED: _____ *PRODUCTIONS*

Date: _____

By: _____ *Signature of talent*

_____ Rep Production co

Title: _____ *Print name:* _____

About the Author

Maxine Trump got her start in radio and television, working for seven years in program development and commissioning for BBC Comedy in the UK. She emigrated to the US in 2003 to become a director of television commercials and has received both Gold and Silver BDA awards for her work.

She went on to direct short documentaries for various TV networks—including TNT, Sundance Channel, TLC—and numerous organizations. Loving the intimate storytelling style of documentaries, Maxine then moved into long-form documentary production for Discovery.

Maxine's feature documentary, *Musicwood*, was a *New York Times* Critics' Pick, a festival award-winner, which played in theaters and on TV networks around the world. Her latest documentary is *To Kid or Not To Kid*.

Maxine is on the selection committee for DOC NYC and Nantucket film festival, a Manhattan chapter leader of the Non-profit film group Filmshop and teaches documentary filmmaking at the New York Film Academy. She holds an MFA from London Metropolitan University. Her BA in Visual Art and background in comedy allow her to bring an entertaining and artistic sensibility to all of her work.

Maxine is a freelance director and documentary consultant. She actively seeks out new stories to tell and enjoys helping new filmmakers bring their documentaries to life. *A Documentary Filmmaker's Roadmap* is her first book.

She lives in Brooklyn NY with her husband and inquisitive cat.

Index

Illustrations are in **bold**.

A Place at the Table 28
A&E 213
Act of Killing 214
AFI Docs 34, 161
Age of Champions 186
Al-Jazeera 212
Aldous, Gethin, *The Work* 33
Amazon 189, 208
AmDoc 165
America Reframed 166–7
archives 6–7, 29, 129
artwork, key 71, 82, 129
ATMOS sound 107
Attenborough, David 29
Auden, W. H. 35
audience: connecting with 15, 153, 174, 180, 205; core 8, 147–8; reactions 16, 24–5, 26, 159
audio 6, 19, 32, 105–9

The Babushkas of Chernobyl 156
Bar-Lev, Amir, *The Pat Tillman Story* 9, 22, 101
Baraka 23
Bazin, Andre, *La Jetée* 34–5
BBC: archives 29; and credible sources 136; Foley sounds 107; mission statement 24; Motion Gallery 130; *Planet Earth* 30; and sponsors 167; Storyville 214–15
behind-the-scenes photos (BTS) 50, 82
Berlin film festival 174–5, 177
Berlinger, Joe 182–3
Bernard, Sheila Curran, *Documentary Storytelling* 17, 18, 111
Big Men 164
Big Sky festival 179
Biopic films 25–6
Blackfish 29, 196

blogs 21, 81, 165, 181, 206
Brain Trust screenings 146–50
Broomfield, Nick 22, 27, 104
budgets 38–45, 152–3, 155
Burns, Ken 23, 26
Burns, Ric, *The Donner Party* 104

Camera Person 3, 18
cameras 18–19, 48–9, 112, 141
Canadian Hot Docs film festival 214
Cartel Land 9, 19, 110–28, **111**
Castaing-Taylor, Lucien, *Sweetgrass* 34, 36
categories, film 158
Catfish 22, 65
Center for Media & Social Impact 132, 135
character led/first person documentaries 30
character led/first person films **21**
characters 15, 17–18, 26, 33, 50–1
Chicken and Egg Pictures 58
Cinema Guild 182, 187, 188, 195
cinematographers 48
City of Ghosts 97
clearance log 139
Cleveland Film Festival, 176, 179
Client 9 24
CNN Films 212, 213, 208
composers 108
consent states 142
controversial films 212
copyright law 129–35, 135–6
The Corporation 23, 28, 29
cost, filmmakers' 38–9, 53
The Crash Reel 214
Creative Capital 59
crews 9, 167
crowdfunding 55, 60–4, 73–95, 180, 194

237

cue sheet, music **132**, 139
Curry, Marshall: films 9, 22, 100, 112, 202; *If a Tree Falls* 24; *Racing Dreams* 6
Curtis, Adam 23, 29

Dark Days 8–9
Daughter from Danang 9, 97
defamation 144–5
deferred funding 56
diagetic sounds 107
Diaz, Ramona 3
Dick, Kirby: *The Hunting Ground* 24, 26; *The Invisible War* 26
Digital Open Call (ITVS) 210–11
digital platforms 187, **193**, 195
digital release windows 189–90
digital streaming 208–11
Directing The Documentary (Rabiger) 35
director, cost of 38–9
Directors of Photography (DP) 48, 57
Discovery networks 213
Distribber 187
distribution, film 159–63, 174–5, 179, 180, 182, 184–95
distributors, international 190–2
distributors, national 187–90
DOC NYC festival 47–9, 60, 112, 157–9, 172, 179
Documentary Core Application 57, 154
Documentary Storytelling (Bernard) 17, 18
documentary types **21**
Dogwoof 190–1, 196
Donaldson + Callif (lawyers) 138, 140
donation, of services 56
The Donner Party 104
door stepping 142
Drew Associates 22
Durst, Robert, *The Jinx* 50
Duvernay, Ava, *13th* 27, 28
DVDs 64, 69, 185, 187, 190

E&O Insurance (errors and omissions) 45, 132, 138, 139–40
editing 52–4, 96–109, 101–2, **106**
educational distributors 160, 190, 195
Encounters at the End of the World 29, 32

Enemies of Happiness 161
Enron 23, 104
environmental films 156
equipment 18–19, 48–9, 112, 141
essay and narrated films 21, **21**, 23, 25–37
ethics 140
European TV networks 214
Every Frame a Painting 103
Exit Through The Giftshop 23
experimental films 23
expository films 23, 29

Facebook 68, **70**, 71, 85–6, 91, 93
Facebook Live 73
Fair Use 133–5, 138–9, 186
Fair Use, Free Speech and Intellectual Property Rights 133
false light publicity 136, 137
feature directors 177–83
fees, screening 175
festivals 130, 161, 169–83, 215 *See also* DOC NYC festival
fiction films 20
film critics 21
film length 96
film panels 202
Filmbuff 187
films, short 12
Final Year 48
finishing, and assembly (editing) 109
finishing costs 39–40
first person/character led films **21**, 27
Fiscal Sponsors 156–7, 162
5 Broken Cameras 191
Fledging Fund 59
flyers 93, 198, **199**, 205
The Fog of War 31
Foley sounds 107
Food Inc 28
footage libraries 129–30
footage, researching 130–1, 133
Fork Films 151–7
formats, footage 109
Foundation Center Library 57
foundation funding 57–60
four-walling 194, 198

4.1 Miles 164
funding 55–66, 57–60, 74, 83–4, 151–7, 165, 167, 210–11
fundraising 54, 60–4, 155

Garbage Dreams 49
Gasland 22
Gathr 194
Gelb, David, *Jiro Dreams of Sushi* 30–2, 36
genres, film 20–37, 164, 209
Getty's Images 130
Gibney, Alex, *Client 9* 24
GIFs 79, 91, 92
Gilliam, Terry, *Twelve Monkeys* 35
Girl Rising 194
Glass, Ira 217
Glass, Philip 31–2
goals, end 58, 62, 63, 67–8, 179
Goodall, Jane 48, 104
Google Play 189
Greenpeace 8, 18, 46, 52, 65, 148
Grey Gardens 22–3
Grierson, John 35, 36

Hamachek, Matt, *Cartel Land* 97, 100, 103, 111
HBO 185, 212, 213
Hegedus, Chris 3
Heineman, Matt: *Cartel Land* 19, 111, 112, 128; *City of Ghosts* 47, 97; films 46
Helvetica 29
Hertzog, Werner: charisma 29; *Encounters at the End of the World* 32; film classes 104; influences 36
Hess, Marilyn 60–1
hidden cameras 141
high-ball budgets 41, 43
Hitman Productions 193
Hoffman, John 204, 212
Hot Docs (Toronto) 175
Hotel 22 164
Huffington Post 186, 206
Hulu 189, 208
Human Rights Watch festival 161, 215

The Hunting Ground 24
Hustwit, Gary, *Helvetica* 30, 69
hybrid films **21**, 23

I Am Not Your Negro 167
IDA (International Documentary Association) 58, 154
IDFA (International Documentary Filmfestival Amsterdam) 161, 174
If a Tree Falls 9, 24, 97, 100, 164
Impact Partners 64
The Imposter 23
in-flight entertainment channels 212
In Transit 33–4
Independent Lens 164, 167, 213
Indie Lens Storycast 210
Indiegogo 80
IndieWire 63, 177, 198, 206
individual funding 60–4
Inside Job 138
Instagram 70, 93
insurance, production 39, 45, 132, 138, 139–40
internships 78–9, 93, 182
interviews 47–8, 50–2, 97, 102, 141
intrusion 136
investigative films **21**, 22
investors, individual 64–5
iPhones 49
issue films 26, 28
iTunes 71, 161, 189, **193**
ITVS (Digital Open Call) 210–11
ITVS (Open Call) 167, 210–11

James, Steve 46
Jane 47, 104, 138
Jason Bourne films 23
The Jinx 50
Jiro Dreams of Sushi 30–2
Johnson, Kristen 3, 18
jokes 142
journalism 136, 140–1

Kanopy and Hoopla 195
Kartemquin films 165
Kate Plays Christine 23
Kenner, Robert, *Food Inc* 27, 28

240 Index

Kickstarter 50, 61, 62, **63**, 64, 77–89, **94**
Kickstarter Live 73, 85
Kings of Pastry 27

launch, crowdfunding 86–7
Leacock, Richard 22
legal action 137
legal insurance 39
lessons learned 93
libel 144
licensing costs 129
likeness, appropriation of 136
LinkedIn 68, 90
LLC (limited liability company) 39, 45
locations 6
low-ball budgets 43, **44**
Lurie, John 183

McLeary, Jairus, *The Work* 33
magazines, film 21
MailChimp 88, 92
Making A Murderer 215
mantras 17, 43, 76, 102, **106**
March of the Penguins 23, 29, 30, 104
Marclay, Christian, "Clocks" 36–7
Marker, Chris 34–5
marketing 40, 202–7, 204–6
marketing, and press 202–7
Marsh, James 26
master recording rights (music) 131
Master Script 97–8
materials, press 202–7
materials, promotion 175–6, 178, 198
The Maysles 22
Maysles, Al, *In Transit* 23, 25, 33–4
Member Database 149, 171
mission statements 24, 152
Moore, Michael 8, 22, 27
Morgen, Brett: influences 47–8;
  Jane 36, 47, 48, 104; *Montage of Heck* 48
Morris, Errol: *A Brief History of Time* 47; films 22, 35; *The Fog of War* 31; as influence 36, 47–8; *My Name Is Lenny* 47; *The Thin Blue Line* 24
Moss, Jesse 3, 19
motivation 79–80

music: copyright law 131–2; performance 17, 31–2, 48; scores 9; and sound 105–9
Music Supervisors 108, 131
Musicwood: audience 76, **76**; budget 41–5, **42**, **44**; copyright law 131; crew **53**; DVDs 192–3; editing 52–4, 97–8, 99; equipment 49; festivals 171–2, 176–7, 185, 187; flyers **2**, **199**; funding 56–65; genre 24, 148; internships 78–9, 93, 182; Kickstarter campaign 61–3, **63**; lawyers for 138–9; music performances 48, 51, **132**; plotting storyline 9–10; press and marketing 203; screenings 89, 148–9, 159, 193; social media 69, 187, **193**; storytelling 1, 3–5, 15–16, 46–7; synopsis 10–11; theatrical tour 197–8, **199**
My Mother's Lost Children 215

Nagan, Justine 163, 165, 166
narrated and essay films **21**, 23
narration 16, 21, 29, 104–5
National Bird 167
National Film Board of Canada (NFB) 36, 54
National Geographic 213
Native Americans 11, 18, 100, 149, 212
Native Corporation 10, 46
Neihausen, Raphaela 157–9
Netflix 161, 189, 208–9, 209
Neumann, Stan 12
Newport Folk Festival 187
newsletters 95
Newtown 167
Nichols, Bill 21, 23
No Film School website 180
Nolan, Christopher 35, 198
non-diagetic sound 107
Non-Fiction Series 25
non-profit funding 65
non-theatrical distribution 194

observational/vérité films 16, **21**, 22–3, 36, 97, 166
O.J.: Made in America 25, 215

Open Call (ITVS) 167, 210–11
The Overnighters 19, 164

parodies 142–3
participatory films 22, 24
The Pat Tillman Story 9, 97, 101
PBS (Public Broadcasting Service) 163–6, 210, 213
PDA (patron driven acquisition) 195
Penn, Sean 1
Pennebaker, D. A. 22
Perez, Chris 140
performative films 22
phone calls, recorded 141–2
phone pre-interviews 50
Pinterest 70
piracy 129
Planet Earth (BBC) 30
plot-driven films 23
plot points 9, 12–15, 113–27
poetic films 23
Poitras, Laura: *Edward Snowden* 24; *Risk* 22, 103–4; voice over 49
POV Digital 168
POV (public television series) 163–6, 167, 213
Powers, Thom 149–50, 157, 172
PR Newswire 207
pre-production 8–19
pre-sales funding 65–6, 161, 209
premieres, film 170, 172–4, **173**, 178
press 80–2, 176–7, 202–7
privacy 135–7, 144
Private Violence 162
producer, cost of 38
production 46–54
Production Assistance Program 159, 162
production, look of 47–8
proposals, film 64–5, 152, 154
public domain 133
public relations (PR) 43, 81, 173, 178, 181, 182, 203
publicity, festival 176–7, 182
publicity, right of 144–5
Pussy Riot 215

Q&A sessions 172, 173, 174, 181, 202, 206
Qatsi Trilogy 23
The Queen of Versailles 137, 138, 191
Quinn, Tom 202

Rabiger, Michael, *Directing The Documentary* 18, 35, 101
Racing Dreams 6, 27
Radio Cut 98
Raiders of the Lost Ark 103
Ramos, Taylor: *Every Frame a Painting* 103; *F Is For Fake* 103
recreations, of real-life events 144–5
Reddit 70, 93
reflective films 21
reflexive films 23
Reggio, Godfrey 23
releases 47, 137–9, 192
researching footage 130–1
Reticker, Gini 153
reviewers 206
Rich Hill 6
rights, copyright owner 130–1
rights, negotiating 130
Risk 22, 103–4
Rottentomatoes 95, 176, 198, 206
rough cuts 89, 149, 171, 178
royalties 189, 209

sales agents 182
Samsara 23
satirical works 142–3
scores, music 9
screening fees 175
screenings, test 89, 146–50, 205
Seed&Spark 80
semi-theatrical distribution 194
semi-theatrical screenings 160, 161, 176, 177, 186, 187
sets, interview 47–8
Sherman's March 22
shooting scripts 12–15
short documentaries 12, 70, 164, 168, 180, 184, 209
Short Film distributor list 180
shot lists 48, 51

Showtime 213
Singer, Marc 8–9
Sky Atlantic 214
Snapchat 70, 168
Snowden, Edward 24
social issue films 24, 57–9, 86, 147
social media 67–71, 90
Soderberg, Steven 103
SOTs (Sound On Tape) 97, 99, 107, 108
sound 6, 19, 32, 105–9
Spellbound 27
sponsors 64–5, 167, 197
spreadsheet, production 52
The Staircase 25, 191
state laws, US 135
statistics, Kickstarter 85
stock footage libraries 129–30
Stories We Tell 22
story beats 15, 98–9, 100, **111**, 112
story elements 15–16, 18
Storyville (BBC) 214–15
Stranger Than Fiction screenings 157–9
streaming, digital 208–11, 213
string-outs 98, 99
Sundance Film Festival 37, 161, 169
Sundance Institute Documentary Program 169
Supersize Me 27
surveys 149
SVOD (Subscription Video on demand) 189–90
Sweetgrass 34, 36
SXSW (South by Southwest) 170, 173, 178
sync rights (music) 131
synopsis, film 10–11, 57, 152

Tangerine 49
Tarnation 22
teams, crowdfunding 77–80
techniques, film 103
test screenings 89, 146–50, 205
theaters 181, 182, 187, 194, 198, 200–1
theatrical marketing 204–6
theatrical releases 196–201
The Hunting Ground 26
Theroux, Louis 22, 25, 27

The Thin Blue Line 24
third-party materials 6–7, 129, 132–3, 138
13th 28
This Is Spinal Tap 23
thriller films 24
Tickled 103
titles, film 155
To Kid or Not to Kid 61, 77, 80–1, 92, 217
Tobias, Scott, *A Place at the Table* 26, 28
tone, film 15
topics, niche 156
Torno, Pam 209–11
Toronto International Film Festival 157, 175
trade press 203–4, 207
trailers 72, 162, 203
trans-media funds 54
transciption 97, 98
trespassing 143–4
Tribeca All Access 59, 170
Tribeca Film Institute Documentary Fund 59
Trint 97
"Trumps Against Trump" 12–15
Tugg 194
TV networks 163–8, 211–15
TV pre-sales funding 65–6
TVOD (Transactional Video on Demand) 184
Twelve Monkeys 35
Twitter 68–9, 90, 93

updates, crowdfunding 89
US Copyright Office 133–5

Vecchio, Kat 154–7
vérité/observational films 16, **21**, 22–3, 36, 97, 166
Vimeo On Demand 163, 184, 186, 187, 209
violation, copyright 131
Virtual Reality (VR) 37
voice overs 99, 103–4, 113
Vox 209
Vudu 189

websites, film 71–2, 147, 186
WEEED (tips for storytelling) 17
Weiner 65, 138, 196
wildlife films 29
Winged Migration 29
Wiseman, Frederick 22
Withoutabox (application platform) 171
Women Make Movies (WMM) 159–64
women, representation of 156, 159–64
The Woodmans 191

The Work 33
Working Films 148

Xbox 189

YouTube 69, 93, 97, 103, 174, 210

Zhou, Tony: *Every Frame a Painting* 103; *F Is For Fake* 103
Zimmerman, Debra 159–63